APOSTLE OF NEW JERSEY

APOSTLE OF NEW JERSEY
JOHN TALBOT

1645 - 1727

By

EDGAR LEGARE PENNINGTON, M.A., S.T.D.

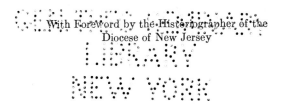

With Foreword by the Historiographer of the
Diocese of New Jersey

PUBLICATION No. 10

THE CHURCH HISTORICAL SOCIETY
PHILADELPHIA

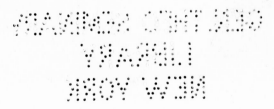

Printed in U. S. A.

RICHMOND:
RICHMOND PRESS, INC.
PRINTERS

To
PAUL MATTHEWS
BISHOP OF NEW JERSEY
1915-1937
INHERITOR OF THE NOBLE TRADITIONS
OF THE STRUGGLING CHURCH OF NOVA CAESAREA
AND
WORTHY SUCCESSOR OF THOSE WHO BORE
THE BURDEN AND HEAT OF THOSE STRENUOUS DAYS
THIS BOOK IS DEDICATED
WITH ESTEEM AND AFFECTION

FOREWORD

THROUGHOUT his episcopate as diocesan of New Jersey (1915-1937), the Right Reverend Paul Matthews manifested a keen interest in the history of the Church in New Jersey. He was determined that the first interstate meeting of clergy and laity from New York, Pennsylvania and New Jersey, in Christ Church, New Brunswick, on May 11, 1784, in the interests of the union of the Episcopal churches following the War of Independence, and the subsequent organization of the diocese of New Jersey, July 6, 1785, should be worthily commemorated. To this end, upon invitation of the bishop and diocesan convention of New Jersey, the triennial meeting of General Convention was held in Atlantic City in 1934. Bishop Matthews commissioned the Reverend Dr. Hamilton Schuyler (April 3, 1862-January 23, 1933), historiographer of the diocese, to write a history of the Church in New Jersey from its beginning. This worthy project, upon which Dr. Schuyler was engaged for some time, was cut short by his untimely death. His manuscript was not sufficiently complete for another, without Dr. Schuyler's knowledge of the whole field and the requisite leisure, to take it up and finish it in time for the commemorations of 1934 and 1935. Upon the appointment of the present historiographer in 1935, it was deemed best to modify the original plan for the time being and in certain particulars, for reasons which will be explained below.

In 1836 the Rev. Francis L. Hawks, D.D., historiographer of the Episcopal Church, was authorized by General Convention to visit England and to secure such documents or copies bearing upon the history of the American Church as the archives of Lambeth Palace, Fulham Palace, and the Society for the Propagation of the Gospel might afford. With the generous financial aid of Trinity Church, New York City, Dr. Hawks was able to undertake the mission and brought back from England seventeen bound folio volumes, now known as the Hawks Transcripts. The work was not exhaustive and the New Jersey volume was particularly incomplete. For this or for other reasons, when Bishop William Stevens Perry published the Hawks manuscripts in his *Historical Collections Relating to the American Colonial*

Church, dealing with the colonial history of Virginia, Pennsylvania, Massachusetts, Maryland and Delaware (in addition to the two volumes concerning the Church in Connecticut, previously published by Drs. Hawks and Perry), New Jersey was almost entirely neglected.

Within the last ten years it has been possible to remedy this neglect as never before. The Library of Congress has collected by transcripts, photofilm enlargements, and photostats, almost everything of a documentary nature in the above mentioned British archives relating to the American colonies. The publication of letters of the missionaries and other documents involving the colonial Church in New Jersey, now so readily available, we deem of immediate primary importance for several reasons:

One, the interests of historical truth in the political, social and economic fields, as well as the ecclesiastical, demand it. For these communications of the missionaries throw considerable light upon matters not strictly ecclesiastical and should be taken into account by the secular historian.

Two, gratitude to the men who bore the burden and heat of those pioneer days, who labored to sow in the face of severe obstacles where we have reaped, constrains us.

Three, the missionaries themselves are well worth knowing better. Five bishops-elect served the colonial Church in New Jersey at one time or another: John Talbot, Samuel Seabury, Thomas B. Chandler, David Griffith, and Uzal Ogden. Of these, only Talbot and Seabury were consecrated, both by Non-Jurors, the former irregularly by one of the English bishops, the latter regularly by three of the Scottish Church.

In addition we have such worthies as Dr. Thomas Wood, physician and priest, who won his spurs in New Brunswick, New Jersey, for his greater work as first missionary in New Brunswick, Canada; Thomas Thompson of Freehold who, by his labors among the negroes there, was inspired to volunteer as the first S. P. G. missionary to Africa; Michael Houdin of Trenton, Wolfe's intelligence officer in the conquest of Canada; Nathaniel Evans of Gloucester and Waterford, a colonial poet of merit and still greater promise; Abraham Beach of New Brunswick, lone active missionary in New Jersey during most of the war years, initiator of the first step looking to the union of the crushed and discouraged Church, peacemaker in Trinity Church, New York

City, when threatened with disruption by Whig and Tory factions, a pillar of steadiness in the critical period of the Church's reorganization, and thrice president of the House of Deputies of the General Convention.

"And what shall I more say? For the time would fail me to tell of" William Ayers, Isaac Browne, Colin Campbell, Samuel Cooke, Leonard Cutting, John Holbrooke, Robert McKean, Jonathan Odell, John Pierson, John Preston, William Skinner, and Edward Vaughan, "who through faith subdued kingdoms, wrought righteousness, obtained promises," "out of weakness were made strong, waxed valiant in fight, turned to flight the armies of the aliens." They "and others had trial of bonds and imprisonment . . . being destitute, afflicted, tormented; of whom the world was not worthy. And these all, having obtained a good report through faith, received not the promise."

We purpose, God willing, to take up the work so long neglected by making available to the general reader and the student the biographies of New Jersey's pioneer missionaries, together with their unpublished letters and other documents bearing upon their life and time. In this plan the first step, obviously, was an adequate biography of John Talbot, "The Apostle of the New Jersey Church," which has been so long needed. The second step should be a definitive life of Thomas Bradbury Chandler, who, if second to anybody in New Jersey, was second only to Talbot.

Upon the recommendation of Bishop Matthews, the Finance Committee of the diocese of New Jersey made an appropriation in 1937 for the search, photostating and copying of the Talbot data in the Library of Congress; and the courteous and efficient assistance of that Library's staff in the Division of Manuscripts is hereby gratefully acknowledged. The copies were turned over to the Reverend Dr. Pennington, who has long specialized in the colonial period and who cheerfully undertook as a labor of love the editing of the letters and the writing of Talbot's biography.

The resulting volume is the fruit of the finest kind of cooperative effort. Bishop Matthews has continued his interest since his retirement from active jurisdiction and has made a generous gift toward its publication. So also has the bishop of Newark, the Right Reverend Benjamin M. Washburn, D. D., whose diocese was originally a part of the colonial Church in

New Jersey. The Right Reverend Wallace J. Gardner, D.D., present bishop of New Jersey, has taken up the mantle of his predecessor in this matter and upon the recommendation of himself and the Finance Committee, the diocesan convention of 1938 authorized an appropriation towards the cost of publication. The Church Historical Society has been glad to sponsor this volume and bear the balance of the cost in line with its policy of publishing constructive contributions to American Church history.

WALTER HERBERT STOWE.
Historiographer of the Diocese of
New Jersey.

INTRODUCTION

John Talbot wielded a considerable influence in colonial America. As one of the original missionaries of the Society for the Propagation of the Gospel in Foreign Parts, his recommendations influenced that body in the planning of its work and the choice of its fields of enterprise. Alert and aggressive, he was a dominant figure in religious affairs in several of the colonies; the force of his personality was recognized by government officials, and his example of industry and consecration was a spur to other clergymen. As a preacher of ability, a zealous pastor, and a man of blameless life, he was undoubtedly an inspiration to innumerable laymen. No man worked harder to secure a resident bishop in the colonies. In his efforts towards that end, John Talbot was moved by no selfish consideration but solely by his enthusiasm for the welfare of the Church.

The want of an adequate biography of this notable churchman has long been felt. It is believed likewise that a publication of Talbot's letters would throw light on American life. During the first quarter of the Eighteenth Century most of the colonies were passing from the period of hardship and insecurity, which marked their pioneer days, into settled communities. They were becoming conscious of their strength and resources, and they were learning to proceed along independent lines. John Talbot may be regarded as typical of the transition. His spirit was energetic and progressive, but he perceived the value of old institutions, such as the Established Church and the episcopate; and he was unwilling that American Christianity should sever its organic connections. Independency was making rapid progress in the sections in which he ministered; but by his untiring labours, Talbot did much to preserve and intensify the popular loyalty to the mother Church.

In the preparation of this volume, the author wishes to express his obligations to Dr. Paul Matthews, until his recent retirement the bishop of New Jersey; to the Reverend Walter Herbert Stowe, S.T.D., president of the Church Historical Society; to the Reverend E. Clowes Chorley, D.D., historiographer of the American Church; to the Reverend G. MacLaren Brydon,

D.D., eminent student of colonial Church history, whose counsel and editorial assistance have been indispensable; to the staff of the Manuscript Division of the Library of Congress, and that of the Rare Book Room of the New York Public Library. The above have given encouragement and help to the author in this undertaking and have thus rendered possible its completion.

EDGAR LEGARE PENNINGTON.

TABLE OF CONTENTS

BOOK ONE

BIOGRAPHY
OF
JOHN TALBOT
1645-1727

Apostle of New Jersey---John Talbot

I. CHURCH OF ENGLAND BEGINNINGS IN NEW JERSEY.

THE territory now known as New Jersey was included in the original claim of the English crown to the whole Atlantic seaboard, from New England to Carolina. This claim was by virtue of the discoveries of the Cabots at the end of the Fifteenth Century; but it was not until permanent settlements had been made in Virginia and New England that undisputed possession was assured to the British. After the explorations of Henry Hudson, the Dutch proceeded to settle the region discovered by him, giving to their holdings the name of New Netherlands. The Dutch included in their claim a part of the Connecticut, the valley of the Hudson and its *hinterland,* and the territory to the south which included what is now New Jersey and Delaware. The Dutch claim was never formally recognized by England; and there was no serious effort made by the Dutch to colonize the present New Jersey, except in the immediate vicinity of Manhattan Island, on the west bank of the Hudson, and the Passaic and Hackensack valleys. A fort was erected on the lower Delaware to defend the Dutch claim to the territory bordering on the river.

The Indians were never very numerous in New Jersey after the advent of the white settlers. It has been estimated that in 1648 there were about two thousand warriors in all throughout the various tribes; subsequently they disappeared.[1]

Following the Dutch, the Swedes came to Delaware; they laid claim to the land on both banks of the river up to the Falls (now Trenton). They built a fort on the west bank near the present site of Wilmington; and there a small settlement grew up. The claim of the Swedes was not recognized by the Dutch; and in 1655, the settlers were attacked and their fortification destroyed. The principal inhabitants were sent prisoners to New Amsterdam, and later transported to Holland; though some of the poorer settlers remained in the country, submitting to Dutch rule. In the southern part of New Jersey, neither Dutch nor Swedish settlers were numerous; and their influence counted for little in the development of the colony. "Such settlements as they had made were confined to a small area, and what few inhabitants remained were gradually absorbed in the English colonization which soon

[1] *Edwin Robert Walker: History of Trenton, pp. 10, 11.*

followed."[2]   The Swedish settlers were served by their own ministers;
churches were built, some of which were afterwards taken over by the
Church of England, for example, the Old Swedes Church of Wilmington, St. George's in Penn's Neck, and Gloria Dei, Philadelphia.   In
northern New Jersey (afterwards known as East Jersey), the Dutch
influence was permanent, especially along the Hudson and in the adjacent country.

On the 23rd of June, 1664, the Duke of York granted to Lord John
Berkeley, baron of Stratton, and Sir George Carteret of Saltrum, all
that territory "lying and being to the westward of Long Island and
Manhitees Island, and bounded on the East part by the main sea and
part by Hudson's river, and hath upon the West Delaware bay or river,
and extending southward to the main ocean as far as Cape May at
the mouth of Delaware bay, and to the northward as far as the northern-
most branch of the said bay or river of Delaware, which is 41° and 40'
of latitude, and crosseth over thence in a straight line to Hudson's river
is 41° of latitude; which said tract of land is hereafter to be called by
the name or names of New Caesaria or New Jersey."[3]   The colony was
afterwards divided into the two separate governments of East Jersey
and West Jersey; Carteret received the former, and Berkeley the latter.
Neither of these men ever visited America; and the boundaries of their
grants having been determined, separate governors were appointed.
Little thought was occasioned by the religious needs of the colonists:
the English, "in their first settlement of this Province, seemed to mind
more the business of their Trade and Plantations, than the great concern of their souls."[4]

Inducements were offered to stimulate immigration.   The first
English settlers of New Jersey were Quakers and Anabaptists; but the
first European settlers had been the Swedes and the Dutch, as we
have seen.   They introduced their own laws, government, and religion.
It is reported that there were some fifty families in Middletown about
1650.   Some English Quakers were brought over from Hull to Burlington, in 1678, by the "Shield".   After the death of Carteret, the
colony of East Jersey was sold to liquidate his debts; and William
Penn, Robert West, and others were the purchasers.   These men, who
composed the Quaker syndicate, took to themselves twelve partners, and
for that reason that portion of Jersey became the colony of the twelve proprietors.   Among these purchasers was James, Earl of Perth, from

[2]*Hamilton Schuyler's Manuscript. (The late Dr. Schuyler began the writing
of a history of the Episcopal Church in New Jersey. The unfinished manuscript
is in possession of the Diocese of New Jersey.)*
[3]*Winsor: Narrative and Critical History, III., p. 422.*
[4]*Jeremiah Bass's account, in Protestant Episcopal Historical Collections, 1851,
pp. 67 ff.*

whom Perth Amboy, the seat of government of East Jersey[5] derived its name. The celebrated Quaker divine, Robert Barclay, was elected first governor; and while he never made a trip to East Jersey, he probably influenced many of the Friends to settle there.

"The colonists of East Jersey, besides original emigrants from England and Scotland, were recruited mainly from New England, Long Island, and Connecticut; and had been attracted thither by the liberal government of Berkeley and Carteret, and by opportunities afforded through the fertility of the soil, fisheries, and commerce. These settlers were of dour Puritan and Calvinistic stock, and brought with them the peculiar religious, civil, and moral equipment which characterized them in the old country or which they had acquired in the New England communities whence they came. They were staunch individualists, intolerant, devoted to the Protestant religion as they understood it, tenacious of their civil rights, and above all bitterly opposed to the Church of England. Their life centered around the town-meeting, the church, and the school; and their chosen leaders were their ministers. These early settlers occupied land in Newark, Elizabeth, Woodbridge and upon the northern portion of the shore of Monmouth county."[6] They began to arrive before 1669; soon afterwards, several towns had sprung into life in the province.

In 1680, the Reverend Alexander Innes came to Middletown; according to old records, he held services in the house of one John Stout, while the public building was in course of construction. He was a native of Scotland, and preached to all denominations; his ministrations continued till his death in 1713.[7]

Lord Berkeley sold his interest in West Jersey, in 1683, to John Fenwick and Edward Billings, who were noted Quakers.[8] The same year a tract was issued to influence settlers, which contained the following language:

> "Libertie in matters of Religion is established in the fullest manner. To be a Planter or Inhabitant, nothing is more required but the acknowledging of one *Almighty* GOD, and to have a Share in the Government, a simple profession of faith of Jesus Christ, without descending into any other of the differences among Christians, only that Religion may not be a cloak for disturbance, whoever comes into the Magistrature, must declare, they hold not themselves in Conscience obliged, for Religion's Sake, to make an alteration, or to endeavour

[5] *W. Northey Jones: St. Peter's Church, Perth Amboy, p. 12.*
[6] *Hamilton Schuyler's Manuscript, cited supra.*
[7] *E. W. Mandeville: Story of Middletown, p. 100.*
[8] *W. Northey Jones: St. Peter's Church, Perth Amboy, p. 12.*

to turn out their partners in the Government, Because they differ in Opinion from them, and this is no more than to follow that great Rule, To do as they would be done by."[9]

The proprietors of East Jersey drew up an act surrendering their share of the province in 1688; they were tired of governing it.[10] The population continued to increase. In 1695, several persons described as "Inhabitants in and about Burlington" purchased a parcel of land as a burial place for themselves and all other Christians so minded to bury their dead. This plot of ground was later enlarged for the purpose of building a church. Burlington was described by Gabriel Thomas three years later as "the chiefest Town in that Countrey."

Besides the advantage of being the seat of government of East Jersey, Perth Amboy was favourably located; hence the town grew rapidly. The Scotch comprised a large element of the population, and there were many Quakers among the residents. Among the prominent members of that body, George Keith is notable, not only because he was an influential leader and a teacher of renown, but also because he became later an important figure in the history of Anglican missions. In the course of this study, a good deal will be said regarding him; at present it may be remarked that he was surveyor-general of the colony, and that he ran the division line between East and West Jersey in the year 1687. There were quite a few English Roundheads at Perth Amboy, as well as some churchmen—men of authority and influence. The proprietors set aside one of the houses erected at public cost for the use of the Church of England; some of the Quaker settlers began to identify themselves with the Church. The building appropriated for Anglican services was repaired and fitted up for a church by subscription. A stone, bearing the date "1685" and supposed to have been the cornerstone of the original church edifice, was taken from this early building and embedded in the rear wall of the present St. Peter's Church (built in 1852).[11]

In the western division of the province there were for some years no settled congregations except those of the Quakers. Divines passed through occasionally, preaching and administering baptism; "and by that means sowed the Seeds of the Gospel, that have since sprung up amongst us, and excited some of the desires of the Inhabitants to make a more diligent enquiry into the true way of worshipping God and had in some measure taken off those prejudices that most of the Inhabitants laboured under, by education, example and reading the Books and hear-

[9]*A Brief Account of the Province of East-New-Jersey in America, 1683; Historical Magazine, 2nd series, I., p. 94.*
[10]*Winsor: Narrative and Critical History, V., p. 217.*
[11]*Archives of the General Convention (edited by Lowndes), VI., p. 349.*

ing the discourse of such as had misrepresented both the Doctrine and Discipline of the Church of England."[12]

Commenting on conditions political and ecclesiastical, the late Doctor Hamilton Schuyler remarked that the times were troublous in Church and State, following in the wake of the great religious upheaval of the Sixteenth Century, and synchronising closely with the English political revolution of 1688. "The fires of religious persecution had then hardly ceased to glow; and the Established Church was still intent upon exacting at least a measure of conformity from those who dissented from its teaching and practice."

> "If the Quakers and other dissenting settlers were not impelled to emigrate from their homes on account of actual physical persecution, at least they suffered from the memory of it, and in any event they incurred in England certain political, social, and religious disabilities. In coming hither, they hoped not only to enjoy full religious liberty, but also to improve their material conditions. In both of these respects they were successful. Without civil interference, they set up their respective ecclesiastical organizations and proceeded to practice their religion according to the dictates of their conscience."[13]

The history of Anglican services in New Jersey begins properly with the arrival of the Reverend Edward Portlock, who came over at the desire of the proprietors of the eastern division, to take charge of Perth Amboy. While Portlock was waiting for the house set apart for worship to be covered, glazed, and fitted with pews, he preached at the governor's house and at other dwellings; he visited the towns of Woodbridge, Piscataway, and Elizabeth Town also, and accompanied the governor to Burlington, where he held services in the public townhouse.[14] He was in New Jersey about 1698, but did not remain long. Not much is known regarding him. He was ordained priest by the Bishop of London, May 11th, 1691; but in his ordination certificate no university was designated. Colonel Robert Quarry of Philadelphia described him as "a great scholar, a very eminent preacher, and a man of good life."[15] The Council of the East Jersey proprietors agreed on March 3rd, 1699, to pay the cost of his passage.[16]

Mr. Portlock moved to Philadelphia and then, from 1702 to 1705, and perhaps longer, he was minister of Stratton-Major Parish, King

[12]*Jeremiah Bass's account, in Protestant Episcopal Historical Collections, 1851, pp. 67 ff.*

[13]*Hamilton Schuyler's Manuscript, cited supra.*

[14]*Jeremiah Bass's account, in Protestant Episcopal Historical Collections, 1851, pp. 67 ff.*

[15]*W. Northey Jones: St. Peter's Church, Perth Amboy, p. 23.*

[16]*Ibid., p. 19.*

and Queen county, Virginia. There the vestry requested that he be inducted as rector.[17] In the memorable controversy between Commissary James Blair, the founder of William and Mary College, and Colonel Francis Nicholson, the governor of the Colony, Mr. Portlock took sides with the governor. We find his name, with the names of several other clergymen, affixed to a letter in 1704, complaining of Doctor Blair; and Portlock was present at a meeting held at Williamsburg, August 29th, 1705, the day before the convention of the Virginia clergy, where he helped draw up a letter sustaining Governor Nicholson and withholding recognition from the commissary.[18]

Immorality was sufficiently prevalent in the new land to cause uneasiness; so we have the proclamation of Governor Bass, of date April 8th, 1698, and intended to bring about "the extirpation of all sorts of looseness & prophanitie & . . . (instead) the frank love of God & of one another . . . (that) all heats & animosities & dissentions may vanish & the blessing of Almighty God accompany our honest & lawful endeavours." The same pronouncement prohibited cursing, swearing, immoderate drinking, Sabbath-breaking, and all sorts of lewdness and profane behaviour in word and action.[19]

The relaxation of moral standards had been observed by others. Colonel Lewis Morris of Shrewsbury, probably the most eminent churchman of the colony, submitted a memorial concerning the state of religion in the Jerseys, which had considerable effect in arousing the English people to their obligation and opportunity. Colonel Morris said:—

"The Province of East Jersey has in it Ten Towns, (viz.) Middletown, Freehold, Amboy, Piscataway, and Woodbridge, Elizabeth Town, Newark, Aqueckenonck, and Bergen, and I Judge in the whole Province there may be about Eight thousand souls. These Towns are not like the towns in England, the houses built close together on a small spot of ground, but they include large portions of the Country of 4, 5, 8, 10, 12, 15 miles in length, and as much in breadth, and all the Settlements within such State and bounds is said to be within such a Township, but in most of those townships there is some place where a part of the Inhabitants sat down nearer together than the rest, and confined themselves to smaller portions of ground, and the town is more peculiarly designed by that Settlement. Those towns and the whole province was peopl'd mostly from the adjacent colonies of New York and New England, and

[17]*Goodwin: Colonial Church in Virginia, p. 299.*
[18]*Fulham MSS., Virginia Box III., #27 (Stevens and Brown Library of Congress Transcript); W. Northey Jones: St. Peter's Church, Perth Amboy, pp. 24-25.*
[19]*W. Northey Jones: St. Peter's Church, Perth Amboy, p. 21.*

generally by Those of very narrow fortunes, and such as could not well subsist in the places they left. And if such people could bring any religion with them, it was that of the Country they came from, and the State of them is as follows:—

"BERGEN, and the out Plantations are most Dutch, and were settled from New York and the United Provinces they are pretty equally divided into Calvinist and Lutheran, they have one pretty little Church, and are a sober people, there are a few English Dissenters mixt among them.

"AQUECKENONCK was peopl'd from New York also, they are Dutch mostly and generally Calvinist.

"ELIZABETH TOWN & NEWARK, were peopled from New England, are generally Independents, they have a meeting house in each town for their public worship, there are some few Churchmen, Presbiterians, Anabaptists, and Quakers settled among them.

"WOODBRIDGE was settled from New England and were generally Independents till about 16 years since, there was a number of Scots Presbiterians amongst them, the People are divided mostly into Presbiterians and Independents, and there is mixt amongst them Baptists, Quakers, Ranters, cum multis aliis.

"PISCATAWAY was settled from New England, and is called the Anabaptist Town, from about twenty in that Town that agree in that Persuasion, the rest of the People are of all, or of no religion.

"PERTH AMBOY the Capital City was settled from Europe, and we have made a shift to patch up the old ruinous house, and make a church of it, and when all the Churchmen in the Province are got together, we make up about twelve Communicants, the People of that town are a mixture of all Persuasion.

"FREEHOLD was settled from Scotland (Mr. Keith began the first settlement there, and made a fine Plantation, which he afterwards Sold, and went into Pensilvania) and about the one-half of it are Scotch Presbiterians, and a sober people, the other part of it was settled by People (some from New England, some from New York, and some from the forementioned towns) who are generally speaking of no religion. There is in this Town a Quaker Meeting-house, but most of the Quakers who built it are come off, with Mr. Keith, they have not fixt yet on any religion, but are most inclinable to the Church, and could Mr. Keith be persuaded to go into those Countrys, he would (with the blessing of God) not only bring to the Church the Quakers that come off with him in East & West Jersey, which are very numerous, but make many Converts in that Country.

"MIDDLETOWN was settled from New York and New England, it is a large Township, there is no such thing as

Church or Religion amongst them, they are p'haps the most
ignorant and wicked People in the world, their meetings on
Sundays is at the Public house, where they get their fill of
Rum, and go to fighting & running of races which are Prac-
tices much in use that day all the Province over.

"SHREWSBURY settled from New England, Rhode
Island and New York, there is in it ab't thirty Quakers of both
Sexes, and they have a meeting house, the rest of the People
are generally of no Religion—the Youth of the whole Province
are very debauch'd and very ignorant, and the Sabbath day
seems there to be set apart for Rioting and Drunkenness. In
a word, a general Ignorance and immorality runs through the
Youth of the whole Province."

Colonel Morris described the settlers of West Jersey in far from
flattering terms; that province was "a hotch-potch of all religions."
He felt that no man should be sent as a governor to any of the plantations but a firm churchman, and, if possible, that none but churchmen
be in his council and in the magistracy; also, that no clergyman be
admitted to any considerable benefice in England, before he has preached
"three years gratis in America."[20]

Local historians have accused Colonel Morris of personal religious
and political bias. It is known that his arraignment was bitterly re-
sented at the time; probably his statements were exaggerated. Edward
Salter, writing in the *Monmouth Democrat,* 1873-4, said:—

"This statement that there was no such thing as religion
or a Church in Middletown was a deliberate falsehood. . . .
This account of Governor Lewis Morris should be received
with considerable allowance not alone because of his animosity
to the Middletown people, who had so frequently prevented
him and ignored his authority, but at the time he wrote this
letter he was anxious to secure the appointment of Governor
from the British Crown. . . . Lewis Morris was an ambitious
and crafty man, and would have put the yoke of priestly titles
on the people of Monmouth without scruples, if he could have
advanced his own interests."[21]

In 1698, Perth Amboy received one of the parish libraries sent
through the efforts of the Reverend Doctor Thomas Bray to America.
The donor's accounts show a gift of thirty books, worth six pounds and
fourteen shillings. Five hundred pastoral letters were also sent to the
town, to be distributed to every family; likewise copies of discourses on

---

[20]*Ernest Hawkins: Historical Notices of the Missions of the Church of England, pp. 22-23.*
[21]*Edwin Salter: Old Times in Old Monmouth, p. 265 (quoted by Hamilton
Schuyler).*

the Covenant of Grace were forwarded for the edification of those preparing for the Holy Communion.[22]

Doctor Bray declared in his memorial to the Archbishop of Canterbury, the Bishop of London, and others, that the Jerseys have some pretty towns, and well people, "but are wholly left to themselves without Priest or Altar." The New England Independents were trying to introduce their cult. "True it is," he said, "Mr. Mathers (Mather) from New England seems now to bestir himself in sending both there and into the other colonies, where he sees us take footing. His Independent Preachers and the Quakers are very numerous in the Jerseys, but I am credibly informed that the people are more affected to our Clergy, could they have them."[23]

Though no definite plan was in operation to supply the American colonies with the ministrations of Anglican clergy, the governors sent to the provinces were given instructions embodying a particular regard for the welfare of the Church. The instructions of Lord Cornbury, licensed as governor of New York and New Jersey, September 9th, 1701, contained the following paragraphs:—

"69. You shall take especial care, that God Almighty be devoutly and duly served throughout your Government. The book of common prayer as by law established, read each Sunday and Holy Day, and the Blessed Sacrament administered according to the rites of the Church of England.

"70. You shall be careful that the Churches already built there, be well and orderly kept, and that more be built, as the Colony shall by God's blessing be improved; and that besides a competent maintenance be assigned to the minister of each orthodox Church, a convenient house be built at the common charge for each minister, and a competent proportion of land assigned to him, for a glebe and exercise of his industry.

"71. And you are to take care that the parishes be so limited and settled, as you shall find most convenient for the establishment of this good work.

"72. You are not to prefer any minister to any ecclesiastical benefice in that our province, without a certificate from the Right Reverend father in God, the Lord Bishop of London, of his being conformable to the doctrine and discipline of the Church of England, and of a good life and conversation; and if any person already prefer'd to a benefice shall appear to you to give scandal either by his doctrine or manners, you are to use the best means for the removal of him and to supply the vacancy in such manner as we have directed.

[22]*Dr. Bray's Accounts, Part I., pp. 19, 26, 28, 29 (Photostat in Library of Congress).*
[23]*Protestant Episcopal Historical Collections, 1851, p. 100.*

"73. You are to give order, that every orthodox minister within your Government, be one of the vestry in his respective parish, and that no vestry be held without him, except in case of sickness, or that after the notice of a vestry summon'd he omit to come.

"74. You are to enquire whether there be any minister within your Government, who preaches and administers the Sacraments in any Orthodox Church or Chapel, without being in due orders, and to give account thereof to the said Lord Bishop of London."[24]

[24]*Samuel Smith: History of the Colony of Nova Caesarea or New Jersey reprint 1890, pp. 230-261 (instructions given in full).*

II. The Founding of the Venerable Society, and the Mission of Keith and Talbot.

The Society for the Propagation of the Gospel in Foreign Parts—known generally as the "S. P. G."—sprang into being largely through the efforts of the Reverend Doctor Thomas Bray, one of the great philanthropists of his time. During his short stay in Maryland as the commissary of the Lord Bishop of London, Doctor Bray had ample opportunity to observe the weakness of the Church in the American colonies and the haphazard, unsystematic way in which clergymen were enlisted for the service and supported while in the ranks. He witnessed the fewness of number which left large areas unshepherded or exposed them to all sorts of dissenting and demoralising religious influences; he recognised the temptations to discouragement and indolence to which the ministers were subjected in their solitary work, far removed from the companionship of educated men and the stimulus of their fellow-clergy, while face to face with unresponsive, apathetic people; he also perceived the precarious nature of their livelihood, the uncertain stipends and the capricious tendencies of the vestries. Returning to England, Doctor Bray sought the means of ensuring for America a steady supply of accredited ministers, sufficient to extend the influence of the Church over a much broader area; these ministers, furthermore, were to be free from anxiety so far as their living was concerned.

By charter granted June 16th, 1701, the Archbishop of Canterbury and ninety-three others (all named) were incorporated as "The Society for the Propagation of the Gospel in Foreign Parts." The instrument of incorporation provided for perpetual succession, the power to purchase and inherit as well as to grant and devise, the right to sue and be impleaded, the authority to have and use a common seal. The annual meeting was set for the third Friday in February, at which time officers would be chosen for the ensuing year; the Archbishop of Canterbury was to be the first president. Business would be transacted on the third Friday of each month; more frequently, if necessary. A yearly reckoning was to be made to the Lord Chancellor or Keeper and two chief justices, or two of them, of all money received and expended.

The design of incorporation was thus expressed in the charter:

"Whereas Wee are credibly informed that in many of our Plantacons, Colonies, and Factories beyond the Seas, belonging to Our Kingdome of England, the Provision for Ministers

is very mean. And many others of Our said Plantãcons, Col-
onies, and Factories are wholy destitute, and unprovided of a
Mainteynance for Ministers, and the Publick Worshipp of
God; and for Lack of Support and Mainteynance for such,
many of our Loveing Subjects doe want the Administration of
God's Word and Sacraments, and seem to be abandoned to
Atheism and Infidelity and alsoe for Want of Learned and
Orthodox Ministers to instruct Our said Loveing Subjects in
the Principles of true Religion, divers Romish Priests and
Jesuits are the more incouraged to pervert and draw over Our
said Loveing Subjects to Popish Superstition and Idolatry

"And whereas Wee think it Our Duty as much as in Us
lyes, to promote the Glory of God, by the Instrucon of Our
People in the Christian Religion And that it will be highly
conducive for accomplishing those Ends, that a sufficient Main-
teyance be provided for an Orthodox Clergy to live amongst
them, and that such other Provision be made, as may be necessary for the Propagation of the Gospell in those Parts:

"And whereas Wee have been well assured, That if Wee
would be gratiously pleased to erect and settle a Corporation
for the receiving, manageing, and disposing of the Charity of
Our Loveing Subjects, divers Persons would be induced to extend their Charity to the Uses and Purposes aforesaid

"Know yee therefore, That Wee have for the Consid-
eracons aforesaid, and for the better and more orderly carrying on the said Charitable Purposes, of our speciall Grace,
certain Knowledge, and meer Mocon, Willed, Ordained, Constituted, and Appointed, and by these Presents, for Us, Our
Heires, and Successors, doe Will, Ordaine, Constitute, Declare,
and Grant, that the most Reverend Fathers in God" . . .
(Here follow the names) . . . "and their Successors to be
elected in Manner as hereafter directed, Be, and shall for ever
hereafter be, and by Vertue of these Presents shall be one
Body Politick and Corporate, in Deed and in Name, by the
Name of, THE SOCIETY FOR THE PROPAGATION
OF THE GOSPEL IN FORREIGNE PARTS: And them
and their Successors, by the same Name, Wee doe by these
Presents, for Us, Our Heires, and Successors, really and
fully Make, Ordaine, Constitute, and Declare One Body
Politick and Corporate, in Deed and in Name."[25]

It is hard to realise how weak the Church of England was in the
colonies at the time that the S. P. G. was founded. Outside the colonies
of Virginia and Maryland (where the English Church was established
by law) there was but the merest handful of Anglican clergymen with
cures. It is estimated that in all the American provinces, there were
fewer than fifty ministers of the Established Church. Various dissenting

[25]*C. F. Pascoe: Two Hundred Years of the S. P. G., II., p. 932. This is the
first printed edition of the Charter in which the original spelling has been followed.*

bodies were making rapid headway, while the English Church had very little prestige. The Anglican colonists were compelled to depend on clergymen sent from England; and this involved expense, loss of time, the dangers of travel, the risk of capture by some hostile power, and the exposure to disease. The existence and activity of the Venerable Society served to put the Church on its feet; and from the time that its activities began, there was steady progress.

After the preliminaries of organisation were over, "the Society did enquire for such Persons in Holy Orders as would cheerfully undertake to go over into those Plantations . . . and for their Encouragement, did supply them with Books and other Necessaries to carry with them and to subsist them in their Voyage; with stated Salaries to support them in their itinerant Missions or settled Stations, to continue at least for three Years, till the Inhabitants should be more able and willing to make and settle some legal Provision for them." Care was taken to find ministers "of a sober and exemplary life," men "moved with a desire of undertaking such an apostolical work, from the principles of conscience and true religion." The Society required of the minister sent to the colonies, information regarding (1) his age; (2) his condition of life, whether single or married; (3) his temper; (4) his prudence; (5) his learning; (6) his sober and pious conversation; (7) his zeal for the Christian religion and diligence in his holy calling; (8) his affection to the present government; (9) his conformity to the doctrine and discipline of the Church of England. Strict care was exercised in the selection of missionaries.[26] All the bishops were invited to canvass for clergymen willing to go to the colonies; provided, "that before their departure, they should wait upon his Grace the Archbishop of Canterbury, their Metropolitan, the Lord Bishop of London, their Diocesan, to receive their Paternal Benediction and Instructions." They were to keep up regular correspondence with the Secretary of the Society; and to send every six months a *notitia parochialis,* or statement of their respective parishes. They were also to communicate whatever was done at the meetings of the clergy and such other matters as might concern the Society.

The missionaries were given the following directions for their guidance:

"*Upon Arrival in the Country whither they shall be sent.*

"First, *With Respect to themselves.*

"I. That they always keep in their View the great Design of their Undertaking, *viz.* to promote the Glory of Almighty

[26]*Account of S. P. G. . . . London, 1706.*

God, and the Salvation of Men, by propagating the Gospel of our Lord and Saviour.

"II. That they often consider the Qualifications requisite for those who would effectually promote this Design, *viz.* A sound knowledge and hearty Belief of the Christian Religion; and Apostolical Zeal temper'd with Prudence, Humility, Meekness, and Patience; a fervent Charity towards the Souls of Men; and finally that Temperance, Fortitude, and Constancy, which become good Soldiers of Jesus Christ.

"III. That in order to the obtaining and preserving the said Qualifications, they do very frequently in their Retirements offer up fervent Prayers to Almighty God for his Direction and Assistance; converse much with the Holy Scriptures; seriously reflect upon their Ordination Vows; and consider the Account which they are to render to the great Shepherd and Bishop of Souls, at the last Day.

"IV. That they acquaint themselves thorowly with the Doctrine of the Church of *England,* as contain'd in the Articles and Homilies; its Worship and Discipline, and Rules for Behaviour of the Clergy, as contain'd in the Liturgy and Canons; and that they approve themselves accordingly, as genuine Missionaries from this Church.

"V. That they endeavour to make themselves Masters in those Controversies, which are necessary to be understood in order to the preserving their Flock from the Attempts of such Gainsayers as are mixt among them.

"VI. That in their outward Behaviour they be circumspect and unblameable, giving no Offence either in Word or Deed; that their ordinary Discourse be grave and edifying; their Apparel decent, and proper for Clergy-Men; and that in their whole Conversation they be Instances and Patterns of the Christian Life.

"VII. That they do not board in, or frequent publick-houses, or lodge in Families of Evil Fame; that they wholly abstain from Gaming, and all vain Pastimes; and converse not familiarly with lewd or prophane Persons, otherwise than in order to reprove, admonish, and reclaim them.

"VIII. That in whatsoever Family they shall lodge, they perswade them to join with them in daily Prayer Morning and Evening.

"IX. That they be not nice about Meats and Drinks, nor immoderately careful about their Entertainment in the Places where they shall sojourn; be contented with what Health requires, and the Place easily affords.

"X. That as they be Frugal in Opposition to Luxury: so they avoid all Appearance of Covetousness, and recommend themselves according to their Abilities by the prudent Exercise of Liberality and Charity.

"XI. That they take special Care to give no Offence to

the Civil Government, by intermedling in Affairs not relating to their own Calling and Function.

"XII. That avoiding all Names of Distinction, they endeavour to preserve a Christian Agreement and Union one with another, as a Body of Brethren of one and the same Church, united under the Superior Episcopal Order, and all engaged in the same great Design of Propagating the Gospel; and to this End keeping up a Brotherly Correspondence, by meeting together at certain Times, as shall be most convenient for mutual Advice and Assistance.

"Secondly, *With Respect to their Parochial Cure.*

"That they conscientiously observe the Rules of our Liturgy in the Performance of all the Offices of their Ministry.

"II. That beside the stated Service appointed for Sundays and Holy-days, they do, as far as they shall find it practicable, publickly read the daily Morning and Evening Service, and decline no fair Opportunity of Preaching to such as may be Occasionally met together from Remote and Distant Parts.

"III. That they perform every part of Divine Service with that Seriousness and Decency, that may recommend their Ministrations to their Flock, and excite a Spirit of Devotion in them.

"IV. That the chief Subjects of their Sermons be the great Fundamental Principles of Christianity, and the Duties of a sober, righteous, and godly Life, as resulting from those Principles.

"V. That they particularly preach against those Vices, which they shall observe to be most Predominant in the Places of their Residence.

"VI. That they carefully instruct the People concerning the Nature and Use of the Sacraments of Baptism and the Lord's-Supper, as the peculiar Institutions of Christ, Pledges of Communion with him, and Means of deriving Grace from him.

"VII. That they duly consider the Qualifications of those adult Persons, to whom they administer Baptism; and of those likewise whom they admit to the Lord's-Supper, according to the Directions of the Rubricks in our Liturgy.

"VIII. That they take a special Care, to lay a good Foundation, for all their other Ministrations, by Catechizing those under their Care, whether Children or other ignorant Persons, explaining the Catechism to them in the most easie and familiar Manner.

"IX. That in their Instructing *Heathens* and *Infidels,* they begin with the Principles of natural Religion, appealing to their Reason and Conscience; and thence proceed to shew them the Necessity of Revelation, and the Certainty of that contained in the Holy Scriptures, by the plain and most obvious Arguments.

"X. That they frequently visit their respective Parishioners; those of our own Communion, to keep them steady in the Possession and Practice of Religion, as taught in the Church of *England;* those that oppose us, or dissent from us, to convince and reclaim them, with a spirit of meekness and Gentleness.

"XI. That those whose Parishes shall be of large extent, shall, as they have Opportunity and Convenience, officiate in the several Parts thereof, so that all the Inhabitants may by turns partake of their Ministrations; and that such as shall be appointed to officiate in several places, shall reside sometimes at one, sometimes at another of those Places, as the Necessities of the People shall require.

"XII. That they shall, to the best of their Judgments, distribute those small Tracts given by the Society for that Purpose, amongst such of their Parishioners as shall want them most, and appear likely to make the best Use of them; and that such useful Books, of which they have not a sufficient Number to give, they be ready to lend to those who will be most careful in reading and restoring them.

"XIII. That they encourage the setting up Schools for the teaching of Children; and particularly by the widows of such Clergy-Men as shall die in those Countries, if they be found capable of that Employment.

"XIV. That each of them keep a Register of his Parishioners Names, Profession of Religion, Baptism, &c. according to the Scheme annex'd N°. I. for his own Satisfaction, and the Benefit of the People.

"Thirdly, *With Respect to the Society.*

"I. That each of them keep a constant and regular Correspondence with the Society, by their Secretary.

"II. That they send every six Months an Account of the State of their respective Parishes, according to the Scheme annex'd, N°. II.

"III. That they communicate what shall be done at the Meetings of the Clergy, when settled, and whatsoever else may concern the Society."[27]

At the second meeting of the Society, held at the Cockpit, July 8th, 1701, it was decided that the motto of the seal should be: *Sigillum Societatis de Promovendo Evangelio in Partibus Transmarinis.* The device chosen was: "A ship under sail, making towards a point of land, upon the Prow standing a Minister with an open Bible in his hand, People standing on the shore in a Posture of Expectation, and using

[27]*Ibid., pp. 24ff.*

these words: *Transiens Adjuva Nos."*

At the meeting held August 15th of the same year, the Society set about ascertaining the religious state of the colonies. Information was sought from the Bishop of London, from English merchants, from colonial governors, and from the congregations. Letters were written to people of distinction in the plantations. Some of the reports were gloomy; the colonies were exposed to atheism and popery. Colonel Lewis Morris's memorial was read at the meeting of September 19th; he gave, as we have seen, a picture of the needs of New Jersey. He likewise described conditions in Pennsylvania. At the same meeting, a report by Colonel Dudley, Governor of New England, was read. He described the population of West Jersey as "Two thousand Souls most Quakers, may yet have one Minister, at present, supported from England;" and East Jersey as "Six thousand Souls in about Seven Towns and Parishes, may at present support Two Ministers, the rest being Dissenters." In conclusion, he said:

> "The Ministers to be sent from England to any of the abovesaid Colonies, must be men of good learning, sound morals, and should not be very young; and where there is not the view of a good support from their hearers, must be supplied from hence that they be not in Contempt, but may be well provided for in those parts where the Governments are immediately dependant upon the Crown and Government of England."[28]

A letter from the Reverend George Keith was brought to the attention of the Society at the same meeting. This letter is of considerable importance, as it probably caused the members to appoint Keith as the first official inspector, to make a personal tour of the colonies and report their actual wants and problems. Keith was a remarkable man. He was born in Aberdeen about 1638; and was educated in the University of that city. Originally a Presbyterian, he became a Quaker in early manhood, achieving great distinction in that sect. In fact, he was the recognised leader of the orthodox party of Friends. In 1682, he moved to America; and from 1685 to 1688, he held the position of surveyor-general of the province of East Jersey. The division line between New York and East Jersey, which he ran, was repudiated by the proprietors; so another line was run. Keith moved to Philadelphia in 1689; and there he took charge of the Friends' school. He was regarded as the greatest preacher among the American Quakers; and,

[28]*This report is printed in Earnest Hawkins: Historical Notices of the Missions of the Church of England, pp. 23-25; also in the Protestant Episcopal Historical Collections, 1851, pp. xiv-xv.*

because of his pronounced views and his fearless speech, he was involved in a good deal of controversy. Quakerism failed to satisfy his orthodox leanings; and at length he sought and obtained ordination within the Church of England.

In his letter to the Society, he wrote (addressing the Secretary):

"According to your desire I send you this short Memorial of the State of Religion in such parts of North America where I have travelled, and which I can give of my own knowledge, especially in relation to Quakerism and some other things by letters from my friends there."

When Keith started living in Philadelphia, in 1689, he told the Secretary, it was evident from the number of men and women who used to attend the yearly meetings from Pennsylvania and West and East Jersey, that there were at least fifteen hundred Quakers. But,—

"After the breach that began in the year 1691 betwixt a party of Quakers that joined with me in opposing some of their errors (especially their notion of the sufficiency of the light within every man to salvation without anything else) and another Party that joyned with Thomas Lloyd then Deputy Governor of Pennsylvania and a great Preacher among the Quakers, all the Meetings in those Provinces aforementioned were broken, and they set up Separate Meetings one from another, on the account of different Principles of Religion . . . so that when I came from Pennsylvania to England, which was in the year 1694, I left behind me fourteen or fifteen Meetings in Pennsylvania, West and East Jerseys, that met apart from the Quakers (on the account of their opposition to their Errors) to the number of above Five hundred persons.

"Since there hath been a Church of England Congregation set up at Philadelphia, the Chief Town in Pennsylvania, a considerable number of those that did come off with me on the account of the Quakers Errors are joyned with the Church of England, both Men and Women of good account, and others of them keep up their Separate Meetings, particularly one at Philadelphia, and some of them have joyned themselves with the Anabaptists in those Parts, as I have had particular Information by letters from my friends there, year after year . . .

"In West Jersey there lyes on the east side of Delaware River, I have several friends that joyned with me in the Separation from the Quakers, especially about Croswicks, which is about Fifteen or Sixteen miles from Burlington (the Chief Town in West Jersey lying by Delaware River); if a Church of England Minister were sent thither it is not to be doubted but he would be received and joyned with, both by some of my friends and some other sober persons. The most proper place to set up a Church would be at Burlington, and another at Croswicks abovementioned.

"In East Jersey I have several friends that came off with me in the Separation from the Quakers, and so continue, and as I have been informed by a worthy gentleman, Colonel Morris, formerly my scholar, who has a family and a good estate in that Province, and is now in London, (being lately come from East Jersey, who knows my friends there) they are well prepared to receive a Church of England Minister among them, and it is not to be doubted but he would have several other persons to joyn with him to set up a Church Congregation; the fittest places to set up a Church Congregation are Amboy and the Falls in Shrewsbury, near where Colonel Morris has his house and estate, for though Amboy has few Inhabitants, yet People would come to it from Woodbridge and other places thereabouts.

"The people of East Jersey who are not Quakers, are generally Independents, having originally come from New England, but the young generation might easily be brought off to the Church, if they have any Church set up among them.

"East Jersey has six or seven considerable Towns in it, as Shrewsbury, Middletown, Woodbridge, Piscataway, Elizabeth and Newark Town; the Inhabitants generally all English that came originally from New England, about Thirty years ago; and Bergen, inhabited generally with Dutch, all Calvinists who have a Dutch Minister.

"There is not one Church of England as yet in either West or East Jersey, the more is the pity; and except in Two or Three Towns there is no place of any public worship of any sort, but People live very mean like Indians."

Keith included some notes regarding the other colonies. In New York, he said, there were very few Quakers; "and some that were, are come off and joyned with the Church there." Long Island did not contain many of the Quaker persuasion. "It is a great place and has many Inhabitants, English and Dutch; the Dutch are Calvinists and have some Calvinistical Congregations; the English some of them Independents, but many of them no Religion, but like Wild Indians; there is no Church of England in all Long Island, nor in all that great Continent of New York Province, except at New York Town. The places where the Quakers have their greatest Meeting in Long Island are Flushing and Oyster Bay, in both which places I have been several times at their Meetings."

"In Road Island where I have been several times, there are many Quakers and Anabaptists, but never had a Church of England until of late.

"In all the Continent of New England there is no Church of England I think, but at Boston, I have travelled through much of it, but never heard of any but that one. Few Quakers are at Boston. There are some at Sandwich, some at Piscataway and other scattered Places, but very few."

Keith, having outlined specific conditions, proceeded to make practical suggestions for the upbuilding of the Church of England in that vast country in which it was scarcely known.

"It seems a good expedient to me that such Ministers as go over into these parts that I have named, should not constantly reside in one place at present, but preach at several places through the whole Province, which they may safely now travel through from one end to another, with little charge or difficulty.

"And that a considerable number of little books, such as the Pastoral Letter, and those against Swearing, Drunkenness, and Sabbath breaking were sent to be spread among them. And if a little book were printed by some able man, to show the sin of Schism, to persuade to the Communion of the Church of England, and sent among them, it would be of good service."

The following postscript was added to the letter:

"Such as go over into those parts for the propagation of the Gospel, should be men of solidity and good experience, as well as otherwise qualified with good learning and good natural parts, and especially exemplary in piety, and of a discreet zeal, humble and meek, able to endure the toil and fatigue they must expect to go through, both in mind and body, not raw young men, nor yet very old, whose godly zeal to propagate true Christianity in life and practice should be their great motive; for people generally of those parts are very sharp and observant, to notice both what is good or bad in those who converse among them."[29]

Such a letter as the foregoing, written by a man of well-known energy and sincerity, must have made a strong impression upon the members of the Society. While the bishops were soliciting contributions in their respective dioceses for the missionary enterprise of the new organisation, it was deemed important that a careful survey of the field be made for the sake of an intelligent regimentation of the Society's

[29]*Ernest Hawkins: Historical Notices of the Missions of the Church of England, pp. 26-29.*

activity. George Keith was the one chosen to make a tour of the American colonies and report his observations in detail. On February 27, 1702, he was appointed the first missionary of the Society for the Propagation of the Gospel in Foreign Parts.[30]

[30]*S. P. G. Journal, I., p. 32.*

III. The Mission of Keith and Talbot.

ON April 28, 1702, the Reverend George Keith and the Reverend Patrick Gordon, recently appointed (March 20th) missionary of the S. P. G. for Long Island, sailed from Cowes on the Isle of Wight in the Queen's ship, "Centurion," bound for Boston. Among their fellow-passengers were Colonel Dudley, Governor of New England, and Colonel Lewis Morris, Governor of New Jersey, and the Reverend John Talbot, chaplain of the ship. The last named was so impressed with Keith's undertaking that he enlisted as a missionary.[31] They landed at Boston on St. Barnabas' day, June 11th; and on the next day, Keith wrote to the Society:

> "Colonel Dudley was so very civil and kind to Mr. Gordon and me that he caused us both to eat at his table all the voyage, and his conversation was both pleasant and instructive, insomuch that the great cabin of the ship was like a colledge for good discourse, both in matters theological and philosophical, and very cordially he joined daily with us in divine worship, and I well understand he purposeth to give all possible encouragement to the congregation of the Church of England in this place. Also Colonel Morris was very civil and kind to us, and so was the captain of the ship, called the Centurion, and all the inferior officers, and all the marines generally, and good order was kept in the ship; so that if any of the seamen were complained upon to the captain for profane swearing, he caused to punish them according to the usual custom, by causing them to carry a heavy woodden collar about their neck for an hour, that was both painful and shameful; and, to my observation and knowledge, severall of the seamen, as well as the officers, joined devoutly with us in our daily prayers according to the Church of England, and so did the other gentlemen that were passengers with us."[32]

Keith and Talbot were soon actively engaged in their mission.[33] When the "Centurion" landed at Boston, the clergy of the city welcomed the three clergymen to their homes. Gordon, who had been appointed to Jamaica, Long Island, proceeded to his post of duty, where he soon died. The other missionaries tarried in Boston, where there was much

[31] C. F. Pascoe: *Two Hundred Years of the S. P. G., I., p.* 10.
[32] S. P. G. A-Series, I., #9.
[33] *The narrative of their American tour was printed in London in 1706, under the title: "A Journal of Travels from New Hampshire to Caratuck, on the Continent of North America." It was reprinted in the Protestant Episcopal Historical Collections, 1851. It is an inspiring document, and a rare and valuable item of Americana.*

to be done. On the Sunday after the arrival of the ship, Keith preached in the Queen's Chapel, before "a large Auditory not only of Church people but of many others;" in his sermon, he laid down "six plain brief rules," which, if "put in practice, would bring all to the Church of England who dissented from her." The Independent pastors at Boston viewed such propaganda with alarm; and Doctor Increase Mather undertook to refute the arguments and thus save his flock from the wiles of the Anglicans. Keith's sermon, which was entitled "The Doctrine of the holy Apostles & Prophets the Foundation of the Church of Christ," was printed at the request of the Boston clergymen and other adherents; in rebuttal of Doctor Mather's reply, Keith published another pamphlet, this time in New York—"the Printer at Boston not daring to print it lest he should give offence to the Independent Preachers there." Other publications followed.

Before setting forth on his journey, Keith lingered in Boston long enough to attend the Harvard commencement. There, said Colonel Lewis Morris, "the good man was met with very little University breeding, and with less learning, but he was most distressed by the theses which were there maintained of predestination and immutable decrees, to which he drew up a long answer in Latin." The Latin letter, sent to the president of the college, was afterwards published at New York in an English translation.

Early in July, Keith and Talbot began their extended missionary travel, which lasted two years and stretched from "Piscataway River in New England to Caratuck in North Carolina." Keith's former identification with the Quakers gave him an introduction to their circles and an understanding of their viewpoint; nor was he sparing in his efforts to turn such an advantage to account in winning them to the English Church. We find him visiting the homes of Quakers and attending their meetings. His *Journal* records abuses and interrupted discourses, for some of his old friends looked upon him as a turncoat and traitor; still there are instances of graciousness and courtesy which are quite touching.

The missionaries went to Lynn, Massachusetts, visiting the homes of the Quakers and attending their religious sessions; they carried on their labours at Hampton, Salisbury, Dover, and Salem, and then returned to Boston. At Newport they had a public disputation with the Quakers; and at Portsmouth, Narragansett, Little Compton, and Swansea, Keith sought to expose the errors of his former co-religionists. New London and other places were included in the journey; leaving New England, the travellers crossed Long Island Sound, and began holding services and conferences at Oyster-Bay, Flushing, and Hempstead. From New York, they moved on to New Jersey.

The beginning of the Eighteenth Century was a time of violent religious prejudice and theological partisanship. Each group seemed disposed to look on the others as steeped in false doctrine, hardness of heart, and viciousness of life. The Quakers were regarded by the Anglicans as enemies of religion. This attitude is revealed in a letter which Talbot wrote concerning Keith in 1702:—

> "Indeed he is the fittest man that ever came over for this Province, he is well study'd Divine, a good Philosopher & Preacher, but above all an excellent Disputant, especially against the Quakers who used to Challenge all mankind formerly, now all the Friends (or Enemies rather) are not able to answer one Geo. Keith, he knows the Depths of Satan within them and all the Doublings & Windings of *the Snake in the Grass;* In short he's become the best Champion agst all Dissenters that the Church ever had, & has Sett up Such a Light in these dark places that by God's blessing will not be putt out."[34]

On October 2nd, 1702, George Keith preached at Perth Amboy; the "auditory was small." His text was Titus II., 11, 12: "For the grace of God that bringeth salvation hath appeared to all men, teaching us that denying ungodliness and worldly lusts, we should live soberly, righteously, and godly, in this present world." Some of his hearers were old acquaintances; and "such as were there were well affected," and desirous that a Church of England minister be settled amongst them. The following Sunday (October 10th), Keith and Talbot attended the yearly meeting of the Keithian Quakers in Freehold; there Keith addressed some of those who had seceded from the other Friends in 1692 and united with him. The audience listened to him without interruption, and the meeting ended peaceably. Keith had made use of some of the Church collects, and had preached on Hebrews V., 9: "And being made perfect, he became the author of eternal salvation unto all them that obey him." The meeting was continued the next day; and Keith had an opportunity to talk to some of the Quaker leaders on their lack of proper ordination.

At Middletown, on the 17th of October, he preached on the subject of infant baptism. There "most of the Auditory were Church People, or well affected to the Church." On the 24th, Keith arrived at Shrewsbury, where the Quakers were holding their annual meeting.

[34]*George M. Hills: History of the Church in Burlington, N. J., pp. 27-28; S. P. G., A-Series, I., #LVI.*

He sent word to them, requesting that they give him a hearing. This favour was refused. Keith remained there at least three days, however; and during that time, he publicly "detected the Quakers' errors out of their printed books," and read "the quotations to the Auditory, laying the pages open before such as were willing to read them, for their better satisfaction." In all places visited in East Jersey, the missionaries were hospitably entertained. Keith observed the work of the Reverend Mr. Innes, that pioneer clergyman of whom so little is known; and he commended the same:

> "Mr. *Innes* being in Priest's Orders, has oft preached among them, and by Preaching and Conferences frequently with Quakers and other sorts of People, as also by his pious Conversation, has done much Good among them, and been very instrumental to draw them off from their Errors, and bring them over to the Church."

From Shrewsbury, Keith and Talbot went to Burlington. There they preached in the town-house, as the Church was not built. They had "a great Auditory of diverse sorts, some of the Church, and some of the late converts from Quakerism." Keith once more "detected the Quakers' errors, out of their great authors, George Fox his Great Mystery, and Edward Burroughs' Folio Book, and others." The missionaries were entertained by Colonel Hamilton, then Governor of West Jersey. From November 1st to the 3rd, they remained in Burlington; then they left for Philadelphia.

In his report to the S. P. G., November 29th, 1702, Keith said:

> "In the two Jerseys those call'd Keithian Quakers were very loving and heard us, professing great Satisfaction, particularly at Middletown, at Shrewsbury, Freehold & Amboy, in East Jersey; and at Burlington in West Jersey."[35]

He recommended the Church congregations at Amboy and the Falls in Shrewsbury to the attention of the Society. In his tour of New Jersey, Keith had learned to admire the good qualities of Colonel Lewis Morris, who had supported him and had exemplified the highest ideals of churchmanship.

> "His family is a little Church. He useth the Common Prayer in his family daily, and on Sundays his neighbours come to his house, as to a Church, and at times Mr. Innesse preacheth in his house. I suppose your Lordship remembereth Mr. Innesse, a good man, but a nonjuror."[36]

[35]*S. P. G. A-Series, I., #50 (Stevens & Brown Library of Congress Transcript).*
[36]*Protestant Episcopal Historical Collections, 1851, p. 27.*

After visiting Philadelphia, the missionaries went to New York; it was there that the clergy convened and drew up "An Account of the State of the Church in Pennsylvania, East and West Jersey and New York." The session of the clergy was followed by a brief stay in the city; and Keith availed himself of another opportunity to address the Quakers at Flushing.

Christmas was spent by the missionaries with Colonel Morris; Talbot administered the Holy Communion, "both Mr. Morris and his wife and divers others receiving." December 27th, Keith preached at Shrewsbury, New Jersey, at the house of a planter; and had "a considerable auditory of Church people lately converted from Quakerism, with divers others of the Church of note in that part of the Country." On the 1st of January, 1703, Keith visited and preached at the dwelling of a former Quaker at Freehold; there he baptised several Quaker converts. On the 10th of that month, he preached at Burlington to a large congregation, before setting out again for Philadelphia and exploring points southward.

A letter from Keith to the Reverend Doctor Bray, dated February 24th, 1703, states that he had travelled among the Keithian Quakers, especially in East Jersey, and with good success; all but a few of the Keithians were "well affected to the Church."

"Betwixt New York and Pennsylvania we continued about a month, viz. from 14th of December to 11th of January travelling among the Friends, call'd formerly the Keithian Quakers esepcially for East Jersey, having been about a whole month travelling among them before that, which was in the month of October; and by God's blessing our labour has had good success among them, so that generally very few excepted, all the Keithians in East Jersey are well affected to the Church, and we baptized twenty-two persons in East Jersey, all eithers Keithians or Keithian children. I am forced to use this name of distinction to distinguish them from the other Quakers who are generally very stiff and averse from the Church, and all principles of true Christianity everywhere, and who decline all discourse or converse with us. Colonel Morris did very kindly entertain us at his house in East Jersey, and both he and his Lady went with us from meeting to meeting in divers places. At Amboy in East Jersey they have contributed about £200 towards building a Church and greatly desire a Minister. The Contributors are some Keithians and some other persons well affected to the Church. At Burlington also several persons (among whom some are Keithians) well affected to the Church have contributed about two hundred pounds towards building of a Church and they are to begin the Building this Spring. In all these new

erectings of Churches in these Northern parts, Governor
Nicholson has largely contributed, and is a mighty promoter
and encourager of them by his Letters and Advice as well
as his purse."[37]

On the feast of the Annunciation, March 25th, 1703, the founda-
tion-stone of the Church at Burlington was laid by the Reverend John
Talbot. The name "St. Mary's" was appropriately adopted. This
beginning was carried on with industry and diligence, till at length
the building was enclosed, covered, ceiled, and glazed. The first mention of the new project by Talbot may be found in a letter written
by him, April 10th, in which he tells of preaching several times in
Burlington.

> "Last Lord's Day I was att Burlington, the Chief Town
> in W. Jersey where I have preacht many times in a house hard
> by the Quaker's Meeting, we shall have one too, I hope when
> we return here again from Virginia, where we think to stay
> but 2 or 3 months, after Sermon I went out with the rest of the
> People, & laid the Corner Stone of St Mary's Church. God
> grant it may rise to be the House of God, and the Gate of
> Heaven to them."[38]

In the same letter, Talbot bewailed the irreligion of the Quakers;
instead of converting the Indians, they were making "Christian
Heathens." He stated that he dreaded the inroads which the Quakers
were making on the Church membership, because of the lack of good
ministers.

> "It grieves me much to see so many People here without
> the Benefit of Serving God in the Wilderness. I believe, I
> have been Sollicited to tarry att 20 Places where they want
> much and are able to maintain a Minister so, thatt he should
> want nothing; they send to N. England, and call any sorry
> young man, purely for want of some good honest Clergy
> Men of the Church of England. Many goe to the Heathen
> Meetings of the People called Quakers because there is no
> houses of God in their Provinces, till at last they come to
> be bewitched & forced out of their Faith & Senses too."[39]

In the same letter, Talbot summed up his work in East and West
Jersey.

[37]*S. P. G. A-Series, I., #87 (Stevens & Brown Library of Congress Transcript); Protestant Episcopal Historical Collections, 1851, pp. 22-23. The reference
is to Governor Francis Nicholson of Virginia.*
[38]*S. P. G. A-Series, I., #CXIX. (Stevens & Brown Library of Congress
Transcript); Protestant Episcopal Historical Collections, 1851, pp. 34-35.*
[39]*Ibid.*

"I have gone with Mr Keith & without him about East &
West Jersey, Preaching, & Baptizing Several Scores of Men,
Women, & Children, encouraging them to build Churches, by
Promising them in time, Ministers from England, and that the
Honble Corporation would take care to send none but sober
good Men, well qualified in all Respects for the work of the
Ministry."[40]

Talbot's earliest preserved letters from America were addressed
to the Reverend Richard Gillingham, vicar of Chigwell in Essex. On
the 3rd of May, he wrote to this friend, and mentioned with gratitude
the patronage so generously accorded the Church by Governor Francis
Nicholson of Virginia.

"Coll. Nicholson Govr here, was the chief founder of
this"—the Burlington Church—"as well as many more, and
Indeed he has been the Benefactor to all the Churches on
this Land of N. America."

He had found the ministers an unworthy sort.

"We want a great many good Ministers here in America
especially in those parts mentioned in the Scheme, but we
had better have none att all than such Scandalous Beasts
as some make themselves not only the worst of Ministers but of
Men."

The want of books—proper reading matter—was an obstacle to
the Church's progress.

"Some good Books would do very well in the meanwhile
I am Sure there is no want of them in England they have
enough & to spare. Indeed we have had many of Dr Bray's
Books, & I could wish we had more But his Way & Method
is not the best for this People that we have to do withal,
Quakers, & Quaker's Friends; to most of them, nothing but
Controversy will serve their turn, 'tis a hard Matter to persuade to the Baptismal Covenant, on which the D^r has writ
3 or 4 Books, one in folio, that they may be ever learning,
& yet never be able to come to the Knowledge of the Creed,
the Lord's Prayer nor the ten Commandments.
"Those that we have to deal with are a sharp and Inquisitive People; they are not satisfied with one D^r's Opinion,
but must have something that is Authentick if we hope to
prevail with them."[41]

[40] *Ibid.*
[41] *S. P. G. A-Series, I., #CXX. (Stevens & Brown Library of Congress
Transcript); Protestant Episcopal Historical Collections, 1851, pp. 36-38.*

The efforts of the missionaries were certainly bearing fruit. A letter from Colonel Morris to Doctor William Beveridge, Archdeacon of Colchester, dated July 12th, 1703, bears witness to the effectiveness of their labours. In Monmouth County, New Jersey, he said, "so many Persons as make a Pretty midling Congregation" had been brought over to the Church by the work of Messrs. Keith and Talbot. In that county, there were above three hundred families; but "the greater part" were "of no Profest Religion, the Prejudices they had against the Church" had been "very much Removed, and their Eyes Opened." If a person, "above fourty, of Piety, of good Learning, well skilled in the various Points of Controversy, and in Circumstances above Dependance were sent over, he would in all Probability make a vast accession to the Church."[42]

On the 22nd of August, 1703, divine services were held in St. Mary's Church, Burlington—five months from the date of laying the corner-stone. Keith preached; his sermon was taken from II. Samuel XXIII., 3, 4: "The God of Israel said, the Rock of Israel spake to me, He that ruleth over men must be just, ruling in the fear of God. And he shall be as the light of the morning, when the sun riseth, even a morning without clouds; as the tender grass springing out of the earth by clear shining after rain." A distinguished group had gathered for the opening service—a group which included Lord Cornbury and many gentlemen who had accompanied the Governor from New York and the two Jerseys.[43] In fact, Lord Cornbury utilised this occasion for the publication of his commission as Governor of East and West Jersey. Keith preached in the new brick Church the following Sunday. After that, the two missionaries started for Philadelphia.

Writing from that city, September 1st, 1703, Talbot said:

"Mr Keith & I have preached the Gospel to all Sorts & Conditions of Men, we have baptized Severall Scores of Men Women & Children, Chiefly those of his old Friends (the Rest are harden'd just like the Jews, who please not God and are contrary to all men) we have gathered Several Hundreds together for the Church of England and what is more to build houses for her Service. Here are 4 or 5 going forward now in this Province and the next. That att Burlington, is almost finisht, Mr Keith preacht the first Sermon in it before my Ld Cornbury whom the Queen has made Govr of Jersey to the Satisfaction of all Christian People. Churches are

[42]S. P. G. A-Series, I., #CXX. (*Stevens & Brown Library of Congress Transcript*).
[43]S. P. G. A-Series, I., #CXXI. (*Stevens & Brown Library of Congress Transcript*).

going up amain where there were never any before. They are going to build 3 at N. Carolina to keep the People together lest they should fall into Heathenism, Quakerism &c. & 3 more in these lower Counties ab^t New Castle besides those att Chester Burlington & Amboy."

Along with the encouraging symptoms, there was the ever-present handicap which attended the shortage of ministers and the absence of a bishop who might ordain and confirm, and in other ways guide and direct the Church in the colonies. Mr. Talbot continued:

"Mr Keith has don great Service to the Church where e'er he has been, by Preaching & Disputing publickly and from house to house, he has confuted many (especially the Anabaptists) by Labor & Travel Night & Day, by Writing & Printing of Books mostly att his own Charge & Cost, & giving y^m out freely, which has been very expensive to him. By these Means People are much awaken'd, & their Eyes open'd to see the good Old Way and they are very well pleased to find the Church att last take such Care of her Children For it is a sad thing to Consider the years that are past, how some that were born of the English, never heard of the Name of Christ, how many others were Baptized in his Name and fallen away to Heathenism, Quakerism & Atheism for want of Confirmation.

"It seems the strangest thing in the World & 'tis thought History can't parallell it, That any Place has received the word of God so many years, so many hundred Churches built, so many thousand Proselytes made, and still remain altogether in the Wilderness as sheep without a shepherd. The Poor Church of America is worse on't in this Respect, than any of her Adversaries.

"The Presbiterians here come a great way to lay hands one on Another, but after all I think they had as good stay att home for the good they do. The Independants are called by their Sovereign Lord the People. The Anabaptists & Quakers pretend to the Spirit. But the Poor Church has nobody upon the Spot to comfort or Confirm her Children. No body to Ordain several that are willing to serve, were they authorized, for the Work of the Ministry. Therefore they fall back again into the Herd of the Dissenters, rather than they will be att the Hazard and Charge to goe as far as England for Orders: so that we have seen several Counties, Islands, and Provinces which have hardly an Orthodox Minister amst 'em, which might have been supply'd had we been so happy as to see a Bishop or Suffragan Apud Americanos."

As much as the Bishop of London deserved to be revered as diocesan, no one could take the place of a resident bishop.

"We are all satisfied that we can't have a greater Friend & Patron than himself. But alas! there is such a great Gulph fixt between, that we can't pass to him nor he to us; but may he not send a suffragan?"[44]

Between the 2nd of January, 1704, and the 13th of February, Keith preached several times in New Jersey, visiting Perth Amboy, Shrewsbury, Freehold, and Burlington. After another visit to Philadelphia, where the presence of the large Quaker population was a challenge and an opportunity, he was back in Burlington on the 26th of March. There he preached twice—his last sermons in Burlington. The same zeal and vigour which had characterised that little flock in building their Church found utterance in the expressed desire for a settled minister. On the 2nd of April, 1704, the Burlington vestry communicated their wishes to the Venerable Society; they testified to the great advantage which they had already derived, and requested that the Reverend John Talbot be settled in their midst.[45] In the meantime, the Reverend John Sharpe, who had served as chaplain of the forces stationed at New York, had ministered to the Burlington congregation.

The action of the Society was favourable. Talbot celebrated the Holy Communion in St. Mary's Church on Whitsunday, June 4th, 1704. Then he began what proved to be a notable and significant ministry among a people where, in the words of Keith, "not long ago, there was little else but Quakerism or Heathenism."

Talbot was reluctant to leave his good friend; but he evidently felt that the object of the mission had been accomplished. The two men had stimulated the struggling, half-hearted groups of churchmen to activity and self-confidence; they had gained a perspective through their travels, from which they were able to submit reliable and intelligent advice to their superiors; they had been able fairly to estimate the problems and needs of the colonial Church. From their letters and reports, the initial policy of the Society for the Propagation of the Gospel in Foreign Parts was largely shaped. Keith returned to England, receiving the living of Edburton, in Sussex, where he remained till his death in 1716. In his *Journal,* published in 1706, he gave the following picturesque summary of the mission:

"I have given an entire Journal of my two Years' Mis-

[44] *S. P. G. A-Series, I., #CXXV. (Stevens & Brown Library of Congress Transcript); Fulham MSS., Pennsylvania, #216 (Stevens & Brown Library of Congress Transcript); Protestant Episcopal Historical Collections, 1851, pp. xxxviii-xl.*

[45] *S. P. G. A-Series, I., #183 (Stevens & Brown Library of Congress Transcript).*

sionary Travel and Service, on the Continent of *North America,* betwixt *Piscataway River* in *New England,* and *Coretuck* in North Carolina; of extent in Length about eight hundred miles; within which Bounds are Ten distinct Colonies and Governments, all under the Crown of *England,* viz., *Piscataway, Boston, Rhod Island, Connecticot, New York, East and West Jersey, Pensilvania, Maryland, Virginia,* and *North Carolina.* I travelled twice over most of these Governments and Colonies, and I preached oft in many of them, particularly in *Pensilvania, West* and *East Jersey,* and *New York* Provinces, where we continued longest, and found the greatest occasion for our service.

"As concerning the success of me and my Fellow-Labourer, Mr. JOHN TALBOT'S, Ministry, in the Places where we travelled, I shall not say much; yet it is necessary that something be said, to the glory of God alone, to whom it belongs, and to the encouragement of others, who may hereafter be imployed in the like Service.

"In all the Places where we travelled and preached, we found the people generally well affected to the Doctrine that we preached among them, and they did generally join with us decently in the Liturgy, and Public Prayers, and Administration of the Holy Sacraments, after the Usage of the Church of *England,* as we had occasion to use them. And where Ministers were wanting, (as there were wanting in many places) the People earnestly desired us to present their Request to the *Honourable Society,* to send Ministers unto them, which accordingly I have done; and, in answer to their request, the Society has sent to such places as seemed most to want a considerable number of Missionaries.

"Besides the general Success we had (praised be God for it) both in our Preaching, and much and frequent Conference with People of Diverse Perswasions, many of which had been wholly strangers to the Way of the Church of *England;* who, after they had observed it in the Publick Prayers, and reading the Lessons out of the Holy Scriptures of the Old and New Testament, and the manner of the Administration of Baptism, and the Lord's Supper, were greatly affected with it, and some of which declared their great satisfaction and the Esteem they had of the Solemn and edifying manner of our Worship and Administration, far above whatever they could observe in other Ways of Worship known to them.

"To many, our Ministry was as the sowing the Seed and Planting, who, probably, never so much as heard one orthodox Sermon preached to them, before we came and Preached among them, who received the Word with Joy; and of whom we have good Hope, that they will be as the good ground, *that brought forth Fruit, some Thirty, some Sixty, and some an Hundred Fold.* And to many others it was a watering to what had been formerly Sown and Planted among them; some of the good Fruit whereof we did observe, to the glory of God, and our great Comfort, while we were with them, even such Fruits of true Piety and good Lives, and sober and righteous Living, as prove the Trees to be good from which they did proceed . . . In all these Countries almost, by the Blessing of God on our Labours, there are good Materials prepared for the Building of Churches, of living Stones, as soon as, by the good Providence of God, Ministers shall be sent among them, who have the discretion and due qualifications requisite to Build with them."[46]

[46]*Keith's Journal, 1706, pp. 82-86.*

IV. THE FIRST YEARS OF TALBOT'S AMERICAN MINISTRY AND THE EFFORT TO OBTAIN A BISHOP.

WHEN the Reverend John Talbot boarded the ship "Centurion," as its chaplain, and sailed from the Isle of Wight on April 28, 1702, bound for America, he had no idea that he was to be a missionary of the newly founded Society for the Propagation of the Gospel in Foreign Parts; and still less that he would spend the rest of his life ministering to the infant Church in colonial America. On shipboard he became interested in the Rev. George Keith and the object of his mission, and when the ship reached Boston on June 11th, he had decided to throw in his lot with Keith and "freely and kindly offered himself" as the latter's assistant and associate in his missionary travels and services. Keith himself was favourably impressed with Talbot and, upon the advice of Governor Dudley and other Boston friends, he wrote to the Secretary of the Society, advising that Mr. Talbot, "known to several worthy persons to be of good ability and fame," should be his "associate and assistant in the service of the Gospel in America, and that he be allowed some honest competency to bear his charges." He recorded in his Journal:

> "Indeed Divine Providence did well order it, for he proved a very loving and faithful Associate to me, and was very helpful to me in all respect, and was well approved and esteemed every where, both with respect to his Preaching and Living, in the several places where we Travelled."

Talbot received his appointment from the Society, September 18th, 1702; but he did not wait for the official notice; indeed he co-operated with Keith in his activities from the time of their arrival.[47]

Keith's Journal recounts the labours of Talbot; in several towns visited by the two missionaries, Talbot's sermons were the first Anglican discourses ever heard by the natives and residents. He made an excellent impression, and undoubtedly attracted many persons who would have been irritated by Keith's strong partisan bias. In a letter written by him from Virginia during the tour, May 3rd, 1703, we find a description of Talbot's methods as well as an avowal of his self-effacing interest in the cause:

> "I use to take a Wallet full of Books and carry them 100 miles about and disperse them abroad and give them to all that desired 'em, wᶜʰ in due time will be of good Service

[47]*Sprague: Annals of the American Episcopal Pulpit, p. 30.*

to the Church, 'tis a Comfort to the People in the Wilderness to see that some body takes care of them. There is a time to sow and a time to reap wh^ch I don't desire in this World. I might have money enough of the People in many Places but I would never take any of those that we goe to Proselyte, especially amongst the Quakers; I Resolved to work with my hands rather than they should say, I was a hireling & come for money, which they are very apt to do."[48]

Talbot's itinerant mission came to an end at Whitsuntide, 1704, when he yielded to the importunities of the people of Burlington, New Jersey, and settled among them. He was already past middle age; but few men have experienced a more active or diversified ministry.

Of Talbot's early life nothing has been said up to this point. He was born and baptised in the parish of Wymondham, Norfolk, England, in 1645. His parents were Thomas Talbot, gentleman, and Jone (Joan), the daughter of Sir John Mede, of Loffts, in the county of Essex. He was educated at Elmden, Essex; and admitted as a sizar in Christ's College, Cambridge, in February, 1660. The following July, he matriculated; he passed Bachelor of Arts, in 1663; became a Fellow of Peterhouse, in 1664; and was admitted Master of Arts by royal mandate from King Charles the Second, in 1671. In June, 1695, he was instituted to the rectory of Fretherne, Gloucestershire. His parish was very small, containing only about twenty houses and 1,125 inhabitants—far too limited a field for a man of such extraordinary force and energy. Hence he became chaplain of the vessel, on which he first became acquainted with Keith. This proved the turning point of his career.[49]

Talbot had no difficulty in entering upon his pastoral duties at Burlington, where he had already called in the course of his mission. He celebrated the Holy Communion in the new edifice, June 4th, 1704. The demand for his services was emphatic, and the people appeared eager to go ahead. Talbot threw his heart and soul into the work, and showed himself a faithful and devoted pastor; still he was far from provincial in his interests and outlook. The needs of the surrounding villages impressed themselves upon him, and he was always responsive to the call of duty; he realised the problems which confronted the provinces outside his own. Thus we find him at work in Pennsylvania, New York, and New England, as well as in the Jerseys. Yet no handicap distressed him more than the fundamental difficulty which faced the Church of England in the American colonies—

[48]*S. P. G. A-Series, I., #CXX. (Stevens & Brown Library of Congress Transcript); Protestant Episcopal Historical Collections, 1851, p. xxxviii.*
[49]*John Fulton's monograph, in Perry: American Episcopal Church, I., pp. 544-545.*

the want of a resident bishop, who might supervise the religious affairs of the people, maintain a high standard for the clergy, administer confirmation, and by means of ordination insure a continuous supply of ministers for extending and carrying on the work.

Early in his Burlington ministry, Talbot began his efforts to obtain an episcopate for America—efforts in which he was engaged for almost two decades. On the 28th of October, 1705, he addressed the Secretary of the S. P. G.:

"As for a Suffragan we are all sensible of ye want we have of one, and pray God send us a man of peace, for otherwise he will do more harm than good, as proud, ambitious, covetous men used to do, troubling the state and perplexing the Church, and then they run away, and leave all in the lurch."[50]

While a bishop clothed with full diocesan responsibility would be preferable, it was argued that at least a suffragan might reasonably be sent.

On the 2nd of November, 1705, fourteen clergymen, representing New York, New Jersey, and Pennsylvania, assembled at Burlington, under the leadership of Mr. Talbot; and gravely pondered the handicaps under which they were struggling because of the lack of a bishop in their midst. It was decided to address their ecclesiastical superiors; and Talbot was endorsed as their spokesman, to present in person their petition for a bishop. The following communication was framed:

"To the most Reverend Father in God, the Lord Abps., the Right Reverend the Bishops, and others Right Honourable Members of the Society Erected for Propagation of the Gospel in Foreign Parts.

"Your Missionaries being convened at Burlington, esteem themselves in duty bound to lay before the Most Reverend, the Right Reverend & Right Honourable Members of the Society, what we conceive to be necessary, with God's blessing on our Labours, to promote the ends of our Mission. The presence and assistance of a Suffragan Bishop is most needful to ordain such persons as are fit to be called to serve in the sacred ministry of the Church. We have been deprived of the advantages that might have been received of some Presbyterian and Independent Ministers that formerly were, and of others that are still willing to conform and receive the holy character, for want of a Bishop to give it. The baptized want to be confirmed. The presence is necessary in the councils of these provinces to prevent the inconveniences

[50]*George M. Hills: History of the Church in Burlington, N. J., p. 59.*

which the Church labours under by the influences which seditious men's counsels have upon the publick administration and the opposition which they make to the good inclinations of well affected persons; he is wanted not only to govern and direct us but to cover us from the malignant effects of those misrepresentations that have been made by some persons empowered to admonish and inform against us who indeed want admonition themselves."

"It is our humble desire that the Custom of the Romans of not Condemning Men before they be heard may be of Force with the most Reverend, the Right Reverend & Right Honble members of the Society, for we find to our Grief that those Characters given of us by those persons have made sad impressions on your minds, as we have in some measure lessened our reputation, which is dearer to us than all Your Encouragements which we have received by Your Bounty. And it is our humble prayer that no Credit hereafter be given to the Society to any Complaints against us but such as are under the hands of three of the Clergy. The Provinces of New York, the Jerseys, and Pennsylvania consist of People of several Nations, & have Preachers among them that speak to them in their own Tongues. The Dutch and the French being of the Presbiterian Perswasion And the former generally tainted with Republican Principles, it is humbly proposed that there be no preacher admitted to preach among them but in the English Tongue; or at least of Episcopal Ordination, that can preach both in English & in their own Tongues, Nor any Schoolmasters to teach any Vulgar Language, but the English without a particular license from the Governor till God bless us with a Bishop. This last Expedient is thought by the Governor to be a likely means of uniting the Country both in their religious and Civil interests."[51]

This petition was signed, by:

"John Talbot
Ericus Biorck
Evan Evans
Sam. Myles
Tho. Moor
Aeneas Mackenzie
Geo. Muirson
Andrew Rudman
Hen. Nichols
Geo. Ross
Tho. Crawford

[51]*Historical Collections, Pennsylvania, edited by William Stevens Perry, pp.* 508-509.

Jno. Sharpe
John Brooke
John Clubb."[52]

The assembled clergymen gave their written recommendation to Talbot; and addressed a letter to the Bishop of London, expressing their great desire for a suffragan bishop, and desiring him to determine whether it would be convenient or not to present their petition to the Queen. They asked that his Lordship have "a particular regard to what (Mr. Talbot) shall say concerning the case of Mr Rudman, Mr Bondet, Mr Eburn and Mr Biorck, whose circumstances are very pressing, and their labours have been very great and successful."[53]

Prior to leaving for England, Talbot had visited several places where the congregations were weak and discouraged for lack of regular ministrations and in danger of lapsing. He left the Reverend John Sharpe, who had served as chaplain of the garrison of New York, in charge of the Burlington field; while he started the rounds of Perth Amboy, Elizabeth Town, Woodbridge, Staten Island, and other points. When he left for the mother country, he put the Reverend Thoroughgood Moor in charge of the vacancy at Burlington, feeling sure that Mr. Moor was "a person of morals, exemplary meekness, piety, and charity."[54]

[52]*JOHN TALBOT is the subject of this study. ERICUS BIORCK was one of the Swedish clergy, in close association with the Anglican missionaries. EVAN EVANS was sent to Philadelphia in 1700; he later served at Oxford and Radnor. SAMUEL MYLES was stationed at Boston. THOROUGHGOOD MOOR was missionary among the New York Indians. AENEAS MACKENZIE was stationed on Staten Island. GEORGE MUIRSON was located at Rye, New York. ANDREW RUDMAN, a Swede, served Oxford and Frankfort, Pennsylvania. HENRY NICHOLS was missionary at Chester. GEORGE ROSS was in charge of Newcastle at the time; the most prominent of the Delaware colonial clergy. THOMAS CRAWFORD was stationed at Dover until 1709, when he was recalled. JOHN SHARPE was an army chaplain. JOHN BROOKE, missionary at Elizabeth Town, was afterwards drowned at sea. JOHN CLUBB served several churches in Pennsylvania.*

[53]*SAMUEL EBURNE was the first S. P. G. resident missionary in New England. DANIEL BONDET was a French minister, who had been driven out of France; ordained by the Bishop of London, he was employed under the New England Company. He was stationed at New Rochelle, New York, from 1709 till 1722. "The Rev. ANDREW RUDMAN, 'Master of Philosophy', was appointed by the Archbishop of Upsal, Sweden, to minister to the Swedes on the Delaware, June 25, 1696, in connection with the Rev. Eric Biorck and the Rev. Jonas Auren. Dr. Clay, in his interesting 'Annals of the Swedes on the Delaware' (second edition, Philadelphia, 1858), gives in detail the story of his ministrations, and records his death on the 17th of September, 1708, at the age of forty years. The fraternal intercourse between the clergy of Swedish ordination and the missionaries of the Church of England continued until after the independent organization of the American Church, when these venerable parishes were absorbed into our own communion, of which they had long been essentially a part."— Historical Collections, Pennsylvania, edited by William Stevens Perry, pp. 504-505.*

[54]*Jeremiah Bass's account, in Protestant Episcopal Historical Collections, 1851, p. 70.*

As we have noted, Talbot's main object in going to England was to represent the need of a bishop for the American colonies. On his arrival, he was prompt in prosecuting his errand. On the 14th of March, 1706, he thus addressed the Society:

"There was a General Meeting of ye Missionaries who resolved to Address the Queen for a Suffragan Bishop, that I should Travel with it, and make known ye Requests of some of the Brethren abroad, whose Case we had recomended formerly by Letter to ye Venerable Society but without Success. . . . I have no Business here but to Sollicite for a Suffragan, Books and Ministers for ye propagating the Gospel, God has so blest my Labours & Travels abroad that I am fully resolved by his Grace, to return the Sooner the better, having done my Business that I came about, meanwhile my Living in Gloucestershire is given away, but I have no reason to doubt of any Incouragement from this famous Society, who have done more in four yeares for America than ever was done before."[55]

A year later Talbot was ready to return to America. In a letter addressed to the Secretary of the Society, April 16th, 1707, he expressed his desire to be sent back.

"I have received several Letters from my Friends in America who think long for my return which I was forward to do once and agen, but Satan hindred me by raising lyes and Slanders in my way, But I have clear'd my self to all that have heard me, and I hope you will satisfy the Honble Society that I am not the man to whom that dark Character did belong, Mr Keith has known my doctrine & manner of life some years and what I have ventur'd suffer'd and acted for the Gospel of Christ abroad and at home. I desire his Letter may be read to the Honorable Board and that they will be pleas'd to dispatch me the sooner the better for the season is far spent and Ships are going out and if I go at all I wou'd go quickly. I know the wants of the poor people in America. They have need of me, or else I shou'd not venture my life to do that abroad which I cou'd do more to my own advantage at home. I shou'd be glad to see somebody sent to North Carolina I hope the Planters Letters is not quite forgot 'Tis a sad thing to live in the Wilderness like the Wild Indians without God in the world."[56]

[55]S. P. G. A-Series, II., #CXLII. (Stevens & Brown Library of Congress Transcript); Protestant Episcopal Historical Collections, 1851, pp. 58-59; George M. Hills: History of the Church in Burlington, N. J., p. 65.

[56]Protestant Episcopal Historical Collections, 1851, p. 59; S. P. G. A-Series, III., #XLV. (Stevens & Brown Library of Congress Transcript).

Looking back across two centuries, the arguments of those who pleaded so persistently and urgently for a resident bishop seem unanswerable; it is hard to understand the strength of the opposition and the procrastinating attitude of the British government. There were several occasions when the granting of bishops, or at least suffragans for the colonies, seemed assured; but somehow the affairs of Church and State were so intimately entwined that nothing came of the efforts. A considerable historical literature has grown up regarding the struggle to obtain a colonial episcopate; and it would be superfluous for us to offer more than a summary review of the matter, even if we had the space. Resolutions, petitions, thousands of letters, bitter controversies, periodicals, and printed books gave contemporary evidence of the intensity with which the campaign was waged. Suffice it to say, that powerful and persistent political and religious elements made it appear inadvisable to the Crown, during a period of foreign warfare and internal strife, to run the risk of alienating any considerable portion of the population. The Puritans—in fact, all the non-episcopal forces, both in Great Britain and America—were staunchly opposed to the spread of episcopal government, and urged reasons against the same which were regarded very seriously at the time. These sectarians constituted a large contingency, and the government dared not offend them. Furthermore, there was a good deal of indifference on the part of Church people. The conscience of the English people as a whole had not been aroused; to most of them, the American colonists were a negligible quantity. Besides, the American Church fell far short of presenting a united front so far as the introduction of a bishop was desired; there were legally constituted vestries which had no idea of yielding their prerogatives and priority to a general overseer imported from abroad. While Talbot and other earnest clergymen realised the fatal disadvantage of marking time and the strength which the Church was losing every day, there were those who were blind to the impending danger and frankly opposed the suggestion of episcopal supervision. The colonial governors were as a rule desirous of retaining their control over the Church.

When we recognize in perspective the hopelessness of the struggle for the episcopate, the letters of Talbot, his colleagues, and those who kept the subject alive for nearly three quarters of a century, ring with pathos. These men, notwithstanding perennial rebuffs, kept appealing to the idealism of their nation, naively confident that the sense of right would sway hard-headed diplomats to subordinate to a spiritual goal considerations of expediency in material things. Their failure constitutes a melancholy chapter; but it redounds to their glory.[57]

During the first part of Talbot's absence from Burlington, there was little alteration in the field. After awhile, however, division and dissension amongst the people "took advantage of his absence, and stirred up such a flame, that had almost broken us to pieces, and occasioned the unhappy removal both of Mr. Moor and Rev. Mr. Brooke, Rector of the Church in Elizabeth Town. . . . If we had had an ecclesiastical governor to have settled differences, mischief would have been cured."[58]

The episode of the Reverend Thoroughgood Moor is important, since it affords a view of Talbot's sympathetic nature and illustrates the friction which often marked the relations between the colonial officials and the priests of the Church. Here it may be remarked, that many of the complaints which reached the Bishop of London and the Society for the Propagation of the Gospel in Foreign Parts came from governors who found that the clergymen were critics of their conduct and policy. The secular authority, though sometimes friendly, was not above resorting to measures to bring the clergy under subjection.

Thoroughgood Moor had been sent by the S. P. G. as missionary to the New York Indians; at the time of his going to that precarious and difficult field, the clergy of the province wrote the Society (October 17th, 1704), protesting that "the *Children* first be satisfied, and the lost Sheep recovered, who have gone astray among Hereticks and Quakers, who have denied the Faith, and are worse than Infidels and *Indians* that never knew it." Talbot communicated his regrets that Moor was to go "so far off as the *Mohocks.* God knows whether we shall see him again. I had the same Call, and had gone to the same Place; but when I saw so many People of my own Nation and Tongue, I soon resolved by God's Grace to seek them in the first place." Another missionary informed the Society that Moor and his assistant dared not venture to the *"praying Indians,* who were so much engaged to the French Interest, that they were our Enemies as much as they could without an open Breach."[59]

[57]*The best discussion of this subject is to be found in Arthur L. Cross: The Anglican Episcopate and the American Colonies.. A splendid bibliography is included. Other excellent bibliographies of the episcopal controversy are found in William Nelson: The controversy over the opposition for an American episcopate, 1767-1774; and E. F. Slafter: John Checkley; or the evolution of religious tolerance in Massachusetts Bay.*

[58]*Jeremiah Bass's account, in Protestant Episcopal Historical Collections, 1851, p. 70.*

[59]*S. P. G. Account, 1706, pp. 47-49; S. P. G. A-Series, II, #XXIII (Stevens & Brown Library of Congress Transcript).*

On Moor's arrival in New York (August 7th, 1704), he had been received by the governor, Lord Cornbury. Shortly afterwards, he had proceeded to Albany, where the Indians had welcomed him, and seemed desirous of instruction. A sachem met him and expressed his pleasure, "that God hath been so propitious to us as to send you to open our Eyes, which have been hitherto shut."[60] For some time, he had been prevented from reaching the Mohawks' Castle, because of snow; finally he attained his destination with great difficulty. There he was courteously received, although he was not urged to reside among the Indians. The influence of the French had undoubtedly been exerted in such a way as to hinder his mission. After waiting nearly a year in the vicinity of Albany, in the hopes of ingratiating himself with the natives, Moor returned to New York. From there he addressed an explanation of his withdrawal to the Society.

The Reverend John Brooke had been sent to Elizabeth Town by the Society, and had been rather successful. He held services in Perth Amboy at various times.

"The Number of People in both Places, was very considerable, and their Ways of Worship various. They were chiefly *Independents,* but many not professing any Religion. However, by diligent Application, he persuaded the better disposed of all Sorts, to consider and attend more, to their spiritual Concernment. He preached to Numbers of *Independents* and Others; they began soon to approve of the Church of *England* Service. The wiser People resolved to settle their Religious affairs, in a more orderly manner."

When Brooke arrived at Elizabeth Town, they had no Place set apart for celebrating divine worship.

"However, he had leave at first, to preach in Colonel Townly's House; that became too small for his growing Congregation, in half a Year's Time; the best Place that could be got was a Barn, and that they were forced to relinquish in Winters. The Members of our Communion were now a large body of People, they resolved to build a Church; and accordingly on St. *John* the Baptist's Day in the year 1706, the Foundation of the Church was laid, whose Name it therefore bears."[61]

Brooke was a very active missionary, and conducted services in no fewer than seven places.

[60]*David Humphreys: Historical Account of the S. P. G., p. 288.*
[61]*Ibid., pp. 188-189.*

With this parenthesis, we return to the Reverend Mr. Moor. That missionary had incurred the resentment of the colonial governor, Lord Cornbury. It seems that the governor had interfered with Moor in the discharge of his ministry; he had ordered him to discontinue the fortnightly sacrament, as too frequent; and he was enraged because the missionary had refused to communicate Lieutenant-Governor Ingoldsby, who was reputedly an evil-doer. Moor showed no disposition to conform to the governor's demands; and he took occasion to reprove the representative of the Crown for his scandalous practice of arraying himself in female attire, and publicly parading in this shameful guise along the ramparts of the fort. Therefore, the offended Lord Cornbury had Moor arrested and confined in Fort Anne.[62]

From his place of imprisonment, Moor addressed a letter to the Secretary of the Society. He declared that he was in confinement in the city of New York.

"I was brought hither by force. . . . About a Month go *(sic)* his Excellency my Lord Cornbury Govr in Chief of ye province of N: Jersey, N: York &c being then at York sent a Summons for me to appear before him at N: York to answer to such things as shou'd be Alleged against me. I was not long considering what to do being only to consult the Legality of the Summons, & whether the Law Commanded my Obedience, wch if it did not, I know of no other Obligation, but had many reasons to the Contrary, as the leaving my Charge without any to supply my place & the incertainty indeed of my return (I being well Satisfyed that my Lord had often declared that he wou'd remove me out of the province for reasons scarce worth while troubling the Society with) &c so that I say I had only to consider whether my Lord had that power to Summons me out of the Province; and a little Consideration was sufficient to satisfy me he had not; N: Jersey being certainly a distinct province from this of N: York as Virginia is; & the power of Governm^t . . . upon the Death or Absence of my Lord Cornbury to be Lodged in the Lieutenant Govr & upon the Death or Absence of the Lieu^t Govr in the Council. But upon my not obeying the Summons His Ex^y the Lord Cornbury sends a Warr^t dated from N: York to ye Sheriff of Burlington to bring me safe to his Lo^{ps} house at Amboy about 50 miles from Burlington in the same province which accordingly he Executed. He took me into his Custody the 15th and brought me to Amboy 16 Instant, being Saturday when we found His Exc^y arrived from N: York. His Exc^y told ye Sheriff he had done very well in bringing me thither, & ordered him

[62]Perry: *American Episcopal Church, I., pp. 166-167; 323.*

by word of Mouth to secure me & bring me before him on
Monday Morning, which accordingly he did; but his Exc^y it is
to be Supposed being otherwise busyed that morning Ordered
I shou'd be brought the Afternoon, and then the next morning, when he was pleased to send for me into a private room
where were only the Lieu^t Govern^r & himself.

"His Exc^y (after some words of Anger not worth mentioning . . .) began to condemn my behaviour to him ever
since my first arrival into America Siding wth his and the
Governments Enemies & that I was a preacher of Rebellion
(which I think he seem'd to intimate I did by my Conversation and not by my Sermons tho' I think he might
have said the one as well as the other) and that I had shown
my rebellious temper particularly in not obeying the Lieu^t
Gov^{rs} Suspension of me."

Moor explained in this letter that, upon his failure to obey the
governor's summons to New York about a month before, Lieutenant-
Governor Ingoldsby had told him before witnesses that for that very
reason he had suspended him from holding divine services in Burlington; but Moor had contended that he did not have the power to sus-
pend him. So the governor next ordered the secretary of the province
to draw up a form, and have it set up at the door of the church; but
the secretary, feeling that he had insufficient warrant, had replied that
he could not safely do such a thing, and that setting up the notice
was the business of the church-wardens. When the paper was delivered to the wardens, they had agreed not to post it.

Lord Cornbury informed Moor that the lieutenant-governor had
acted well in suspending him, and that he himself confirmed the sen-
tence and discharged him from preaching any more in that or the
neighbouring province. In response, Moor begged that the governor
judge favourably of him; he insisted that he had acted from a sense
of duty, and not from sheer obstinacy, and that he was ready to
accept the best advice and to proceed according to his conscience. An
unpleasant altercation followed.

"He told me that he wou'd be obeyed, that my Conscience shou'd not rule him; I told him I cou'd not expect
that, but beg'd I might be excused if it did me. He told me
that he wou'd be obey'd and that if I did not, he wou'd use me
like other Rebels; He ask'd me farther who I thought myself
to bee: I told him a Minister of the Church placed in Burlington, both by the Laws of God and Man; a being placed
there by my Lord of London. He told me my Lord of London did not place me there; I told him I humbly conceived

he did by a Letter I had from the Secretary of the Society of wch my Lord of London was a Member."

Then the governor declared that the Bishop of London "had no power to place (him) there or any where else in his Government, neither ever did he place any & that the Queen had invested him with that sole power, & that he was Ordinary."

When Moor replied that if the governor was indeed ordinary, he would make no opposition, but that he was not convinced of the fact, the governor told him that "since (he) was so uncertain, he wou'd secure (him) from disobeying." So he ordered the sheriff to take him into custody.

Moor was continued a prisoner till the following Saturday; then he was commanded to attend the governor in his barge for New York. He refused to enter the barge except by force. The Amboy sheriff thereupon seized him by the sleeve, against his protest. "When I was come pretty near the Barge, I told his Ex^y that I wish'd him a good Voyage & that I design'd to go not farther unless I was forced to it." The governor, "in great anger bid the Sheriff again do his Office, & the Lieut^t Govr or rather more probably by other reasons he leaves me again to the Sheriff, who encouraged by my L^{ds} Example & the earnestness of ye Lieut^t Govr to him to take me did so, & took hold of my Gown and went before me into my Lords Barge, in wch my Lord brought me to York, being 40 Miles from Amboy."

Arriving at the fort in New York, Moor was conducted to a room; and the officer of the guard was informed that he was a prisoner, and that his escape must be prevented. When the Reverend John Sharpe, the chaplain, asked the governor if he would be permitted to attend church, he received a negative answer; Moor should not go without the walls until he was sent to England.

It is only fair to say that Moor was not cruelly treated while in confinement. "I thank God I fare very well here," he said in his letter; "his Lo(rdshi)p having given orders that I shou'd want nothing." He added, in conclusion:

> "I hope my present and late Sufferings will be no dis-
> advantage to ye Church. I am well satisfyed in my mind of
> the Contrary, & that I shall have reason to bless God for
> inabling me to Act as I have done in relation to my L^d
> Cornbury & the Lieut^t Govr."[63]

When the Reverend Mr. Brooke learned of Moor's detention, he

[63]*S. P. G. A-Series, III., #CXLIV. (Stevens & Brown Library of Congress Transcript).*

made frequent visits to him in New York, "tho' at the same time he neglected his Churches in East Jersey." On the 12th of September, 1707, Lord Cornbury left for Albany, though giving directions that Moor should want for nothing in his absence. About ten days later, he learned that Moor had made his escape from the fort, leaving in company with Brooke. In fact, the day that the governor went away, Brooke and Moor dined with the officer of the guard; after dinner, Brooke left, but returned about four o'clock in the afternoon; he went to Moor's room, and the two walked out separately, the sentry not recognising the prisoners. Forthwith they hurried to New England, so as to take a boat back home.[64]

On reaching Boston, Messrs. Moor and Brooke met the Reverend Mr. Talbot, who had returned from England, and was surveying the religious wants of New England. Talbot was deeply impressed by the sad story of the persecution; and he took the two men under his charge, and sought to persuade them to remain in America and serve the New England Church. When he visited Marblehead, Massachusetts, he carried the two missionaries with him; and they were invited to preach before they departed.

Moor and Brooke were lost at sea. Talbot, nine months after he saw them for the last time, wrote the Society the circumstances of their departure.

> "They told me what hardships they met with from the Gov[r] of N. York and Jersey and how they escaped out of their hands, I was for converting them back agen, telling them the dangers of the Sea and the Enemy but poor Thorowgood said he had rather be taken into ffrance than into the Fort at New York, and if they were sunk in the Sea, they did not doubt but God wou'd receive them since they were persecuted for righteousness that is for Christ's sake and his Gospel and doing their Duty to the best of their knowledge. Truly as it was in the beginning so I find it in the end, all that will live godly in Christ Jesus shall suffer persecution, but somebody must answer for these things at home or abroad; if I cou'd have given them any hopes of a Bp or Suffragan to direct or protect them, I believe they wou'd not have gone; nay, I wou'd have hindred them but alas I had no such hopes myself. . . . As for Thorowgood I never knew his Fellow of his age, nor ever shall agen I fear, nothing can make this Country amends for their loss but a good Bp but alas! that is *rara avis in terris* &c."[65]

[64]*S. P. G. A-Series, III., #CLV. (Stevens & Brown Library of Congress Transcript).*
[65]*S. P. G. A-Series, IV., #LII. (Stevens & Brown Library of Congress Transcript).*

Talbot and the rest of the clergy were convinced that the presence of a resident bishop would protect the cloth from arbitrary interference and indignities of this sort. While Lord Cornbury had his defenders, it cannot be denied that the typical colonial governor was a man exceedingly jealous of his prerogatives, eager to impress his superiors back home with his efficiency, and somewhat patronising in his attitude towards religion. Furthermore, this episode shows Talbot in his true light, as a man ready to champion the cause of the unpopular and the oppressed, and glad to risk the imputation of disloyalty, if need be, rather than sully his ideals of right.

Once more in Burlington, Talbot was discouraged. He was probably of too restless a disposition to feel content in one place. During his absence, the Church had suffered; and the state of the province was worse than before. On the 20th of August, 1708, he wrote:

"We have lost our labour and the Society their cost, there being several Churches and no Ministers in all East Jersey to supply them, so that they fall away apace to heathenism, Quakerism and Atheism, purely for lack of looking after."

Of course, the presence of a bishop would remedy matters, in a land where the "Bodies and Souls of men . . . (are) ruin'd and undone, and the Bounty of the Society lost, for lack of an Overseer of the poor Church in America, without which the Gospel can't be Planted nor any good work propagated in the World."[66]

On the 24th of August, 1708, he wrote the Secretary of the Society:

"Ye are my witnesses that I pleaded with all my Soul, to send an Overseer of the poor Church but you wou'd not hear, therefore is this evil come upon us."

The particular evil to which he referred was the loss of Messrs. Moor and Brooke.

"We Christians in Jersey are most miserable; we have Churches now but no Ministers to open them and if the Gate of Heaven be shut, the Gates of Hell will soon prevail against us."

Since Brooke had gone, no one had visited Elizabeth Town and Amboy.

[66] *S. P. G. A-Series, IV., #LI. (Stevens & Brown Library of Congress Transcript); Protestant Episcopal Historical Collections, 1851, pp. 50-60.*

"I am forced to turn Itinerant agen for the care of all the Churches from East to West Jersey is upon me; what is the worst I can't confirm any nor have not a Deacon to help me; My Clark is put in Prison and was taken from the Church on the Lord's day upon a Civil Action of Meum & Tuum, I don't know how soon I may be served so myself, but I bless God I fear no evil so long as I do none."[67]

On the 30th of June, 1709, Talbot forwarded another gloomy report.

"The Churches in East Jersey are falling to the Ground for lack of looking after, I can't go there above once or twice a year to administer Holy Sacraments, that they be not quite Starved. It had been better not to have put these poor People to the Charge of building Churches, than have no body to supply them. I can't get so much as a Reader here for any of them and it were to save their Souls."

The need of bishops for ordaining ministers and keeping the churches supplied was surely urgent. Talbot's plea waxed eloquent.

"You that live at home at ease and Plenty, little do you know what they and we do bear & Suffer here, and how many thousand Souls are legally lost while they at home are legally supplying them. . . . Is it not strange that so many Islands shou'd be inhabited with Protestants, so many Provinces planted, by them, so many hundred thousand Souls born and bred up here in America; but of all the Kings, Princes, and Gov^{rs}, all the Bishops and Archbishops, that have been since the Reformation, they never sent any body here to propagate the Gospel,—I say to propagate it by imparting some spiritual gift by Ordination or Confirmation?"

But Talbot was doing his best to provide for the comfort of one who might appear. He said that he had secured "the best house in America for a Bishop's seat; the Archbishop told me he would contribute towards it and so I hope will others." As for Burlington, the Church was flourishing, and should soon be out of debt."[68]

[67]*S. P. G. A-Series, IV., #LII. (Stevens & Brown Library of Congress Transcript).*
[68]*S. P. G. A-Series, V., #XIX. (Stevens & Brown Library of Congress Transcript.).*

V. TALBOT'S BURLINGTON MINISTRY—ZEAL AND IN-
DUSTRY; PROBLEMS AND CONTROVERSY.

IN 1710, Robert Hunter became governor of New York and New Jersey. A strong-minded and imperious man, it was inevitable that sooner or later he would clash with the more positive members of the clergy. The story of his quarrel with the Reverend William Vesey, of Trinity Church, New York, is a painful chapter in colonial history. Soon after his arrival, Governor Hunter began to impute disloyal tendencies to the Reverend Mr. Talbot.[69] Nevertheless, he could not disregard the high esteem in which the New Jersey priest was held; and we find him writing to the Society, May 7th, 1711, that "Mr. Talbot I have found a perfect honest Man, and an indefatigable labourer; If he had less warmth he might have more success but that's the effect of Constitution." [70] Others who knew Talbot arrived at the same estimate. Jeremiah Bass, for example, church-warden of Burlington and a distinguished official, intimated to the S. P. G. that in some things Talbot might be more moderate, but "his conversation is unblameable and his care and concern more for the interest of the Church and the glory of God than for anything that can concern himself."[71] The appraisal made by Doctor Hamilton Schuyler, after a study of Talbot and his environment, is probably fair.

> "Talbot was a man of wide vision and tremendous energy. He was looked up to and trusted by his brother clergy and was moreover influential in political as well as religious circles. . . . As is often the case with men of Talbot's energetic disposition and abounding enthusiasm, he was wont to exalt his office and to be impatient with those who disputed his authority and thwarted his projects. Thus at times he came in conflict with the civil powers in the Colony and incurred their displeasure. His troubles were largely due to his zeal for the welfare of the Church and his rugged independence, which led him at times into opposition to those whom a more affable treatment might have conciliated."[72]

Steps were taken even before Governor Hunter's arrival to provide a house for the bishop who might be sent to America; Talbot

[69]John Fulton's monograph, in Perry: American Episcopal Church, I., p. 546.
[70]S. P. G. A-Series, VI., #70 (Stevens & Brown Library of Congress Transcript).
[71]George M. Hills: History of the Church in Burlington, N. J., p. 92.
[72]Hamilton Schuyler's Manuscript, cited supra.

showed in his correspondence of the year 1709 that he had been busy in this regard. When he reported to the Society that he had found suitable living quarters, it was decided to arrange the business details through the new governor. The following is quoted from the official Abstract of Proceedings of the S. P. G.:

> "It having been frequently represented to the Society, that there is a very great want of a Bishop to govern those Missionaries, whom the Society has, or shall, from time to time, send over to New-England, New-York, Pennsylvania, and other parts of the Continent of North-America, as well as the rest of the Clergy in those and the adjacent Colonies; and to ordain others, and to Confirm the children of the Clergy and Laity; this matter has been most seriously considered of, and is yet depending before the Society; and in the mean time, and till they can bring it to bear, they are looking out for the best and most commodious place, as near the centre as possible of the above mentioned Colonies, to fix the See for the said Bishop; and having been informed, that at Burlington, in New-Jersey, there is a spacious and very convenient House, with some Land belonging to it, (fit for the purpose) to be disposed of upon good terms, they have empowered the Hon. Col. Hunter, Her Majesty's Governor of New-York and the Jerseys, to treat with the Owner for the purchase thereof."[73]

Negotiations for the purchase of a site for a bishop's house came to a head on the 29th of October, 1712, when a deed was executed by John Tatham of NewYork, gentleman, and Mary his wife, to Governor Robert Hunter, for the Society of the Propagation of the Gospel in Foreign Parts. The Society paid six hundred pounds for the Tatham house, together with fifteen acres of ground and twelve acres of meadowland. The Reverend Mr. Talbot, at Governor Hunter's direction, secured the estimate of a carpenter for repairing the dwelling. The prospect of a bishop in America seemed most encouraging.[74]

On the 16th of January, 1713, the Society's Committee for Bishops and Bishoprics in America reported "that it is highly Expedient There be two Bishopricks Established in her Majesty's Dominions on the Continent of North America." The seat of one should be at Burlington; the other at Williamsburg, Virginia. The district of the former should extend from the east side of the Delaware River to the utmost bounds of her Majesty's dominions eastward, including Newfoundland; the district of the latter should extend from the west side of the Dela-

[73]*Abstract of Proceedings of S. P. G., 1711, p. 36.*
[74]*S. P. G. A-Series, VIII., pp. 212-219 (Stevens & Brown Library of Congress Transcript).*

ware to the utmost bounds of her Majesty's dominions westward. Likewise, two bishoprics should be established in the islands of America: the seat of one was to be in Barbados and the seat of the other was to be in Jamaica. The district of the former should comprise the two governments of Barbados and the Leeward Islands; the district of the later should be the governments of Jamaica, the Bahama Islands, and the Bermudas. Not less than £1000 sterling should be allowed for the maintenance of the said bishops, considering "the Great Extent of the Districts of the Bishopricks on the Continent and the Expensiveness of the Bishops Travelling in the Discharge of their Pastoral Care." Considering the greater dearness of provisions in the islands and the necessity of travel from one island to another, £1500 should be allowed the insular bishops. The two islands in the Delaware River near Burlington, supposed to be in the gift of the Crown, were to be sought for the maintenance of the bishops; furthermore, the bishops should be entitled to the tenth of future grants and escheats, as well as other provisions for their support.[75]

The plans for a resident bishop came to naught. With the death of Queen Anne, the hope for the immediate appointment of a bishop for the American colonies was dissipated. The House of Hanover was beset with political troubles; its very existence was in jeopardy, owing to Jacobite plots. As for the see-house in Burlington, the S. P. G. subsequently seemed to lose interest in it; and the building fell into decay. On November 1st, 1722, the church-wardens of Burlington wrote to the Society:

> "We are extremely sorry that your House at the point is so miserably out of repair and almost torn to pieces, since it was repaired by the care of one of us by the direction of Brigadier Hunter your Honors having taken the Charge out of our hands and put it into others who have done nothing. . . . We shall at all times be ready in that or any other thing to show our readiness to serve you."[76]

Talbot reminded the Society, November 22nd, 1722:

> "The Bishop's house here at the point is in the worst condition of all; tis nothing but a baudy-house, a sheep's cote and play house . . . tis in vain to repair it any more, unless some family be put in to guard it, I think . . . I would not live in the point house, if they would give it to me, but I am loathe to see it fall down as the coach house and

[75]S. P. G. A-Series, VII., pp. 105-109 (Stevens & Brown Library of Congress Transcript).
[76]Hamilton Schuyler's Manuscript, cited supra.

stables have already; and what will they do for the meadows, they will be lost if not claimed speedily; the witnesses will be dead that know where the lands lie."

He suggested that the house might be used for a free school or college: "it is very well contrived for that purpose."[77] On the 20th of September, 1723, Daniel Coxe and William Trent advised the Society that they had persuaded, "with much difficulty," an honest gentleman, the deputy secretary to the province and a justice of the peace, to live in the bishop's house at Burlington; repairs had been made.[78] Seventeen years later (May 3rd, 1740), the Reverend Colin Campbell, rector of St. Mary's Church, Burlington, wrote the Secretary:

> "I am heartily sorry the Society takes so little notice of their house here, which if not timely looked to will inevitably go to ruin and decay."[79]

In 1748, the house was destroyed by fire. Thus came to a melancholy end the ambitious project to establish a colonial see at Burlington.[80]

Governor Hunter's evident interest in the Church did not convince the clergy of his sincerity. We find the Reverend Mr. Talbot complaining of the conditions that prevail. The Churches in New York, New Jersey, and Pennsylvania never wanted patronage so much as now, he wrote, August 31st, 1713.

> "The Rights of the Church are invaded and Possest by her Enemies, Affidavits are procured and dispersed by the worst of men against the best Missionaries, the plate and Books given by the Society and other Benefactors are violently carried away, and those who Pretend to be Promoters of the Gospel use all wayes and means amongs, and have perswaded one unworthy Brother to carry affidavits from Province to Province ag^t another, And as I have allways Said wee cannot Expect any better Treatment till we have a Superior Pastor to Order and Establish the Church. This is the one thing necessary, which I have been Solliciting these ten Years. I find it all in vain for them or us to offer to propagate the Gospel or Erect the Church without Bishop or Deacon, which I humbly offer to our Superiors at home for the burden is too hard upon us poor Presbiters, who labour under all Sorts of Perils and Difficulties which we are not able to bear any longer."[81]

[77]*Ibid.*
[78]*Ibid.*
[79]*Ibid.*
[80]*Ibid.*
[81]*S. P. G. A-Series, VIII., pp. 181-182 (Stevens & Brown Library of Congress Transcript).*

The differences between Doctor Vesey of Trinity Church, New York, and Governor Hunter reached such a state that the former decided to go to England to seek relief. In this unpleasantness, he had the sympathy and support of his brother clergy; and Talbot and others supplied his parish during his absence. The trip proved successful; and Vesey returned with the commendation of the Bishop of London and an appointment as commissary. Colonel Hunter felt the sting of the rebuke, however; and while he maintained an outward friendliness, he felt little affection either for Vesey or for those who had sided with him.

An act passed in New Jersey about this time enabled Quakers and other dissenters (even those who abstained from taking oaths) to occupy positions of trust and profit in the government, as well as to serve on grand and petit juries. This procedure was regarded with gloomy forebodings by the Anglicans, who were keenly aware of their numerical disadvantage and saw the aggressiveness of those outside their fold. Hence they complained about the act in no uncertain terms. The rector, wardens, and vestry of St. Mary's Church, Burlington, addressed the Queen; and declared that "this unrighteous Act delivers up the Church to the Power of her Implacable Enemies the Quakers and of all Sects of Dissenters the most dangerous to Christianity." They added:

> "This Impious Act gives them (by the Laws they shall make and by the Judgments they shall please to give) a liberty to dispose of the Estates & Libertyes of your Majestys Subjects and to controle or persecute the Church purely upon the Credit of their bare Affidavits without any lawfull Obligation injoyned upon them to the contrary, upon wch sacred Obligation of Religious Oaths depend all the Laws of Great Britain both Ecclesiastical and Civil."

They prayed that such law would receive no sanction from her Majesty: "Wee are more aggrieved to see the Church of Christ in the Power of Quakers;" and they hoped for protection "from ye Power of Schismaticks and Quakers, from the Priest Hood of Micha, from ye Snare of the Hunter, from the Counsellors of Zoane, from the Statutes of Omri."[82] It is obvious that Talbot, who undoubtedly was the author of this address, used the biblical expression, "ye Snare of the Hunter," with very specific intention.

In their appeal to the Society for the Propagation of the Gospel of Foreign Parts, the wardens of St. Mary's, Burlington, contended that

[82] S. P. G. A-Series, IX., pp. 192-202 (Stevens & Brown Library of Congress Transcript).

"all those good designs" would not be endangered by laws meant "to discourage and ruin our Infant Church and propagate false and Erroneous Principles destructive to the Interest both of the Church and State," if there had been a resident bishop, who might put a stop to those growing mischiefs. "From the Apostles day to this time," there was never a period "when so many thousand souls as the Northern Colonys alone have inhabiting in them and the greatest part of them professing themselves members of an Episcopal Church have no Bishop residing amongst them to Rule and Govern." Hence there could be no wonder, if the members grew "careless Remiss and Slack in their duty if many fall into Scandalous and damning Errors If Atheism Deism, Quakerism Freethinking & other Heresies increase amongst us, If Scandals are both given and taken when the Ecclesiastical Sword is wanting to punish Evil doers to Reduce the Erroneous & Cast of(f) the Heretiques."[83]

That churchmen, who were few and disorganised in the colonies, and cordially disliked by the Quakers and other religious bodies in those days of bigotry and intolerance, had reason to fear injustice and oppression when their cases came before judges and jurors of hostile persuasion, was the thought in the minds of those who signed these addresses. Governor Hunter, who approved the act and affixed his signature to the same, must have been considerably annoyed when he heard that a protest had gone to England against a measure which he favored. The clergy of the Established Church in the colonies certainly incurred the resentment and displeasure of the political heads, who strove hard to discredit them. When no other ground was available, they could be accused of disloyalty to the present government and of cherishing Jacobite sympathies. This was a charge easy to make and hard to deny convincingly, in those days of bitter partisan feeling. Such an accusation was especially calculated to arouse the suspicion of the civil authorities. Talbot and other clergymen suffered from this insinuation.

Mindful not only of what he considered a dangerous life but also of the humiliations which his brother clergymen had suffered because of the civil authorities, Talbot wrote the following complaint (May 11th, 1714):—

> "Who that has any sense of Religion (who teaches us Duty to our God, Loyalty to our Sovereign and love to our Country) can with any Patience behold ye Doctrines of the Gospel ridiculed and Vilified, the Church of Christ undermined and Shaken, and the Laws of England intirely Subverted. The most Impious and Atheistical Books and Tenets

[83]S. P. G. A-Series, IX., pp. 98-100 (Stevens & Brown Library of Congress Transcript).

are not only cunningly and privately but Impudently and publickly spread abroad and promulgated & even Acts of Assembly past (containing most abominable ffalsitys to make them the more pallatable) in order to Countenance the Quakers those Enemies to our Church and Holy Religion, and Enable them to act in all places of Trust and proffit in the Government as well as to serve on Grand and Petty Jurys, by wch means they are capable by Indictments &c to destroy the Reputation of or at least to cast an! Odium on ye Ministers and Members of the Church of England."

He also deplored "the frequent and Scandalous Reports against many sober and Religious Divines, and threatening even the very Lives of others."[84]

But Talbot's concern over political issues did not impair his effectiveness as a clergyman. On the 28th of October, 1714, the industrious missionary, then almost seventy and at last impaired by the prevailing sickness, gave a summary of his activities. During the epidemic, he had busied himself; but many Church people died that had nobody to visit them when sick, nor bury them when dead. He had been obliged to give up preaching because of his own physical condition.

"I have been long enough in these Parts to see Iniquity established by Law and that by some of your own Members, and what good can Your Missionaries do. . . . In all this Province of West New Jersey there never was any Minister of Christ's Church settled but myself. I have built 3 Churches since I came here, but have no body to help them nor myself neither. We have had a very hard time this year, I have buried more than in ten before and many Christian People dyed that had no body to visit them when sick nor bury them when dead."

He upbraided the Society for not sending deacons as school-masters, in accordance with their original resolution. If the Society had done so, the deacons could have kept the church-doors open; they could have read the prayers and homilies, and baptised and catechised the youth; they could have visited the sick and buried the dead. Now, alas, the people must bury one another.

"They have no where to go but to Quakers meetings which are as bad as Indians there's nothing but Pawawing and Conjuring to raise a Devil they cannot lay again and now this Wickedness is Establisht by Law."

[84] *S. P. G. A-Series, IX., pp. 202-204 (Stevens & Brown Library of Congress Transcript).*

In the same letter, Talbot told of the opening of the church at New Bristol, under the Reverend Francis Phillips.

"I went now and then to preach there on Sundays in the afternoon before I was sick, but since that I have not been able, so the Church has been shutt up, almost ever since it was Opened."

The church there was begun by the late Thoroughgood Moor; and, said Talbot,—

"When he was taken away by this same Cursed Faction that is now Rampant, I was unwilling that any of his good Works should fall to the Ground, so I crost the Water at my own Cost to serve these poor People who lived in Darkness and the Shadow of death in the Midst of Heathenism, Atheism, and Quakerism; but it pleased God by our preaching the word in season and out of season, some came to believe and were baptized they and their Children."

Talbot had presented the New Bristol congregation with a gift of of five pounds and a pulpit of black marble. Since the work was discontinued, the Quakers are asking, "Where is your Church, it may serve us for a meeting house."[85]

Governor Hunter could not long regard with complacency a clergyman who took such an uncompromising stand wherever the Church and its rights were involved, and who seemed so little awed by the power of the secular arm. In looking for some vulnerable point to attack, he took advantage of that issue which was causing no end of bitterness in Great Britain—the strife between the Crown and the adherents of the dispossessed heir of King James the Second. The struggles of the Pretenders to gain the English throne were long and bloody; and insinuations of disloyalty, once more, were difficult to refute. Merely to intimate that a person holding a position of trust was a Jacobite sympathiser was sufficient to incite resentment as well as suspicion. On the 9th of April, 1715, the governor notified the Board of Trade that "Mr Talbot has Incorporated the Jacobites in ye Jersies under ye name of a Church in order to Sanctifie his Sedition & Insolence to ye Governm^t;" and he suggested that "if ye Society take not more care for ye future y^n had been taken hitherto in ye Choice of their Missionaries, instead of Establishing Religion they^ll destroy all Governm^t & good Manners."[86]

[85]S. P. G. A-Series, IX., pp. 167-169 (Stevens &Brown Library of Congress Transcript); Protestant Episcopal Historical Collections, 1851, pp. 66-67.
[86]S. P. G. A-Series, X., p. 178; S. P. G. A-Series, XI., p. 301 (Stevens & Brown Library of Congress Transcript).

The complaint promptly reached the Society; and on the 23rd of August, the same year, the Secretary wrote Mr. Talbot that serious charges had been made concerning his behaviour. Talbot replied with an indignant denial; he declared that Governor Hunter does not visit the church in Burlington once in three years, and has no personal knowledge on which to base his accusations. Still the royal governors were hostile in their attitude towards the Church and its members. Mr. Bass, the chief church-warden at Burlington, "as diligent and faithful a servant of the Church and Crown as any, has been belied out of his Secretary's Office, and fined, and confined in the Common Gaol, for nothing but defending the Royal Law of King George, against an idol of the heathenish Quakers. Mr. Alexander Griffiths died heart-broken, being falsely accused." The school-master at Burlington, Rowland Ellis, "is very much discouraged in his business by a Quaker school-master being set up in opposition to his license." Such hardships had been mentioned by royal governors, who had been made members of the Society.

> "God help us for Governm^t here—especially your outlying members, I don't know one of them good. I am sorry I should be accused of sedition in my old age after I have travelled more than any body to keep the peace in church and state."

As for his loyalty to the present government, Talbot suggested, "please to ask Mr Secretary Hall and he will tell you that I was a Williamite from the beginning"—that is, a supporter of King William instead of King James the Second.

> "Let them consult the admiralty office and they will find I took all the oaths that were necessary to qualify me for the service which I have performed faithfully abroad and at home. As soon as I have time I will call the Church together to answer for themselves and me too to the illustrious Society for propagating the Gospel, &c. Meanwhile the Lord rebuke that evil spirit of lying and slander that is gone out against the Church. Here and there they spare none. I suffer like my Lord and Master between two at Philadelphia and New York, but God has been my succour and I doubt not but he will still deliver me from the snare of the Hunter."[87]

(The reader will note the pun.)

The wardens and vestry of Burlington endorsed Mr. Talbot's denial. They informed the Society that they had had "ye happiness at

[87]*Protestant Episcopal Historical Collections, 1851, p. 77; Historical Collections, Pennsylvania, edited by William Stevens Perry, pp. 93-94; S. P. G. A-Series, XI., pp. 328-329 (Stevens & Brown Library of Congress Transcript).*

your Expence, of being Educated under ye Care, of a truly Pious &
Apostolick Person, the Revd Mr Talbot the fervour & excellencies of
whose discourses and ye Piety of whose Life are ye best Recommendations, of ye Religion he professes." For twelve years Talbot had cared
for them and for the neighbouring congregations.

> "In all y^t time we are bound to assert, y^t we never heard,
> either in his publick Discourses, or Private Conversations,
> anything y^t might tend towards Incouraging Sedition, or any
> wiles Insolencing ye Goverm^t."

They avowed their resentment of Colonel Hunter's insinuations:
"what could conduce this Gentleman to Endeavour to fix so Barbarous
& Groundless, is to us altogether unaccountable." Finally, they expressed their own loyalty to the reigning house, and said that they daily
offered up their prayers for the royal family.[88]
The Society evidently felt that Colonel Hunter had registered his
accusations without sufficient knowledge of the facts, and that he had
been unjust in not affording Mr. Talbot an opportunity to present his
side when the charges were made. Accordingly, on the 14th of May,
1716, the Secretary addressed the governor, as follows:

> "The Society for the propagation of the Gospel in fforeign
> parts make it their request to your Excellency that you Would
> inform them if any of their Missionaries within your Excel-
> lencys Governments of New York or New Jersey are disaf-
> fected to the Governm^t of his Majesty King George & if there
> be any Such that your Excellency would be pleas'd to Specifie
> the Matter upon which the Charge of Such Disaffection is
> Grounded and Cause a Coppy of Such Accusation to be De-
> livered to the persons Accused before it is transmitted hither,
> that if they have any thing to offer in defence of themselves
> they may have a Speedy Opportunity of transmitting it to the
> Society."[89]

A little later, Talbot learned that his bills against the Society for
his services had been ordered to lie unpaid for half of a year, doubtless
due to Colonel Hunter's slanders. Such a postponement was very em-
barrassing to the missionary; and he wrote the Society:

> "I don't know any thing y^t I have done Contrary to my
> Duty either in Church or State, But if it be Resolved y^t no

[88]*S. P. G. A-Series, XI.*, pp. 300-304 (*Stevens & Brown Library of Congress Transcript*).
[89]*S. P. G. A-Series, XI.*, p. 373 (*Stevens & Brown Library of Congress
Transcript*).

English man Shall be in Mission or Commission, Apud Americanos I dont know what we have done y^t we should all give place to Scotch, Irish, but I am Content to Suffer with good Company. . . . The Poor Church of God here in ye Wilderness, Thers none to Guide her by ye hand of all the Sons y^t she has brought up."

He recalled how the Apostles went to the rescue of the converts of Samaria, and how Paul and Barnabas were sent out, and how Paul journeyed to Macedonia; "but we have been there these 20 Year Calling till our Hearts Ake," but without response.

"I must say this if ye Honble Society dont do more in a short time than they have in a long, they will I fear loose their Hon^r & their Charact^r to, I dont pretend to prophesy but you know how they said the Kingdom of God shall be taken from y^m & given to a Nation y^t will bring forth ye fruits of it."[90]

When the Reverend Mr. Talbot, in a former letter, spoke of suffering like his Lord and Master "between two at Philadelphia and New York," he had in mind the opposition not only of Governor Hunter but also of the Pennsylvania governor. In 1715, the Reverend Evan Evans of Philadelphia visited England; and during his absence, his place was filled by the Reverend Francis Phillips, a man of ingratiating personality from all accounts but one of the most immoral men in colonial Church history. His conduct did a great deal of harm, but he succeeded in getting the support of Governor Charles Gookin. When complaints were made of his behaviour (which involved nothing short ot a charge of seduction), the Bishop of London placed the Philadelphia parish in the care of Mr. Talbot. Phillips and his friends were not easily vanquished; they tried to hold on in the face of local feeling and a strong public opinion. When at last the Bishop decided against them, they were compelled to give up possession of the church. But they retaliated by making Talbot's ministry as difficult as possible. Governor Gookin proceeded to charge the New Jersey priest with Jacobite sympathies.[91] He refused to attend the church as long as Talbot held services, going instead to the Swedish church.[92] He even averred that Talbot had refused to take the oath of allegiance to King George—an ac-

[90]*S. P. G. A-Series, XI., pp. 334-335 (Stevens & Brown Library of Congress Transcript).*

[91]*Perry: American Episcopal Church, p. 232.*

[92]*Historical Collections, Pennsylvania, edited by William Stevens Perry, p. 93.*

cusation which once more inclined the Society to suspect their missionary's loyalty to the Crown. In fact, the Secretary (August 2nd, 1717) instructed Mr. Talbot, that "if you have not already taken the Oaths to his majesty King George that you do without delay, by the first convenience transmit to the Society an authentic Certificate of your having so done."[93]

On June 2nd, 1718, a petition addressed to the archbishops and bishops of the Church of England, and signed by prominent clergymen and laymen of Pennsylvania, New Jersey, and Maryand (including the Reverend George Ross of New Castle, the Reverend Mr. Talbot, and Attorney-General Bass of the Jerseys), was forwarded, in the desperate hope that a bishop might be obtained for America.

"The representation and humble petition of many of the faithful in the communion of the Church of England in North America, Most humbly sheweth:

"That whereas, the British colonies and settlements in America have now for many years been blessed with the pure and primitive doctrine and worship of our mother, the Church of England, of which you are happy at this day in (being) the great ornaments and rulers;

"And whereas for want of Episcopacy's being Established amongst us and that there has never been any Bp sent to Visit us, Our Churches remain unconsecrated, our Children are grown up and cannot be confirmed; their Sureties are under Solemn Obligations but cannot be absolved & our Clergy sometimes under Doubts and cannot be resolved.

"But whereas more Especially for the Want of that Sacred Power which is Inherent to Your Apostolick the Vacancies which daily happen in our Ministry cannot be supply'd for a considerable time from England whereby many congregacons are not only become desolate and the light of the Gospell therein Extinguished but great Encouragement is thereby given to Sectaries of all Sorts which abound and Increase amongst us, and some of them pretending to what they call the power of Ordination the Countrey is filled with Fanatick teachers debauching the good inclinations of many poor Souls who are left destitute of any Instruction or Ministry;

"May it therefore please your lordships, in your great piety and regard for the government of the Church by bishops, to think of some means whereby these sorrowful complaints and most grievous misfortunes may be heard and redressed, and that Almighty God may, of his infinite mercy, inspire your thoughts, and assist your pious endeavours to accomplish this evident necessary work, is the most earnest and daily prayer

[93]*George M. Hills: History of the Church in Burlington, N. J., p. 152.*

of, may it please your lordships, your lordships' most humble petitioners and most obedient sons and servants.'[94]

Talbot was probably beginning to smart under the rather cautious and restrained attitude which the Society displayed towards him; he felt that he had been an indefatigable worker in the service of the Church, but that he had been the target of powerful critics. On the 3rd of May, 1718, he had written to the Secretary of the Society:

"All your missionaries hereabouts are going to Maryland, for the sake of themselves, their wives and children; for my part, I cannot desert my poor Flock, that I have gathered, nor will I, if I have neither money, credit, nor Tobacco. But if I had known as much as I do now, that the Society have not been able, for their parts, to send Bishop, Priest, nor Deacon, no Lecturer, nor Catechist, no hinter, nor holderforth, I would never have put the good people in these parts to the charge and trouble of building Churches; (nay, now they must be stalls, or stables for Quakers horses, when they come from market or meeting) as I said before, but some people will not believe till it is too late. Dr. Evans himself is gone to Maryland, for he says nobody will serve the Church for nought, as I do; for my part, I cannot blame the People in these parts, for they do what they are able."[95]

The Burlington parish register of 1719 shows a list of books "belonging to Burlington Library revised by Mr. John Talbot Incumber & Mich: Piper (Michael Piper) ye 25th day of March 1719." In this early parish library, there were 252 titles given, including classics, scientific works, theology, and devotional items. Talbot wrote the Secretary of the Society, September 7th, 1724, a letter which would indicate that the collection was a private one, designed for the use of the parish. "There is no parochial library yet, for I never had any, from the Society, but I design to leave mine, and Mr. Thorogood Moor's, when I die, to that use."[96]

In 1720, Talbot went to England, where he applied for the interest on a legacy of £1000, which Archbishop Tenison had left towards the settlement of bishops in America, and for the maintenance of deserving missionaries of the province of Canterbury until such time as bishops

[94]S. P. G. A-Series, XIV., pp. 144-147 (Stevens & Brown Library of Congress Transcript).
[95]S. P. G. A-Series, XIII., p. 370 (Stevens & Brown Library of Congress Transcript).
[96]George M. Hills: History of the Church in Burlington, N. J., pp. 156-160, 190.

were lawfully appointed.[97]   He was supported by the testimonial of the Burlington wardens and vestrymen, who wrote:

> "We should justly accuse o^{r}selves of ye highest ingratitude did we not take this opportunity by o^r worthy pastor the Revd Mr John Talbot to return You o^r hearty thanks for the inexpressible benefit that we have received by the Mission of him amongst us;
> "A true and unfeigned Zeal for the Glory of God & ye good of his Church hath during his time with us influenced the whole of his life & conversaċon & his exemplary piety hath as much adorned (wth grief we may say) the unguarded lives of some y^t hath been Missionaries amongst us."[98]

In April, 1721, the interest on Archbishop Tenison's legacy was directed by order of chancery to be paid to Mr. Talbot, on account of his long service as a missionary of the Society, the true pains he had exhibited in his holy function, his zeal, his exemplary life and conversation, and his great service to the Church.[99]

Talbot returned to Burlington, in 1722, full of zeal for his work, and evidently very much pleased over the mark of confidence that he had received. He wrote the Secretary from Burlington, November 27th, 1722, that he and the Reverend William Skinner (missionary to Perth Amboy) had arrived in safety—"never better Weather nor so good a passage as the Capt. said (who was a Quaker) they & the Sailors Used to say they had no good luck when ye Priests were on board but now they are prettily Convinced—& finely converted to say so no more." He was cordially received. "All Sorts & Conditions of men women & Children were glad to see us return for they had given me over." The house purchased for a bishop's residence at Burlington was found in bad shape.

There was plenty of work awaiting Mr. Talbot; he had fifteen miles to travel from the capes of Delaware to the hills and mountains in East Jersey, with none to help him but a Swedish minister, who was planning to leave. During one month, he visited Trenton, Hopewell, and Amwell; and preached and visited the sick. In one day, he had nineteen baptisms.[100]

Talbot was able to report, December 9th, 1723, that the Society's house at Burlington had been restored to order.

[97]*S. P. G. A-Series, XIV., pp. 44-45 (Stevens & Brown Library of Congress Transcript).*
[98]*S. P. G. A-Series, XIV., p. 151 (Stevens & Brown Library of Congress Transcript).*
[99]*Protestant Episcopal Historical Collections, 1851, pp. 79-80; John Fulton's monograph, in Perry: American Episcopal Church, I., p. 550.*
[100]*Protestant Episcopal Historical Collections, 1851, pp. 81-82.*

"The Gardens, Orchard and pasture are fenced all round and, what is more than ever was done, they have got an honest man . . . to live there as Adam did in Paradise to dress it and keep it so 'tis fit now for any Governor in Church or State."

In fact, Governor William Burnet of New York had said that it was more pleasant than Salisbury. That gentleman had succeded Colonel Robert Hunter.[101]

[101]*George M. Hills: History of the Church in Burlington, N. J., pp. 176-177.*

VI. TALBOT'S LAST YEARS, AND THE QUESTION OF HIS CONSECRATION TO THE EPISCOPATE.

THE Indian summer of Talbot's life was of short duration; the storm-clouds surged upon him soon after his return to America. In December, 1723, he visited Philadelphia for medical treatment; and while recuperating, he supplied Christ Church. But that parish was in a state of turmoil, because of the dismissal of the Reverend John Urmstone, a priest of contemptible character who had involved himself in serious difficulties wherever he had gone. Urmstone had filled the vacancy created by the death of the Reverend Mr. Vicary; but during his stay at Philadelphia, as Peter Evans, a lawyer, said, "the misfortune that drove him from Carolina & other places still attended him & his behaviour became such at Philadelphia as is not proper to be mentioned or allowed in any sober society."[102] Leaving Pennsylvania, he had gone to Maryland, from whence he wrote letters seeking to vindicate himself and incidentally to damage the reputation of the Philadelphia vestry and all who might have stood in his way or helped supplant him. He complained that he had been "kicked out very dirtily by the Vestry." But, he added, "I was not sorry for my removal from so precarious and slavish a place, where they require two Sermons every Lord's Day, Prayers all the week, and Homilies on Festivals, besides abundance of Funerals, Christenings at home, and sick to be visited; no settled salary, the Church-wardens go from house to house every six months, every one gives what he pleases."[103]

In June, 1724, the Reverend Doctor Robert Welton arrived in Philadelphia, a stranger. The circumstances of the parish were very melancholy; there was no regular minister, and since Talbot had returned to Burlington, there had been no services for months. As Peter Evans described the scene, there was a "numerous congregation, which if kept together were not only able but willing to raise a handsome support for a Missionary." So the vestry extended a call to Doctor Welton, so as to prevent the dwindling of the congregation; and requested that he officiate until the coming of a missionary.[104]

But Doctor Welton had a past history, which, without involving his moral character, certainly rendered him obnoxious to the Establish-

[102]*Historical Collections, Pennsylvania, edited by Williams Stevens Perry, p. 141.*
[103]*Historical Collections, Maryland, edited by William Stevens Perry, pp. 236-237.*
[104]*Historical Collections, Pennsylvania, edited by William Stevens Perry, pp. 129-142.*

ment. He had been deprived of the rectorship of Whitechapel, London, for his adherence to the Non-Jurors, who were in great disfavour at the time because of their allegiance to the Stuart line. In 1723-4, Doctor Welton had even been consecrated bishop by Ralph Taylor, of the Non-Jurors. This act of consecration, by Taylor alone and on his own authority, was so irregular that neither Taylor nor Welton was ever recognised as bishop by any of the English Non-Jurors.[105] But Welton's identification with interests antagonistic to the Crown and to the English Church prevented him from serving long in Philadelphia; in January, 1726, an order was received recalling him. The writ was served; and Welton left soon afterwards. He was last heard of in Lisbon.

In the meantime, however, an anonymous letter, dated July 29th, 1724, and sent from Cecil County, Maryland—doubtless from John Urmstone—was addressed to the Reverend Doctor Thomas Bray, one of the most influential clergymen of the Church, complaining of the Reverend Mr. Talbot's disaffection to the present government.[106] In August, the same year, the Reverend Jacob Henderson, of Maryland, probably relying on Urmstone's information, wrote home that "Mr Talbot, minister of Burlington, returned from England about two years ago in Episcopal orders, though his orders till now of late have been kept a great secret."[107] That month, Governor Burnet wrote that Talbot "had the folly to confess to some that have published it that he is a Bishop."[108]

Concerning Henderson's and Burnet's letters, the Reverend John Fulton, who made an exhaustive study of the question, remarked that "Henderson and Burnet were evidently repeating Urmston's slander, so that Urmston alone is absolutely the only contemporary witness to prove that Talbot ever pretended to be or ever admitted that he was, a bishop by non-juror consecration."[109] It may be remarked at this juncture that more evidence has come to light since Fulton's able and conscientious investigation was made; in the meantime we shall take up the order of events and later consider the light which has recently been thrown on the subject.

Urmstone's own signed letter was written September 29th, 1724, to Philip Stubbs, who transmitted the information to the Bishop of London. He said:

[105]John Fulton's monograph, in Perry: American Episcopal Church, I., pp. 542-543. This whole monograph ("The Non-Juring Bishops in America"), pp. 541-560, will repay study.
[106]S. P. G. Journal, V., p. 19.
[107]Historical Collections, Maryland, edited by William Stevens Perry, p. 243.
[108]George M. Hills: History of the Church in Burlington, N. J., p. 188.
[109]John Fulton's monograph, in Perry: American Episcopal Church, I., p. 553.

"Mr Talbot did me no diskindness in causing me to be
turned out of Philadelphia to make room for himself. He convened all the Clergy to meet, put on his robes & demanded
Episcopal obedience from them. One wiser than the rest refused, acquainted the Govr with the ill consequences thereof,
the danger he would run of losing his Gov^{mt}, whereupon the
Govr ordered the Church to be shut up."[110]

The same embittered clergyman renewed the charges which others
had made against Mr. Talbot, and which the poor minister had tried so
zealously to deny—the charges of disloyalty. The letter written to Doctor Bray in June, 1724, from Maryland, accused Talbot of poisoning
all neighbouring clergy with rebellious principles.

"They dare not pray otherwise than he does when he is
present . . . Some of his confidents have discovered that he is
in————————orders, as many more rebels are. I have
heard of no ordination that he has made as yet, but doubtless
he'll perswuade all the clergy who are his creatures to be ordained again by him.'"[111]

Furthermore,

"Govr Burnet hath been long displeased with (Talbot),
by reason he is a notorious Jacobite, & will not pray for the
King & Royal Family by name, only says the King & Prince,
by w^{ch} 'tis obvious whom he means. He hath often endeavoured
to perswaude me to do so too."

When Talbot returned from England, the letter stated, he came
fraught—

"with some of the most virulent & scandalous pamphlets he
could pick up; one I met with by chance whose title was the
case truly stated, proving that all ordained by Bishops consecrated since or such as conformed & approved of the revolution are imposters, & the divine service is only to be performed by those who have been re-ordained by non-jurors."[112]

The accusations had their effect. Talbot's loyalty had been questioned more than once; and the Society, anxious to get rid of any seditious elements and to prove their allegiance to the Crown, acted ad-

[110]*Historical Collections, Pennsylvania*, edited by *William Stevens Perry, pp.
142-143.*
[111]*Protestant Episcopal Historical Collections, 1851, p. 91.*
[112]*Historical Collections, Maryland*, edited by *William Stevens Perry, pp.
236ff.*

versely to the missionary's interests. On the 16th of October, 1724, the following order was recorded:

> "The Society being informed that their Missionary at Burlington, in New Jersey, would never take the oaths to the King, and never prays for him by name in the Liturgy— Ordered that the Secretary acquaint him that the Society have received the said information from a Person of very good credit, and therefore have suspended payment of his salary till he can clear himself of those facts laid to his charge."

At the same time steps were taken to prevent any further payment to Talbot of the interest in the Archbishop's legacy.

> "Ordered that the Secretary wait on Mr. Bennett the Master of the Chancery to know how far the said Mr. Talbot has received the interest of the £1000 left by the late Archbishop Tenison for the Establishment of Bishops in America; and to desire him to put a stop to any future payment of the same."[113]

Unfortunately for Talbot, the true character of Urmstone was not yet known to his correspondents, as Fulton remarks. "Unfortunately, too, the Bishop of London, under whose patronage Talbot had received the Tenison legacy was dead. Still more unfortunately, the members of the board of managers of the S. P. G. were new men, unacquainted with his previous history, and ignorant of his previous vindication from false charges of disloyalty. . . . The allegations against Talbot went to the new bishop, and from the new bishop to the new board, with all the startling freshness of novelty." It is apparent that they acted hastily.[114]

On the 29th of November, 1724, the minutes of the Society state that "the Secretary acquainted the Board . . . he finds that Mr. Talbot has received the interest of the £1000 . . . to Midsummer last, and that Mr. Bennett has promised that no further payment shall be made to him."[115]

With an efficiency which the Society never seemed to apply to the matters so near the poor missionary's heart, the following action was taken and recorded, December 18th, 1724:

> "Upon reading the Minutes of the Society at last meeting relating to Mr. Talbot, and a letter without name to Dr.

[113]*John Fulton's monograph, in Perry: American Episcopal Church, I., p. 554.*
[114]*Ibid., p. 553.*
[115]*S. P. G. Journal, V., p. 12.*

Bray dated Cecil County in Maryland 29 July 1724 sent to the
Board by the Lord Bishop of London complaining of Mr. Talbot's Disaffection to the present Government, etc., and the
Board being informed that Dr. Welton is arrived in Philadelphia, in Pennsylvania: Ordered that letters be wrote to the
Governors of New York and Pennsylvania acquainting them
with the accounts the Society have received of the behaviour
of Mr. Talbot and Dr. Welton and particularly acquainting
Governor Burnet that the Society have, upon the first information they received of Mr. Talbot's disaffection to the Government, suspended the payment of his Salary from this Board and
stopt the further payment of the Interest of the late Archbishop Tenison's Thousand Pounds bequeathed for settling
Bishops in America."[116]

The Governor forthwith ordered Talbot to desist from holding
religious services. On the 2nd of July, 1725, the distressed clergyman
wrote the Bishop of London: "I know nothing about it; nor any body
else in all the world. I could disprove it by a thousand witnesses."
He appealed to the bishop to do him the right, as he had done him the
wrong; and to allow him to remain *in statu quo.*

"As your Lordship has done me the wrong, so I hope you
will do me the right upon better information, to let me be in
statu quo,—for indeed I have suffered great wrong for no offence of fault that I know of. A long, long penance have I done
for crime, alas! to me unknown, but God has been with me,
and made all things work together for good; meanwhile I
hope your lordship will hear the right, and do nothing rashly,
but upon your authority for the edification and not for the destruction of this poor Church."[117]

On the 8th of July, Talbot wrote the Society, acknowledging their
letter telling him that he was out of quantum with the Society, and that
a bill of thirty pounds had been protested. He asserted that he was entitled to three quarters' salary; "for I never knew any Board discard
ye officers but they paid em for the time being in their Service."

But Talbot's pleas were of no avail. The Society, on the 15th of
October, 1725, noted his letter, praying that he might be paid his salary
to Lady Day; but "agreed that this matter be suspended till the Society
can be informed where his residence has been and how he has performed
Divine Service since Lady Day 1724 and that Mr. Tovey to whom the
bills are payable be acquainted that the Society expect before any money
be paid to Mr. Talbot he should transmit proper certificates of such

[116]*S. P. G. Journal, V., p. 19.*
[117]*Protestant Episcopal Historical Collections, 1851, pp. 83-84.*

his residence and performance of Divine Service."[118] The month before (September 17th), they had received a letter "intimating what's necessary to be done to discharge the order in chancery for the payment of the Interest of the late Archbishop Tenison's legacy to Mr. Talbot;" and had agreed "that it is not proper any more interest should be paid to Mr. Talbot, and that Mr. Edwards be desired to proceed in the proper manner in the Court of Chancery for discharging said order."[119]

Memorials were sent from the wardens and vestrymen of Christ Church, Philadelphia, from St. James's Church, New Bristol, and from St. Mary's, Burlington, expressing regret at Mr. Talbot's discharge from the Society. He "for nigh thirty years past has behaved himself with indefatigable pains, and good success in his Ministry," it was declared. "By his exemplary life and ministry, he has been the greatest advocate for the Church of England, by Law Established, that ever appeared on this shore."[120] Another and quite significant tribute came from the new rector of Christ Church, Philadelphia, the Reverend Archibald Cumming, who submitted his testimonial of the high regard in which Talbot was held, at the risk of incurring the displeasure of his superiors. He wrote the Bishop of London, October 19th, 1726, exonerating Talbot from sharing the disaffection and disloyalty of Doctor Welton. "Welton attacked the Establishment, urging people not to receive those who came among them." Cumming had been importuned by the people of Burlington and of Pennsylvania to write to his Lordship in favour of Talbot.

> "They made me promise to mention him, otherwise I would not presume to do it. He is universally beloved, even by the Dissenters here, and has done a great deal of good. Welton and he differed and broke off correspondence, by reason of the rash chimerical projects of the former long before the Government took notice of them. If he were connived at and could be assisted by the Society (for I am told the old man's circumstances are very mean), he promises by his friends to be peaceable and easy, and do all the good he can for the future."[121]

But Talbot's end was near. He passed away on St. Andrew's day, November 30th, 1727. Before his death he made over in trust to the wardens of St. Mary's Church, Burlington, certain tracts of land and buildings in Burlington, to which he held a title, retaining a life-interest

---

[118]*S. P. G. Journal, V., p. 58.*
[119]*Ibid., p. 57.*
[120]*Protestant Episcopal Historical Collections, 1851, pp. 85-86.*
[121]*Historical Collections, Pennsylvania, edited by William Stevens Perry, pp. 148-149.*

in the income of the property,. which after his decease was to be applied "to the use, benefit, and behoof of a presbyter of the Church of England as by law now established, that hath received episcopal ordination and is admitted to the cure of St. Mary's Church at Burlington." Before enjoying the income, his successors were required, after admission to the cure, "upon Easter day or Whitsunday," or certain holy days following, "publickly before the congregation (to) read the Thirty-nine Articles . . . and publickly testifie his assent and consent to all and every one of them and thereupon subscribing his name in said Common Prayer Book belonging to the said Church."[122]

Of Talbot, the Reverend Doctor Francis Lister Hawks declared: "The Society never had, at least in our view, a more honest, fearless, and laborious Missionary."[123] We feel that Talbot was one of the most admirable men in American colonial history. He was eager and alert, indefatigable and energetic; uncompromising in his convictions, and courageous. Besides he was kindly and sympathetic, and won the affections of the people among whom he laboured. Somewhat guileless and unsuspecting, he never seemed to grasp the political entanglements which impeded the introduction of colonial bishops; less scrupulous and more sophisticated men, like Urmstone, were able to appraise the situation immediately and to make capital of it.

And now we come to the much discussed question, Was Talbot ever consecrated a bishop? It has been argued that he received orders from the Non-Jurors during his last visit to England; and Urmstone circulated a rumour to that effect, in the hopes of proving Talbot's disloyalty to the Crown and to the Establishment. That Doctor Welton was ordained, though irregularly, there is little or no doubt; but the evidence of Talbot's consecration, while ardently received by certain students, has been treated by others with great caution.

Doctor George M. Hills, in his *History of the Church in Burlington, New Jersey,* asserts that Ralph Taylor, singly, consecrated Doctor Robert Welton, who had been deprived of the rectorship of Whitechapel, London, for his adherence to the Non-Jurors; and that Ralph Taylor and Robert Welton together consecrated John Talbot as bishop.[124] The only authorities cited by Doctor Hills in substantiation of the above statement are Percival, on the Apostolical Succession, and Lathbury's *History of the Non-Jurors.* John Fulton notes that "a glance at the works of Percival and Lathbury suffices to show that

---

[122]*George M. Hills: History of the Church in Burlington, N. J., pp. 180, 185.*

[123]*Francis L. Hawks: Contributions to the Ecclesiastical History of the U. S., II., p. 182.*

[124]*George M. Hills: History of the Church in Burlington, N. J., p. 168.*

they do not say so. . . . The Christian name JOHN does not appear in either of them." Percival's table of Non-Juror consecrations gives the name of Robert Welton, as consecrated "1723-4" by Ralph Taylor; and "........ Talbot," consecrated "1723-4" by Ralph Taylor and Robert Welton. It contains no record of Talbot's Christian name. Lathbury speaks of the person consecrated simply as "Talbot". Says Fulton:

"To suggest the identity of Percival's '........ Talbot' and Lathbury's 'Talbot' with John Talbot of Burlington, there is absolutely nothing except that Percival says that 'Welton and *Talbot* both went to the colonies in North America . . . and exercised the episcopal functions;' while Lathbury says that '*Taylor* and Welton . . . both exercised the episcopal functions in the American colonies.' Beyond these contradictory statements there is no evidence that any of the three 'exercised episcopal functions' in America."[125]

In Doctor Rawlinson's Manuscripts in the Bodleian Library at Oxford, there is a list of Non-Juror consecrations and ordinations; and the following is stated:

"Ric. Wilton, D. D., was consecrated by Dr. Taylor alone in a clandestine manner. . . . Talbot, M. A., was consecrated by the same person, at the same time, and as irregularly."[126]

Beside the appeal to the authorities, there is the story told by Bishop William White of Pennsylvania, as recounted to him in his youth by his elder brother. It seems that a Congregationalist minister from Connecticut, Whittlesey by name, expressed doubts regarding his ordination, and was troubled. He left home about the time that Welton and Talbot were in Philadelphia. The minister returned afterwards, saying he was satisfied with his orders; he said he had been to some of the southern colonies. It was soon whispered that he had visited the non-juring bishops and been ordained; and this was believed among the churchmen.[127]

Summing up the evidence, Fulton says:

"Of Dr. Welton's irregular consecration, and of his visit to Philadelphia, there is no doubt; that a person bearing the surname of Talbot was consecrated at the same time as Welton, or shortly afterwards, is not denied; but that John Talbot of

[125]*John Fulton's monograph, in Perry: American Episcopal Church, I., p. 557.*
[126]*Ibid.*
[127]*Francis L. Hawks: History of the Church in Maryland, p. 185.*

Burlington was in sympathy with the political principles, or an adherent of the schismatical sect of non-jurors, can only be proved by admitting the unsupported accusations of a few malignant enemies, and at the same time rejecting the evidence of his friends and his own solemn protestations of loyalty to the sovereigns of the Protestant succession and fidelity to the Church of England as by law established, both of which asseverations are supported by the unbroken testimony of his whole life."[128]

Talbot went to England in the latter part of 1720; he remained there nearly or quite two years. It is during this time, when he was seventy-six or seventy-seven years old, that he is alleged to have received consecration from the Non-Jurors. Fulton continues:

"Indeed, it is the only time at which he could receive such consecration. It is not denied that a person named Talbot (Christian name unknown) was consecrated in 1723 or 1724, that is, a year or two after Talbot's return to America; but even supposing that the consecration of that person had taken place in 1721 or 1722, it would require the strongest evidence to identify him with John Talbot of Burlington, an original Williamite and Hanoverian, at the very time when he was seeking and obtaining from the Hanoverian government, through the Bishop of London and the S. P. G., a sum of money in lump and a pension for life besides. Independently of the duplicity towards the government, the bishop, and the Society, which such a proceeding would have involved, it is obvious that the instinct of self-interest alone would guard a man so old as Talbot was from a course which was not only contrary to his principles, but likely to involve him in serious difficulties."[129]

All honour to Fulton's painstaking and scholarly treatment of the subject; but since his time, evidence has come to light which decidedly points to the conclusion that it was John Talbot of Burlington who was consecrated bishop, though irregularly. While it is likely that he never exercised his espiscopal functions in America, he may none the less be considered the first Anglican bishop in this country.

A recent work on the later Non-Jurors [130] quotes freely from the manuscript of the eminent Thomas Brett (1667-1743), himself a Non-Juring bishop. Henry Broxap, the author, speaks first of the conse-

[128]*John Fulton's monograph, in Perry: American Episcopal Church, I., p. 542.*
[129]*Ibid., pp. 550-551.*
[130]*Henry Broxap: The Later Non-Jurors (Cambridge University Press, 1924).*

cration of Ralph Taylor, D. D., and Hilkiah Bedford, M. A., at Gray's Inn, on the 25th of January, 1720-21.

"The newly consecrated bishops may be said to be old and broken men. Bedford had only recently been released from prison and Taylor is always spoken of as greatly weakened both in body and in mind. Neither of the prelates long survived his consecration. . . . The death of Dr. Taylor took place on the 26th December, 1722, but in the summer of that year, he had taken upon himself to consecrate two bishops, *solus* and contrary to the advice of his colleague."

The following is Thomas Brett's own account of the matter, as quoted by Broxap:

"Dr. Taylor proposed to his colleague to consecrate Dr. Robert (sic) .... Welton and Mr. John Talbot, who for some years had been a Missionary in one of our English plantations in America, particularly at Burlington in New Jersey. But they refused Dr. Welton because, though he had been deprived of his living at Whitechapel for refusing the oaths, yet they thought his morals not unexceptional, and thought his behaviour had been imprudent, and Talbot they rejected as no Non-Juror. However, Dr. Taylor by himself alone, proceeded to consecrate Welton, and he and Welton consecrated Talbot, but the other Non-Jurors never acknowledged either of them as bishops. However, Welton got himself an Episcopal seal and went to Pennsylvania, and getting subscriptions began to build a church and to act as a bishop. But Dr. Edmund Gibson, Bishop of London, being informed of Welton's proceedings, procured an order from King George to oblige him to return to England. The Doctor retreated to Portugal and died at Lisbon in the year 1726. I cannot say what became of Talbot. The newspapers spoke of him as being commanded to return from America to England at the same time as Welton received such a command, but he was mentioned no more. I suppose therefore, he made a submission to the Bishop of London, laid aside his pretences to the episcopal Character, and as he had taken the oaths and was ready to take them again, it is probable he was permitted to continue where he was."[131]

A memorandum was made in 1766 by Nicholas Brett, younger son of Thomas, on the back of the sheet which contained his father's record:

"Talbot was a Non-Juror in the State but not in the Church, and continued in the plantations to the day of his death. He was, as Mr. Owen tells me, a quiet, inoffensive, jocose man.
[131]*Quoted in Broxap: The Later Non-Jurors, p. 88.*

The Governors always winked at him, and he received a pension from the Society to the last as one of their missionaries. He was sent over in Queen Anne's time by Mr. Nelson's interest, who did it because he would not take the oaths, but whether he practised as a bishop after Welton was recalled, I know not. Burnet, the Governor of New York, knew he was a bishop. He never prayed for the King by name. Being asked by Burnet one day in a large company why he did not pray for King George, he answered he thought him old enough to pray for himself. Notwithstanding this answer Burnet was not angry with him and always made him welcome. . . . This I had from Mr. Orem, many years Chaplain to the garrison of New York, and now (1766) Rector of Conington in Hunts."[132]

There are several inaccuracies in the entries just quoted; but they are no more than one would expect where word of mouth was principally relied on. Nicholas Brett's notes were made more than forty years after the events occurred of which he speaks; and while his memorandum is to be used cautiously so far as the particulars of Talbot's career are concerned, it is convincing so far as establishing the matter of identity.

Broxap is of the opinion that Talbot came more and more into touch with the sentiments of the Non-Jurors during the latter year of the reign of Queen Anne. He notes the "striking fact that although many subsequent letters of Talbot are extant he never again referred to the question of the episcopate. On the other hand there are, henceforward, repeated references made by others to the fact that Talbot had himself received episcopal consecration." Here he refers to the correspondence of Governor Keith of Pennsylvania, Governor Burnet, and the Reverend John Urmstone. But in the face of the contemporaneous statements of Thomas Brett and the mass of circumstantial evidence, "the only intelligible inference to be drawn from these facts is that John Talbot of Burlington is to be identified with the man who received episcopal orders from Bishop Taylor in 1722, and he may therefore be regarded in some sense, as an irregular predecessor of Bishop Seabury."[133]

There is other evidence which points to the fact of the consecration. On the 1st of February, 1725 (N. S.), the Reverend Samuel Johnson, of Stratford, Connecticut, wrote the Bishop of London:

[132]*Quoted in Broxap: op. cit., p. 89. The name "Owen" is an error; the Rev. James Orem was commissioned chaplain under Gov. Burnet in 1723, and continued at the New York fort for several years. A letter signed by him at the same station in 1742 is in existence.*
[133]*Broxap: Op. cit., p. 91.*

"There are two nonjuring Bps in America one of them travelled thro the Country last fall & not knowing who he was, but professing himself a minister of ye Chh of England, I invited him to preach for me. . . . The Tuesday following he let me know what he was, whereupon I was very much surprised & begged of him not to come into these parts of ye Country again. . . . The people are mightily taken with him & if he should come this way again as I fear he will I doubt I shall find difficulty enough to keep many of them in the unity of the Church."[134]

Johnson did not give the name of the visitor; but he wrote that the Newtown (Connecticut) people were inclined to ask him to ordain a minister for them; but he (Johnson) protracted their patience in the hopes of another bishop being sent.

It is not impossible that Talbot himself was the clergyman who visited Johnson. Welton arrived in Philadelphia in the summer of 1724, and was probably engaged in his work there; we have no evidence of his absence during the fall. On the other hand, the season coincides with that in which Talbot was being dispossessed of his living at Burlington. There is mention of his being so indiscreet as to reveal that he was a bishop; this may have been such an occasion.

On the 15th of March, 1725, one Joseph Browne, of New Haven, who introduced himself to the Bishop of London in his letter as "not only a perfect stranger to your Lordship, (having never been out of this country,) but also a plain man, and therefore unworthy to presume so far," wrote that "the non-jurors have sent over two bishops into America, and one of them has travelled through the country. . . . I had accidentally a little acquaintance with him." He used this fact as the basis of a plea for the sending of bishops, without whom the Church was "daily languishing."[135]

A statement from a distinguished Congregationalist divine and educator of the Eighteenth Century is of interest. Doctor Ezra Stiles, President of Yale College, made the following entry in his Diary, July 23rd, 1785:

"In 1768 I had a Conversation with the Revd Noah Hobart in Fairfield, who about 1730 was sent by the Boston Convention of Pastors to preach as a candidate to a Pres. Chh. in Philad^a where he resided & preached some time. While in those parts he became acquainted with the Presb. ministers at Trenton, Burlington &c in Jerseys. From him in my Itin^y Sept. 1768 I minuted thus—

[134]*Hawks Papers, N. Y. Historical Society, Box 2, #52.*
[135]*Hawks and Perry: Church Documents, Connecticut, I., p. 98.*

" 'Rev. Mr. *Talbot*, missionary at Burlington, died there
about 1725. He was a BISHOP of the NON-JURORS.
Rev. Mr. Vaughan of Elizabeth Town told Mr. Dickinson
of Norwalk that he found his Letters of Consecration among
Mr. Talbots Papers.'

" 'Another Episcopal Minister the Rev^d Mr. *Welton* at
Philadelphia was also ordained a Non Juring Bishop. He was
sent for home as such, but he escaped & died in Portugal,
declaring himself a Non Juror, about 1730.' "

Another entry in the Diary is of value as evidence:

"Mr. Hubbard the Episc^o Minister with me; he told
me Dr Seabury was consecrated by three Non-Juring Bishops
in Aberdeen in Scotland & that he had his consecration
sermon printed by anonymous—that Dr Seab^y had brought
over with him a List of the Succession of non-juring Bps. from
Abp. Sancroft & Dr Hicks at the Revolution in 1680 to the
present time—that it was said there were Bps for every See
in Engld, upon my asking how many Nonjuring Bps there
were now in being:—that Mr. Talbot of Burlington was a non-
juring Bp."[136]

In view of such evidence, there is little doubt of Talbot's consecration. But when we accept the fact, as we feel bound to do, we find
ourselves a bit perplexed—not so much by the historical sequence as
by the enigma which Talbot's own life presents. Here we find a man
who emphatically avowed his loyalty to the royal family, yet accepted
consecration from those of contrary allegiance; it would appear that his
protests were hollow, to say the least, and that his conduct was neither
straightforward nor consistent. Furthermore, a suspicion arises from
the apparent secretiveness of his conduct in securing consecration; he
may have been impelled by worthy motives, but the scant records lead
us to conjecture that he did not act openly. He expected to continue
in the service of the Venerable Society and to enjoy the favour of the
Establishment, in spite of an act which his superiors would certainly
regard with displeasure.

We are not able to deal with such problems exhaustively because
the records are extremely fragmentary; from the standpoint of source
material, the last years of Talbot's life are not satisfactorily attested.
His letters were few; and the note of anxiety and despair takes the
place of cool, deliberate reasoning and explanation. We must, therefore, gather such threads as we possess, and see if the warp and woof
of the aged clergyman's character produce an harmonious whole.

[136]*Literary Diary of Ezra Stiles, D. D., President of Yale College*, ed. by
Franklin Bowditch Dexter, Vol. III., pp. 173, 175.

Talbot seems to rise superior to the charges of his critics. His long years of untiring service and self-sacrifice, his patient pursuit of an ideal, his indefatigable efforts to extend the Church and make it a vital influence throughout the eastern colonies, his irreproachable integrity and morality, have established a name which will not be marred perceptibly by a single mistake committed at the age of nearly eighty. For it may be admitted that the acceptance of Non-Juror consecration was a mistake, an indiscretion; yet there is not the slightest reason to suspect that the old man had any selfish or disloyal intention in mind. He believed that the very existence of the Church in America depended on the presence of a resident bishop; he knew at first hand—far better than the Anglican hierarchy or the Society knew—that the Church was suffering because of its handicaps; that ministers were scarce and hard to obtain, that disorganization was a present menace, and that the dissenting bodies were rapidly overtaking the Church. The need of such a bishop was a constant theme of his correspondence; at his instance, conventions drafted resolutions appealing for a colonial episcopate; he spared himself no pains in the matter of a bishop's dwelling. The long delays and the lack of any response on the part of the government and the Society must have given him untold anxiety and disappointment. Is it not probable that he turned to the Non-Jurors in desperate hope that he might be permitted to do even a little bit in America to aid the cause?

Talbot never apparently realised that his conduct was inconsistent. He denied all disaffection to the Establishment or the royal family; and emphatically declared that he had done nothing to merit the stern measures taken by the Society. The letter of the Reverend Mr. Cumming is evidence that he did not keep company with Welton, when it came to any act of disloyalty. And we may accept the testimonials of the wardens and vestrymen of at least three parishes—including those where he was best known—that he had always proved himself exemplary in his life and ministry and been a great advocate for the Church of England. Talbot lived in a time of political stress and strain; the reigning house felt insecure; charges of disloyalty were easily made, while exoneration was difficult. In a calmer period, he would doubtless have been recognized back home for his heroic qualities of soul and mind and for his stupendous industry.

BOOK TWO

———

LETTERS
OF
JOHN TALBOT

THE MANUSCRIPT SOURCES.

THE following letters and entries are largely transcribed from the archives of the Society for the Propagation of the Gospel in Foreign Parts. There we find reports and letters of the Society's missionaries and foreign correspondents, and the manuscript Journal of the Society, dating from 1701. Of these the Library of Congress has collected, by transcripts, photofilm enlargements, and photostats the following groups:

1. SERIES A (Transcripts). Twenty-six volumes of contemporary copies from 1701 to 1736. Most of the Talbot letters are in this series. The same are designated in this study by the name of the series, with the volume in Roman numerals, and the letter with its consecutive number or page according to the original numbering. (For example: "S. P. G. A-Series I., No. 87.)

2. SERIES B (Transcripts). Twenty-five volumes of original letters and documents, from 1701 to 1786. There is very little Talbot material in this series.

3. MANUSCRIPT JOURNALS. The original Journals of the Society have been photofilmed for the Library of Congress. The first four volumes contain references to Talbot.

4. MISCELLANEOUS UNBOUND DOCUMENTS.

The archives of the Bishop of London, at Fulham Palace, contain over two thousand letters and miscellaneous papers relating to the Church of England during the colonial period in America. The manuscripts are kept in pasteboard boxes; they too have been rendered available to American students by the Library of Congress. Talbot references in the Fulham documents are very rare.

E. L. P.

LETTERS OF JOHN TALBOT.

(1)

Mr John Talbot to Mr Richard Gillingham
New York 24 Novr 1702.

My dear friend.

I take all opportunities to let you know that I live, & shall be glad to hear as much of you. ffriend Keith & I have been above 500 miles together visiting the Churches in these parts of America viz New-England, New-Hampshire, N. Bristol, N: London, N. York, & the N. Jerseys as far as Philadelphia. We preach'd in all Churches where we came and in severall Dissenter's Meetings such as own'd the Church of England to be their Mother Church, & were willing to communicate with her, and to submit to her Bishops if they had opportunity. I have baptized severall persons whom Mr Keith has brought over from Quakerism, & indeed in all places where we come, we find a great Ripeness & Inclination amongst all sorts of people to embrace the Gospel, even the Indians themselves have promised obedience to the Faith, as appears by a Conference that my Lord Cornbury the Govr here, has had with them at Albany, 5 of their Sachems or Kings told him they were glad to hear that the Sun shined in England again since K. Wm^s Death, they did (not?) admire at first what was come to us, that we should have a Squaw Sachem vizt a woman King, but they hoped she would be a good Mother, & send them some to teach them Religion, & establish Traffick amongst them that they might be able to purchase a Coat & not go to Church in Beaver skins, and so they send our Queen a Present, 10 bear Skins to make her fine, & one for Muff to keep her warm, after a many Presents & Compliments they sign'd the Treaty and made the Covenant so sure that they said Thunder & Lightning should not break it on their part, if we did not do as the Lord Bellamont did, throw it into the Sea. The Papists have been very Zealous and Diligent to send Priests and Jesuits to convert these Indians to their Superstitions, tis wonderfully acted, ventur'd, and suffer'd upon that Design, they have indeed become all things and even turn'd Indians as it were to gain them, wch I hope will provoke Some of us to do our part for our holy Faith & Mother the Church of England, one of their Priests lived half a year in their Wigwams (i e Houses) without a shirt and when he petition'd my Ld Bellamont for a couple he was not only deny'd but banish'd, whereas one of ours in discourse with my Lord of London said who did his Ldp think would come hither that had a Dozen Shirts. If I had their Lan-

(Marginal notes:)

Mr T. relates his Travels with Mr K. & success

The Indians are disposed to embrace the Gospel.

A Treaty with them, & Presents for ye Queen.

The Zeal of the Papists to Convert the Indians.

The Jesuits manner of doing it.

guage; or wherewith to maintain an Interpreter it should be the first thing I should do to go amongst the thickest of 'em. Mr Keith sais if he were younger he would learn their Language & then I'me sure he might convert them sooner than the Heathen

He gives a fine character of M^r K.

call'd Quakers. Indeed he is the fittest man that ever came over for this Province, he is a well study'd Divine, a good Philosopher & Preacher, but above all an excellent Disputant, especially against the Quakers, who use to Challenge all mankind formerly, now all the Friends (or Enemies rather) are not able to answer one Geo: Keith, he knows the Depths of Satan within them and all the Doublings & Windings of *the Snake in the Grass;* In short he's become the best Champion ag^st all Dissenters that the Church ever had, & has Sett up Such a Light in these dark places that by God's Blessing will not be

The Clergy of those parts meet at the charge of Coll. N.

putt out. The Clergy here have had a Sort of Convocation at the instance and charge of his Execllency Col. Nicholson Govr of Virginia we were but 7 in all, & a week together we sat considering of ways & means to propagate the Gospel, and to that end we have drawn up a Scheme of the present State of the Church in these Provinces, which you shall see when I have time to transcribe it, and I shall desire you to send it afterwards to my good Brother Kemble. We have great need of a Bishop here to visit all the Churches, to ordain some to confirm others & bless all we pray for my good Lord of London, we cannot have better than he whilst he lives, therefore in the meantime we shall be very well content with a Suffragan. Mr Keith's Mission will be out ab^t a year hence, by that time I hope to get some tokens for my good friends and Benefactors. But as for my self I am so well Satisfyed with a prospect of doing good that I have no Inclination to return for England, however be so kind as to let me know how you do wch will be a Comfort to me in the Wilderness. You know all my friends, pray let them especially my Mother & Sister Hannah know that I am well God be praised & shall be glad to hear so much of them. I cannot write many Letters, much less one 2, or 3 times over as when I had nothing else to do. I pray God bless you & all my friends, I desire the Benefitt of their Prayers tho' I can't have that of their good Company. I know you'll take all in good part that comes from,

your old ffriend

John Talbot.

P. S. I have many places offer'd me but I know not where I shall settle, in the mean time you may direct your Letters for me to be left with Mr Bridge of Boston N: E., Mr Vesey at N. York, Mr Evans at Philadelphia, & Mr Wallace in Virginia.

Cloaths are very dear here, a Gown & Cassock here will cost above 20^li. I go yet just as they do at Whitehall but they wont last me long unless you send me a Recruit. I hope the Corporation will allow me travelling charges & that you'll receive

this Bounty & send me Cloaths from head to foot. I want nothing else I thank God.

yᵣˢ &c. J. T.

You may direct a Chest of Goods for me to be left
at any of the places within mention'd but especially to
Mʳ Vesey Minister of New York for that is the center
of our Circuit.

The Directions are

To the Revᵈ Mʳ Richᵈ Gillingham. To
be Left at Mʳ Toveys near Bosvil in Lincoln's
Inn ffields
London.

(S. P. G. A-Series, I., #LVI. This important letter, more than once
reprinted, gives Talbot's first impressions. RICHARD GILLINGHAM
was vicar of Chigwell in Essex, and a personal friend. RICHARD
COOTE, EARL OF BELLAMONT, was Governor of New York.
COLONEL FRANCIS NICHOLSON, prominent among the colonial
governors, was an ardent patron of the Church. WILLIAM VESEY,
1674-1746, was rector of Trinity Church, New York. CHRISTOPHER
BRIDGE, assistant at King's Chapel, Boston, later became S. P. G.
missionary at Naragansett, and at Rye, N. Y.; he died in 1719. JAMES
WALLACE was minister of Elizabeth City Parish, Virginia, from
1691 to 1712. In that parish Hampton was located, and Mrs. WALKER,
the daughter of George Keith, resided.)

(2)

Mʳ Talbot to Mʳ Gillingham

New Castle 10 April
1703

Dear Sʳ.

God be praysed we are come thus far in health and Safety   A Descrip-
in our way towards Virginia, we are to goe abroad a Sloop   tion of New-
on Munday Morning, and hope to be at James' Town next week.   castle
This is a Pretty Town in Delaware River between Pennsylvania & Maryland. Here is no Church as yet, neither ever
was an Orthodox Minister Settled here, but one Mʳ Wilson a
Presbiterian, that Preaches to the People in the Court House,
he has left them this last Winter, but finding it not for the   He hopes to
better he means to come again this Summer, he has much dis-   Found a
obliged some People thereby which makes them the more favour-   Church
able to the Church, which I hope by God's Blessing to found   there.
here very Speedily.

The Place is very Pleasant and agreeable as most in America
& would be very populous, but that there is no Settled Ministry
nor Government, for what good does it do People to live in a
Place void of Gospel & Law too, so that several People have

He goes
about
Preaching
thro' E & W.
Jersey.

The sending
Mr Keith a
great ad-
vantage to
the Church.

An account
of the
Quakers and
particularly
of Mr Pens
writings and
principles.

The Quakers
incourage all
that believe
in one God
to come
among them.

He has seen
comissions
from them
to Kill &c.

He says
they are
subject
to the Penal
Laws not-
withstanding
the Tolera-
tion

moved and gone elsewhere to the Church seeing the Church does not come to them.

I have Sent you a scheme of the Present State of the Church in these Parts, as we have found in our Travels; Since it was drawn up, I have gone with Mr Keith & without him about East & West Jersey, Preaching, & Baptizing Several Scores of Men, Women, & Children, encouraging them to build Churches, by Promising them in time, Ministers from England, and that the Honble Corporation would take care to send none but sober good Men, well qualified in all Respects for the work of the Ministry. I look upon it that the Sending Mr Keith, in Quality of a Missionary to travel for the good of Churches, has been the Best Service that has been done yet for the Church of England in these Parts of the World; for he is a general Scholar, an able disputant and a Perfect honest man. He is in a Word Hereticorum Malleus, & so he had need, having to deal with some of the worst that ever troubled the Church or the World. Here is little or no Government & People in many places take the Liberty to say there be three Gods, or no God, & nothing is done to them. Certainly tis better to live where nothing is lawful, than where all things are. Since I came to be more acquainted with the Quakers I have much worse Opinion of them than ever I had. It appears by Wm Pen's Book, that he is a greater Anti-Christ than Julian the Apostate. He has said that Christ is a finite, Impotent Creature, and Faith, in the History of Christ's Outward Manifestation, is a deadly Poyson these later ages have been infected withal to the Destruction of holy Living. who was Defender of the Faith when this Lewd Heretick was made Governor & Proprietor of a Province? Certainly God gave this Land into the hands of the English that they might Publish the Gospell and give Knowledge of Salvation to these People, & I am sure, the King gave this to Wm Pen with Injunction expressly in his Patent, that he should Endeavour to Convert the Indians to the Faith, but instead of that he Labours to make Christians Heathens, & Proclaims Liberty & Privilege to all that believe in one God, & yet when they come here, they say there are three, or none, & yet be born out by the Quakers against the Christians. They Pretend they ought not to fight; yet I have seen severall Commissions, under several of their Govrs Hands to kill &c. God bless Queen Anne & defend Her that She may defend the Faith; & her faithfull Councellours if they have any Piety or Policy, I'm Sure will take Some Course with these Heathens, & Hereticks, for if they be let alone to take the Sword (which they certainly will when they think they are strong enough) we shall perish with it for not opposing them in due time. Notwithstanding the Tolleration they are subject to all the Penal Laws, as you'l find if you read the Act, & were I in England and had as much Knowledge in Law as you, I would bring

Statutes & Judgem^ts against them. I have done So att N. York
where there is a good governour my Ld Cornbury.

Last Lord's Day I was att Burlington the Chief Town in
W. Jersey where I have preacht many times in a house hard by
the Quaker's Meeting, we shall have one too, I hope when we
return here again from Virginia, where we think to stay but
2 or 3 months. after Sermon I went out with the rest of the
People, & laid the Corner Stone of St Mary's Church. God
grant it may rise to be the House of God, and the Gate of Heaven
to them.

It seems the Honble Gentlemen of the Corporation have
considered my Travels for the Service of the Church, and have
given me a handsom allowance to bear my charges wth M^r
Keith. Pray give them my Hearty Service & thanks & let them
know that by the Grace of God I shall make it my Business to
fullfill my Mission. Pray, Remember my Duty & Love to my
Good Mother: I hope she is alive and well, let her not want 10£
p an: as long as I have 60£ coming to me, which will be due
the 12th June next ensuing. It grieves me much to see so many
People here without the Benefit of Serving God in the Wilderness. I believe, I have been Sollicited to tarry att 20 Places
where they want much and are able to maintain a Minister so,
thatt he should want nothing; they send to N. England, and
call any sorry young men, purely for want of some good honest
Clergy Men of the Church of England. Many goe to the
Heathen Meetings of the People called Quakers because there is
no houses of God in their Provinces, till at last they come to be
bewitched & forced out of their Faith & Senses too. The Country is a good Land in all Parts of it, bating the Sudden change
of heat & cold, which, if People be not carefull, they are many
times the worse for. The Air is generally clear, & pure, no body
complains here of the Spleen unless he has allso an evil Conscience attending. I saw Mr Bewley Mr Scot's Friend att
Philadelphia. I was att his house, he lives very well & entertained me very civilly & was glad to hear of his old friends.
I am but poor att present, being rob^d by a Negro of all my
Money out of my Portmanteau; the young Slut did not leave me
one Token for my Self, only I got the Bag again. But blessed
be God I never wanted meat nor drink, nor Cloaths neither,
as yet; but if you don^t send me some Cloaths next shipping,
instead of going as they do in White Hall, I shall go as the Indians do. I shall be content let it be as it will. I might have
had money enough here, if I would have taken what People have
offered me, but lest the Quakers should say truly, as they do
falsely, that we come for money, and preach for hire, I preach
the Gospel as freely as the Apostles did to the first Churches.

Marginal notes:

& that he has prosecuted them accordingly at N. York. He assisted to lay the corner stone of St Mary's Church at Burlington.

He desires him to thank ye Society for the Allowance of 60£ per annum.

The People want Ministers at many Places & are able to maintain 'em.

A Description of Pensylvania.

He is robb'd by a Negro &c.

He refuses to take any Mony of the People.

Virginia 8th June.

When I writ this, I miss'd the Opportunity to send it, so I brought it hither with me, so you must take it rough as it runs, we have been now att our Journey's End in N. Carolina as far as we could goe. now we tak about, and stand t'other way to Philadelphia again, thus G. Keith's home & mine is every where. Governor Nicholson has been very kind & generous to me. I

A Caracter of
Gov: Nichol-
son.

pray God prosper him long in his Government, he has some Enemies, as well as other men, but none of them can deny, but he is a Just Magistrate in his Place. I have sent the Scheme of our Church Affaires by one Mr Beverly an honest Gentleman of this Country, who is bound for England very Speedily, you'l hear of him att Mr Perry's the Virginia Merchant George Keith comes home next year, then if I can get anything worthy sending, I shall have a carefull hand to deliver it. There is one Mr Keyes My Ld of London's Taylor; you may deal with him to send me a chest of cloathes new or old once a year. Direct them or any thing else for me to be Left att Geo: Waker's att Kecoughtan in Virginia. I am

Semper idem

J. T.

(S. P. G. A-Series, I., #CXIX. NEW CASTLE was established as a missionary station of the S. P. G.; and the Rev. George Ross did effective work there, dying about 1754. WILLIAM PENN, proprietor of Pennsylvania, was one of the most prominent figures in the colonisation of America; he employed his literary talents in behalf of Quaker principles).

(3)

Mr Talbot to Mr Gillingham.

Virginia 3d May. 1703

Dear Friend

Now att last (God be praised) we are arrived att the Haven where we would be. Mr Keith is got to his Daughter's House & I am got amongst my old Friends and Acquaintance in these Parts who are very glad to see me, especially those of the

An account
of his Ar-
rival in Vir-
ginia.

Ministry, who came over along with me. Here has been great Alterations in these 10 years, Since I was here, many of my old Friends are dead, but I have found some new in their stead amongst which is the Bearer Mr Robt Beverly who has one of the Best houses & plantations in this Country, where I reckon my self as it were att home: He has been so courteous & civil. But there is some Dispute in Law concerning the Title & he is come over to see abt it, wherein I hope you will and can be Serviceable to him, and I shall take it as done to my self. I have sent you several Letters but have none yet from no Body.

I hear the honble Gentlemen of the Society att Bow have Ordered 60 £ p. an. for travelling Charges: 30 £ I have Recd upon Bill. I desire you will receive the other 30 £ & let this

Gentleman Mr Beverly have 10£ to buy Books for a friend of mine here who will repay me. I desire you to lay out 10£ more in Cloaths & Shirts which I desire Neighbour Levitop to buy for me & send them in some ship to N York directed to me to be left att Mr Vesey's Minister there. I shall be glad to hear how all our Friends do, especially my good Mother, pray let me know where she is & how she does, let her have decem Minas upon My acc^t as long as she lives, I have sent the present State of the Church apud Americanos as far as we have gone the first year, from Dover 80 Miles Eastward from Boston in N. England, to Philadelphia in Pensylvania; Since that Scheme was finished, I have gone up and down in E. & W. Jersey, preaching & Baptizing, & preparing the way for sev^eral Churches there. att Amboy they are going to build one, att Hopewell another & at Shrewsbury Coll. Morris is going to build one att his own Cost & charge and he will endow it as he sayes, which I don't doubt, for he is an honest gentleman, and a Member of the Honble Society for Propagating the Gospel in forreign Parts. I was att Burlington last Lady day and after Prayers we went to the ground where they were going to build a Church and I laid the first Stone, which I hope will be none other than the House of God and Gate of Heaven to the People. Coll. Nicholson Govr here, was the chief founder of this as well as many more, and Indeed he has been the Benefactor to all the Churches on this Land of N. America, God bless this Church and let them prosper that love it. we called this Church St Mary's, it being upon her day. Janu^ry last I was att the opening of a Church att Chester: I preached the first Sermon that ever was there on Sunday the day before the Conversion of St Paul, and after much debate what to call it, I named it S^t. Paul's. This is one of the best Churches in these American Parts and a very Pleasant Place but they have no Minister as yet, but Mr Evans of Philadelphia officiates there once in 3 weeks. The Governour of Virginia is building Several more Churches; Two at N: Carolina where we are going next week, & one att New-Castle; where in all Appearance we shall have a considerable Congregation of Christian People. The Place is very well planted for trade both by Sea & Land it being almost in the Midway between Philadelphia & Mary-Land upon Delaware River; where God Willing I intend to spend some Labour & Pains; tho' I can't find in my heart to settle in any Place for my own, but to Travel, as I told you for the Good of the Church in general. I should be glad to hear how you did about the Centurion; and how matters of Acc^t stand between us; 'tis good to reckon sometime, if we never intend to pay, th' I hope to be out of Debt to the World. Yet I shall allways count my Self obliged to my Friend. I have been with Geo: Keith a year next June ye 12th. Then my 60£ becomes due. This has been a sickly year apud Americanos, but (God be praised) I have had

He mentions the Several places in E & W. Jersey where they are ab^t building Churches one of wch Coll. Morris undertakes at his own expense.

Coll Nicholson the Founder & Benefactor of Many Churches. a Church open'd at Chester and nam'd St Paul's. Mr Evans officiats there every 3^d week. Gov: Nicholson is building two Churches in N. Carolina & one at Newcastle.

His Zeal for
the Service
of God apud
Americanos.

He is going
by land to
Pamplico in
N. Carolina
where one
Bret a
Scandalous
Fellow had
been the
Minister.

The want of
books in
those
Parts &c
He objects
agst D^r
Brays
method of
Comenting
on the Ch.
Catechism.

The People
of those
parts Sharp
& inquisitive.

Comon
Prayer
Books &c
wanted.

good health all this Time. And I believe, I have done the
Church more service since I came hither than I could in seven
Years in England. Perhaps when I have been here 6 or 7 years
I may make a trip home to see some friends (for they won't
come to me) but then it will be animo Reversendi for I have
given my self up to the Service of God & his Church Apud
Americanos and I had rather dye in the Service than desert it.
Pray give my Service and Thanks to the Honble Society for their
generous Allowance to bear my Charges. I shall take care to
fullfill my Mission and goe as far with it as any body, that they
shal send forth. we came hither in a Sloop from Pensylvania.
When we were out of Delaware River a North-west wind took
us & carried us out to Sea and lost us 10 or 12 hours so, as I
was never lost in my Life, 'tis true sometime as the Saylor
sayes the last Storm was the worst. The Sea never got any
thing before by my sickness but then I was so sick that I had
much adoe to keep my Bowels within my Belly; we arrived
safe att last God be praised, but I shall be hardly catch^d on
board so small a vessel again a good while. we are going now
by Land to Pamplico in N. Carolina a Place where there never
was any Minister, but only one Dan: Brett a Scandalous fellow,
that has done more harm than good everywhere, he was the
worst I think that ever came over.

We want a great many good Ministers here in America
especially in those parts mentioned in the Scheme, but we had
better have none att all than such Scandalous Beasts as some
make them selves not only the worst of Ministers but of Men.
if you know none so good as to come, I hope you will find them
that are willing to send. Some good Books would do very well
in the meanwhile I am Sure there is no want of them in England
they have enough & to spare. Indeed we have had many of D^r
Bray's Books, & I could wish we had more But his Way &
Method is not the best for this People that we have to do withal,
Quakers, & Quaker's Friends; to most of them, nothing but
Controversy will serve their turn, 'tis a hard Matter to persuade
to the Baptismal Covenant, on which the D^r has writ 3 or 4
Books, one in folio, that they may be ever learning, & yet never
be able to come to the Knowledge of the Creed, the Lord's
Prayer nor the ten Commandments.

Those that we have to deal with are a sharp and Inquisitive People; they are not satisfied with one D^r's Opinion, but
must have something that is Authentick if we hope to prevail
with them.

We should have some Common Prayer Books new or old,
of all Sorts & Sizes, with the 39 Articles & some books of
Homilys to set up the Worship & Service of God till we have
Ministers. Some of Dr Comber's Books would be of right good
Use here to give those that ask a Reason of all things contained
in our English Liturgy which has still stood the best Test of all

Adversaries that were not blind & deaf. Above all Mr Lesly the Author of the Snake in the Grass has given Quakerism a deadly wound I hope never to be healed, & his 5 Discourses about Baptism and Episcopacy have brought many to the Church. We want 1000 of them to dispose of in the way that we goe. I use to take a Wallet full of Books and carry them 100 miles about and disperse them abroad and give them to all that desired 'em, wch in due time will be of good Service to the Church, 'tis a Comfort to the People in the Wilderness to see that some body takes care of them. There is a time to sow and a time to reap wch I don't desire in this World. I might have money enough of the People in many Places but I would never take any of those that we goe to Proselyte, especially amongst the Quakers; I Resolved to work with my hands rather than they should say, I was a hireling & come for money, which they are very apt to do. The Govr of Virginia my old friend has been very generous to us, and has taken care that nothing be wanting to us while we are in his Territories if there were such another Governour in America it would be much cheaper travelling for the Missionaries. But alass! I am afraid we shall loose him before we get such another. There are a Parcel of Men in the World that are given to change and don't know when they are well themselves, nor can't let others alone that do. But more of this another time I have writ enough to tire you and myself too, you must take it as it is. I have Something else to do now than write Letters twice over, rough as it runs I hope you'l take it in good Parts with my Love and Service to all Friends

His Manner of Distribut- ing Books as he Travels. He refuses to take Money of ye People. The Gover- nor of Vir- ginias kind- ness to Mis- sionaries.

 I desire your Prayers & rest
    yor Real Friend
     & Servt
       J. T.

P. S.
 Pray give my Service to all Friends for Indeed that's all I have to give 'em having my Portmanteau plunder'd by a Negro. I lost all the money I had in the World, but God be praised I have lack^d nothing since I came ashoar. I found such Welcome att some friends or others, that I have been as it were att home, & could command much more than if I had been there, so that tho' I am one that has nothing, yet I possess all things y^t the Country affords.

The People of ye Country very kind to him.

 I want Bands Shirts & Shoes very much they are 9^s a pair here and not half so good as in England; a girdle or 2. would do very well such as Mr Barnaby sells. I wish they would send me a Chest of Cloaths yearly to New York or Philadelphia & you could pay them for me. pray do so much as write out a Copy of this fair, & send it to my honest friend & Brother John Kemble att the Vicaridge house in Standish, I have sent him a letter wth some advice of it; Pray seal it & send it as directed.

(S. P. G. A-Series, I., #CXX. ROBERT BEVERLEY, clerk of the Virginia Council and historian, published *The History and Present State of Virginia* in 1705; he was involved in litigation. COLONEL LEWIS MORRIS was one of the most prominent of the colonial governors. EVAN EVANS, D. D., was sent to Philadelphia by the Bishop of London in 1700; later he was stationed at Oxford and Radnor, Pa.; he died in Maryland in 1721. DANIEL BRETT, the first Church of England minister sent to North Carolina, was probably an S. P. C. K. missionary; he remained only about half a year, and did the cause more harm than good. THOMAS BRAY, D. D., 1656-1730, was commissary of the Bishop of London in Maryland, the founder of the S. P. C. K. and the S. P. G., the promoter of the parochial library and other philanthropic enterprises. THOMAS COMBER, 1645-1699, published his *Short Discourse upon the whole Common Prayer* in 1684. CHARLES LESLIE, 1650-1722, Nonjuror and controversialist, was the author of *A Short and Easy Method with the Deists,* 1698, and *The Snake in the Grass,* 1696—an attack on the Quakers).

(4)

Mr Talbot to the Secretary

Philadelphia 1st Sept.
1703

S^r
We have been the grand Circuit from N. England to N. Carolina, & are now return'd to the Center of our Business. Mr Keith shewed me a Letter wch menton'd the allowance that the Honble Corporation were pleased to appoint me for my travelling Charges. I am much obliged to them for their Extraordinary Bounty, & return them my hearty thanks for it, Resolving by God's Grace to go as far with it as anybody for the Service of the Church in the Wilderness to which I have given my Self entirely. Yours came to me in a very good time, for just before, a Negro stole out of my Portmanteau all the Money that I had in the World, and since I have had another Loss (more irreparable in these Parts) my Chest of Books & Box of Cloaths were overset by a Storm in the Bay of Mary-Land. Indeed I recov^d both again but the Books were spoiled wth Salt Water, three Bibles am^st the Rest, so that I have not one left. Only St Antony Escaped by as strange a Miracle as most is in his Life writ by St Athanasius the great. The Cloths will serve agen, because they are very dear here, black is hardly to be had att any Rate. It would cost a man 40 £ perAnn to goe decently here in the habit of His Order wherefore I have written to a Friend of mine Mr Richd Gillingham Vicar of Chigwel in Essex to buy me some things such as I want I desire you would let him have what is coming to me. Tho' I should Anticipate your Bounty this year. I hope the Honble Gentlemen will excuse it considering these Accidents. Now tho' we have

He gives account of his Journy

and Thanks for the Allowance from the Society.

His Losses,

and the Dearness of Ministers Cloaths in the Plantations.

had such ill Luck by the By yet God be praised we have had
very good Luck in the Main.

Mr Keith & I have preached the Gospel to all Sorts &
Conditions of Men, we have baptized Severall Scores of Men
Women & Children, Chiefly those of his old Friends (the Rest
are harden'd just like the Jews, who please not God and are
contrary to all men) we have gathered Several Hundreds together for the Church of England and what is more to build
houses for her Service. Here are 4 or 5 going forward now
in this Province and the next. That att Burlington, is almost
finisht, Mr Keith preacht the first Sermon in it before my L^d
Cornbury whom the Queen has made Govr of Jersey to the
Satisfaction of all Christian People. Churches are going up
amain where there were never any before. They are going
to build 3 at N. Carolina to keep the People together lest they
should fall into Heathenism, Quakerism &c. & 3 more in these
lower Counties ab^t at New Castle besides those att Chester Burlington & Amboy.

And I must be so Just to a Member of your's, his Excellency Francis Nicholson Govr of Virginia as to acknowledge
him to be the prime Benefactor & founder in chief of them all;
so generous has he been to the Church; so just to the State,
so far from taking of Bribes, that he will not receive a present
from any, great or small. Therefore we have hopes that it will
please God and the Queen, to give him time to perfect the good
Works that he has begun that he may see the Church prosper
& prevail agst all her Enemies, wch I dare say is all that he
desires being Zealous for the Honor of the Church of England
which is the Mother of us all. Upon her Acc^t it was that I
was willing to travel with Mr Keith. Indeed I was loath he
should goe alone now he was for us, who I'me sure would have
had followers enough had he come agst us Besides I had another End in it, that by his free Conversation and Learn'd Disputes both with his friends & enemies, I have learn't better in a
year to deal with the Quakers, then I could by Several years
study in the Schools. We want more of his Narratives which
would be of good Use here where we often meet wth the
Quakers & their Books. More of his Answers to Robt Barclay
would come well to the Clergy of Maryland & Virginia &c.
Barklay's Book has done most Mischief, therefore Mr Keith's
Answer is more Requisite & Necessary. Mr Keith has don
great Service to the Church where e're he has been, by Preaching & Disputing publickly and from house to house, he has confuted many (especially the Anabaptists) by Labor & Travel
Night & Day, by Writing & Printing of Books mostly att his
own Charge & Cost, & giving y^m out freely, which has been
very expensive to him. By these Means People are much
awaken'd, & their Eyes open'd to see the good Old Way and
they are very well pleased to find the Church att last take such

Marginal notes:

Mr K. and
he have
Baptiz'd
many
Quakers.

4 or 5
Churches
Building in
Jersey &c

and several
in N Caro-
lina &c.

Coll. Nichol-
son's Zeal for
the Church
&c.

An account
of Books
written agst
the Quakers
& much
wanted in
those Parts.
Mr K. has
printed sev-
eral Books
agst the
Anabaptists
& given
them away
at his own
charges.

Care of her Children For it is a sad thing to Consider the years that are past, how some that were born of the English, never heard of the Name of Christ, how many others were Baptized in his Name and fallen away to Heathenism, Quakerism & Atheism for want of Confirmation.

He laments
the Want of
a Bishop in
those Parts.

It seems the strangest thing in the World & 'tis thought History can't parallel it, That any Place has received the word of God so many years, so many hundred Churches built, so many thousand Proselytes made, and still remain altogether in the Wilderness as sheep without a shepherd. The Poor Church of America is worse on't in this Respect, than any of her Adversaries.

The Advan-
tage of the
Presb In-
dep: & other
Sectaries in
that Respect.

The Presbiterians here come a great way to lay hands one on Another, but after all I think they had as good stay att home for the good they do. The Independents are called by their Sovereign Lord the People. The Anabaptists & Quakers pretend to the Spirit. But the Poor Church has nobody upon the Spot to comfort or Confirm her Children. No body to Ordain several that are willing to serve, were they authorized, for the Work of the Ministry. Therefore they fall back again into the Herd of the Dissenters, rather than they will be att the Hazard and Charge to goe as far as England for Orders: so that we have seen several Counties, Islands, and Provinces which have hardly an Orthodox Minister amst 'em. which might have been supply'd had we been so happy as to see a Bishop or Suffragan Apud Americanos.

The Indians
wonder at a
Squa
Sachem.

When we brought over the News that King William was dead, & Queen Anne reigned in his Stead The Indian wonder'd what was come to the English that they should have a Squaw Sachem as they s^d a Woman King, how ever they sent her a Present, & hop'd that she would prove a Good Mother to this Church, and send us a God-Father or rather a Father in God with Apostolical Gravity & Authority to bless us, that we allso may be a Church for I count, No Bishop no Church, as true as No Bishop No King.

We count ourselves happy and indeed so we are under the Protection and Fatherly Care of the Right Revd Father in God Henry L^d B^p of London, & we are all satisfied that we can't have a greater Friend & Patron then himself. But alas! there is such a great Gulph fixt between, that we can't pass to turn nor he to us; but may he not send a Suffragan? I believe & am sure there are a great many learn'd, & good men in England, & I believe also did our gracious Queen Ann but know the Necessities of her many good Subjects in these Parts of the World, she would allow 1000£. p an. rather than so many souls should suffer; and then 'twould be a hard case if there sh^d not be found one amst so many Pastors, and Doctors (de tot millibus unus Qui transiens adjuvet nos), meanwhile I don't doubt but some learn'd & good man would goe further and do the

Church more Service with 100 £ p an : than with a Coach & Six, 100 year hence.

The Rev[d] Author of the Snake in the Grass has don great Service here by his Excellent Book, nobody that I know since the Apostles dayes has managed Controversie better ag[st] all Jews, Heathens & Hereticks : many here have desired to see the Author, however I hope we shan't want his works, especially ag[st] the Quakers, & y[e] 5 discourses which have convinced many & are much desiderated. Those Boxes of Books that were sent over last year M[r] Keith has disposed of in their several Places as directed. I have carried several of the Smaller Sort in a wallet some hundred miles, & distributed them to the People as I saw need. They have been long upon the Search of Truth in these Parts, they see thro' the Vanity & Pretences of all Dissenters and generally send directly to the Church. Now is the time of Harvest, we want a hundred hands for the work, meanwhile 2 or 3 that are well chosen will do more good there than all the rest. for we find by sad Experience that People are better where they have none, than where they have an ill Minister. Next unto God, our Eyes are upon the Corporation for help in this heavy Case. I daresay nothing has Obtained more Reputation to the Church & Nation of England abroad than the Hon[ble] Society for Reformation of Manners, and the R[d] & Hon[ble] Corporation for propagating the Gospel in forreign Parts.

The Quakers Compass Sea & Land to make Proselytes, they send out yearly a parcel of Vagabond fellows that ought to be taken up, & put in Bedlam, rather than suffer[d] to goe ab[t] railing & raving ag[st] the Laws & Orders of Christ & his Church, for why? their Preaching is of Cursing & Lyes, poysoning the Souls of the People wth Damnable Errors, & Heresies, and not content with this, in their own Territories of Pensylvania, but they travel wth Mischief over all parts as far as they can goe ; over Virginia and Maryland, and agen thro' Jersey & N. York as far as N. England, but there they stop, for they have prevented them by Good Laws & due Execution; Fas est et ab hoste doceri.

S[r] The Inclosed with all Submission is offer[d] to your Discretion by the hands of our good Brother M[r] Jo[n] Thomas, who has done good in the Church, and is well testified of all, he can tell more particularly the affairs of the Church here, and how we do, so that I need not be further tedious to you att p[r]sent. hoping you will take in good parts what has past. M[r] Keith thinks to return home in the Spring, but my call is to stay here still, & wait for yo[r] Instructions, if in anything I may be Serviceable, I shall be diligent, to do my Best by the Grace of God for the Good of Souls, and shall be very glad to embrace those that come over upon that design. Pray be so kind as to present my humble Duty & Service to my Bene-

The Works of the Author of the Snake in the Grass are much wanted—

He has disperst the Books sent over by M[r] K. with great success

The Credit of the Societies abroad.

The Quakers Zeal to make Proselytes.

He refers to M[r] Thomas whose Caracter he gives &c.

factors the R^t R^d my Lords the Bishops and the other Honble Members of the Noble Corporation particularly my very good Lord the Bishop of London, whose Prayers & blessing are humbly and heartily desired by

S^r

> yor most humble & Obedient
> Servant
> John Talbot

The Directions are
To John Chamberlayne Esqr
in Petty-France
Westm^r

(S. P. G. A-Series, I., #CXXV. JOHN CHAMBERLAYNE was the first secretary of the S. P. G.; he was a man of some literary distinction, Fellow of the Royal Society, and author of *Dissertations on the Most Memorable Events of the Old and New Testaments,* as well as of several miscellaneous pieces; he resigned in 1712. ROBERT BARCLAY, 1648-1690, Scotch Quaker, was the author of *An Apology for the true Christian Divinity . . .,* published in 1676. The Bishop of London alluded to was HENRY COMPTON, 1632-1713, who had been translated to that see in 1671. JOHN THOMAS was schoolmaster at Philadelphia and assistant to the Rev. Evan Evans; after ordination to the priesthood, he served at Hempstead, Long Island, 1704-1724).

(5)

Mr Talbot to the Secretary.

Philadelphia 7 Apr: 1704

Worthy S^r

He gives a Great Caracter of Mr Keith & Account of his Labors.

Mr Keith has fought the Good fight, finisht his Race, bravely Defended the Faith, Done the Church of Christ true & Laudable Service, wch I trust will be regarded here, and Rewarded hereafter. ——— I may say he has done more for the Church than any. Yea than all that have been before him. He Came out worthy of his Mission & of the Gosp^{ll} of Christ. Taking nothing of the Heathen that he came to Proselyte; besides his Ordinary or rather Extraordinary Travells, his Preaching Excellent Sermons upon all Occasions, his Disputes wth all sorts of Heathens & Hereticks, (who Superabound in these Parts, Africa has not more Monsters than America) He has written & Printed 10 or a Doz: Books & Sermons, much at his own Charge, & Distributed them freely, wch are all Excell^t in their kind, and have done Good service all along shoar. Now since Friends must part, I wish, I pray God, shew some token upon him for Good, that he may arrive safe in England where he would be, that all his Adversaries may see it and be Asham'd of their Impious Omens &c. I have one Vote more to God for the sake of his Church in the Desert, viz: That the Rev^d & Honble Corporation, may find one amongst the Thousands of the Rev^d & Learned Clergy of England, worthy, Honest & Willing to Succeed, that the People of the Lord may not be Scatter'd abroad in the Wilderness like sheep without a Shepherd.

As for the Affairs of the Church here, we have s^d much formerly in Schemes & Letters, but have hear'd no great Matter how or whither rec^d therefore I dont Mean to be tedious at present, something I think I should say because you desir'd me to keep a Journall. To begin then where we began our Travells at Boston N. England———There is one Church & there were 2 Ministers, both sober & Discreet Men in the Main, & I believe would have done Good Service att a Distance, they were both our friends, and I could wish they had been so to one another, or that those Rep^{r}sentations were true that are now Gone to his Grace & to the R^t R^d Bps of the Corporation, wch say they parted Good Friends, but to say the truth as it is, There is such a Variance that the Church Can't flourish between them. Mr Vesey does very well wth his People at New York. Mr Honyman is arrived but not yet Settled, because he has been Scandaliz'd by an Evill Report wch we have no Reason to believe. —— I should not have forgott my Honest Brother Lockier of Rhode-Island who is very Industrious when well. The Quakers themselves as far as I can hear have no Evill to say of that Priest. Nova Caesarea or N. Jersey has been most unhappy, there is not nor ever was an Orthodox Min^r settled amongst them. But there is one Mr Alex^r Innes a Man of great Piety & Probity, who has by his Life and Doctrine preacht the Gospell & rightly & Duly Administer'd the H. Sacram^{ts} We hope he will find fav^r wth the Noble Corporation, because he is Worthy & has need of it, as the People have need of him & are not so able or willing as we Could wish to Support the Ministry, 'tis Pity those hands should be putt to Dig, that are fitt to Cultivate The Vineyard. I come now to Philadelphia, where there is now none but Mr Evans a very Sober Discreet Man, who has Doubled his Diligence since Mr Thomas Departed, he does the whole Service of the Church now, & is more Constant and frequent in preaching & performing Divine Service, than any that I know upon the Continent, But the School is supplyed here by a Swede, untill one Can be sent from England, wch I hope will not be long, now there is a good Salary fix'd, & would be a very good School, were there but a Good Master, 'tis hard that the Heathens should have 3 Schools in the Town, & the Christians not one—The Church at Chester is allmost finish'd, & one at N. York is going to be rear'd—both by the Care & Industry of Mr Jasper Yeates, & all by the Generous Bounty of Govr Nicholson, God send us such a Publick Spirited Min^r in the Church here, as he is always & every where the best Friend & Patron of the Church, the Crown & Country, that ever Came over; I dare say this because I know it to be

He begins ye Acc^t of his Travels: Two Church Ministers at Boston

But they can not Agree.

Mr Vesey at N. York Mr Honyman not y^{et} setled. Mr Lockier in Road Island. Mr Innes in New Jersey.

Mr Evans at Philadelphia.

The School supply'd by a Swede. a schoolmaster now expected from Engl: there being a good Salary fixed.

The Charity and Generosity of Coll: Nicholson.

true, having had the Honor to know his Exc^y Many Years, tho' I know he has many adversaries as the Church herself, & the More I dare say upon her Account.————We rec^d a Box of Books by the Hands of his Hon^r Govr Evans, written by the Revd Author of the Snake in the Grass, we know not who sent them, but being Directed for Mr Keith we Ventur'd to Lend them abroad for the Public Good, & pray God to Bless the Authors & the Donors. There were the first & second Defences of the Snake &c but not the Snake itself, & 4 of his 5 Discourses, but not that of Episcopacy, wch are most Desiderated here, we Cannot purchase either of those Books at any rate, we want 1000 Com̄on Prayer Books, we can hardly get one in America & when we do find one, it Costs 5 times as much as 'tis worth in England, The Church wants to be Publisht here, wch Can't be done wthout her Liturgy & something to shew for w^t we say. Mr Tate's & Mr Brady's Psalms have obtaind here & would do so every where if they had in y^m the B^p of Londonderry's book of the Inventions of Men in the Worship of God, & Dr Beveridge's Sermon of the Excell^{cy} &^{c} of the Com̄on Prayer which have gone a great way here to serve the Church— I Can't tell what would do more Except the Doctors should Come themselves, however I hope they will send these books we Mention'd wth some others in the Scheme, as Mr Brent's of Bristol ag^t: Lying, wch is not to be forgotten at this time & Place. I'm sorry Mr Barclay return'd so soon from his Post at Brain tree in N. England, the Poor Christians are mightily opprest there by a sort of Hypocrites, who pretend to receive the Church, but indeed are her mortal Enemies, their Colledge also has gone a great way to Poison this Countrey wth Damnable Doctrines, wch appear by the Learned books of the Revd Mr Keith to be worse than Heathenism or Atheism, we hope that Care will be taken In this heavy Case, that some Grave & Wise Tutor & Philosopher will be sent to Preside at the Colledge of Cambridge in N. Engl^d to teach them humanity in the first Place that in time they might be brought to Christian Principles & Practises, for at Present they are not much better than the Quakers, & in the Latter much Worse. But I must not forgett that this Comes by Mr Keith who Can give the Revd Board an Acc^t of all things much better, God send him well home that he may receive Double Hon^r some Ease & rest in the End of his Days that worthy Men May see it & be Zealous to serve the Church of God where there is Most Need & where they may do most Good. If I had an Estate I could not have laid it out better than in the Service of God *apud Americanos,* along with Mr Keith who is a True Son of the Church of England, sound in faith & holy in Life whom I love & Rev^{r}ence as my Father & Mast^r & shall be as Loath to Part with him as if he were so Indeed, Therefore I am The More obliged to the Rev^d and Honble. Society for their Generous Allowance to me, that

Marginal notes:

They lend ab^t the Books of ye Author of the Snake, &c, agst Quakers.

Com̄on prayer books much wanted.

B^p of Londonderry's Book of ye Inventions of Men in the worship of God, and Dr Beveridge on the usefulness of the Com̄on prayer are much wanted. As also Brent of Bristol agst Lying.

Mr Barclay.

Description of the Colledge at Boston.

I might not be Burdensome to him nor to others, but beneficial to all as far as we Could goe. God be praised a Door is Open'd to the Gospell, & the true light shines to them in the Wilderness, but here are many Adversaries, and now our Champion is gone, we must make a running fight on't, by God's Blessing & his Books I shall do my best, I mean to gather up the Arrows that he has shot so well at the Mark, & throw y^{em} agen where there is most Need. Pray S^r please to offer my humble Duty Service & thanks to the Rev^d & Noble Body of our Patrons & Benefactors, to my Good Lord of London in Particular. I pray God Comand the Dew of his Blessing upon them all for the Good of his Church & the Glory of Christ. I humbly Desire their Pray^{rs} & Blessing that I may do my Duty where it has pleas'd God to Call

Your most humble
& Obedient Serv^{tt}

Jno Talbot.

The Directions are
For
John Chamberlayne Esqr

(S. P. G. A-Series, I., #CLXXXI. Talbot refers to the dissension between SAMUEL MYLES, 1663?-1728, of Queen's Chapel, Boston, and his assistant, CHRISTOPHER BRIDGE. JAMES HONYMAN was missionery at Jamaica, Long Island, 1703-1704, and was transferred to Newport, R. I., where he served from 1705 to 1750, when he died. JOHN LOCKYER began his Rhode Island ministry about 1697; he served Newport till his death in 1704. ALEXANDER INNES arrived in Middletown, N. J., in 1680; he died in 1713. As in other letters, there is mention of GEORGE KEITH'S controversial pamphlets. NAHUM TATE, 1652-1715, and NICHOLAS BRADY, 1659-1726, collaborated in the production of *A New Version of the Psalms of David*, 1696—an important event in the history of English hymnody. WILLIAM KING, 1650-1729, published *A Discourse concerning the Inventions of Men in the Worship of God*, in 1694. WILLIAM BEVERIDGE, 1637-1708, Bishop of St. Asaph, was the author of numerous works. The BRENT referred to was probably SIR NATHANIEL BRENT. WILLIAM BARCLAY was S. P. G. missionary to Braintree, Mass., 1704-1705).

(6)

Mr Talbot to Mr Keith

N. York. October. 20th.

Reverend S^r

We received Advice from Barbado's that yor Fleet was arrived, a confirmation of wch we shall be glad to have from yo^{r}self. We the Clergy in these Provinces, Pensilvania N. Jersey and N. York being conven'd here by the directions of my Lord Cornbury & his Excellency Govr Nicholson, to make a Rep^{r}sentation of the p^{r}sent State of Affairs of the Church wch we have drawn up in a Scheme and transmitted to ye venerable Society sign'd by their 12. Apostles apud Americanos. I mean

Clergy con-
ven'd to
rep^{r}sent the
State of the
Church.

to do in this Letter as I do in my Travels touch and go from place to place and tell you such things as I thought not so proper for yᵉ Publick view. I got some hundreds of Fʳ Buggs Bombs printed, wᶜʰ I had endorsed wᵗʰ a Challenge & so was bound to answer it, but I could not quote the Friends to it by no means. No. they say as they use to do that they will Answer in Print. Then I offer'd to take the 2. Almanacks by Dan: Leeds & Caleb Pusey & prove them by Friends books. I challeng'd yᵉ latter at yᵉ head of his Regiment to come forth & see himself proved a Lyar, in yᵉ very same Book and Page where he most impudently changed G: K: D. D. and yᵉ 8 Ministers of yᵉ Church of England. But all I could get of them at pʳsent was this Sorry Paper, False News from Gath, wᶜʰ I intend to answer wᵗʰ true News to Gath, Ashdod and yᵉ rest of the uncircumcised, unbaptiz'd Philistins At length I appointed a meeting at Church whether they would come or no, & there I exposed their Errors before all Men, Women and Children that were there, but none answered a word, tho' several Quakers were there, whilst I Mʳ Sharp and Mʳ Nicols examined yᵉ Bomb, yᵉ Serious and D. L. Almanack by their Books, and proved yᵉ Questions true. I have hired a Chamber at Burlington where I keep the pretious Collection of Friends Books, several of them came to me there and were satisfied, but some desired me to set down my Quotations Book & Page wᶜʰ I promised to do at my Leisure, pticularly to one of their Friends of yᵉ Ministry who I believe will come off, I have forgot his name, he lives near Pet: Chamberlains in Pensilvania, Mʳ Sharp was very zealous to bring yᵉ Quakers to stand a Tryal, he carried one of yᵉ Bombs into their Meeting and read a new Challenge wᶜʰ I sent them to answer what they had printed, but all in vain, Sam: Jenings stood up and said Friends let's call upon God, then they went to prayer and so their Meeting broke up. Since I have read several scandalous Letters from several Quakers whereby I see they are pʳparing War agᵗ me, one was from W. Rakeshaw, the same Villain that pulled yᵉ Paper out of your hand last yearly meeting at Philadᵃ, he said there was not a word of truth in the Bomb & he would answer it, but never appear'd. Mʳ Nicols Mʳ Sharp & I preacht in our turns proper Sermons to warn yᵉ people of their Errors and Heresies, So we kept up yᵉ Christian yearly meeting so happily begun by you at Philada, Mʳ Nicols gives his Service to you, he is indeed an Ingenious man, & will prove in all appearance an able hand agᵗ Quakerism. I have promis'd to set him up with Friends goods, & we mean to go down to Chester and give them a Broadside there, if the Governor will give us leave. They are all out at Philada as much about Governmᵗ as ever they were abᵗ Religion. There is Charter agᵗ Commission, and Major agᵗ Govᵗ. The y have 2 Sheriffs Capᵗ Fenny ap-

he appoints
a time for
Argumᵗ wᵗʰ
yᵉ Quakers.

appoints another time.

examine the
Bomb &
other Books.

Mʳ Sharp
zealous to
bring yᵉ
Quakers to
stand a
Tryal.

Mʳ Nicols
an Ingenious
man likely
to be an able
hand agᵗ
Quakerism.

Quakers disagree abᵗ
Govermᵗ at
Philadelphia.

pointed by G^r Evans, and young John Budd by ye Major Now
G. Jones, the Govr proclaim'd their proceedings null & void,
but G. Jones told him it was not he nor his M^r neither that
shou'd take away their charter, So much for State affairs, You
may hear all phaps one of these days in Westm^{r}hall, meanwhile here's a Gov^t divided ag^t itself, God p^{r}serve his Church—
and let them that have the Watch look out. There is a New
Meeting house built for Andrews, & almost finish'd since you
came away, wch I am afraid will draw away great part of the
Church, if there be not ye greater care taken of it. Mr Rudman
serves there some times but chiefly at ye Country Ch (in Oxford
near Franckfort) with good Success, but he has met with some
disturbance from Edw: Eaton who has been very peevish &
scandalous in words and writings, for wch he was p^{r}sented to
ye Grand Jury, but it was hard to pswade them to find the Bill,
what will come of it I know not.

a new Meet-
ing house at
Philad. w^{ch}
wthout care
may be
dangerous

Mr Sharp and I have gon ye rounds several times from
Burlington to Amboy to hopewell to Eliz: Town to Staten
Island in our Turns with good Success God be blessed, in all
places. He has gathered a Church himself at Cheesquake where
he preach't several times, & Baptiz'd about 40 psons. Now I
am alone for my Lord Cornbury has p^{r}ferr'd him to be Chaplain of her Maties Fort and Forces at N. York I saw his Com-
ission sign'd this day, in ye Room of Mr Mott who dyed about
3 months agoe. I was loth to part with my good Friend and
Companion in Travel, but considering how he had been dis-
appointed at home I would not hinder his p^{r}ferment abroad.
Hoping that ye good providence of God, and ye venerable Society
will supply his Place.

Mr Sharp
& Mr Tal-
bot gone the
rounds wth
good Suc-
cess.

Mr Sharp
p^{r}ferr'd by
ye Lord
Cornbury.

The Assembly sat Burlington in Sep^t but did nothing
that my L^d desired them so he dissolved them and call'd
another there in O^{ber} now I hear that Mr Wheeler our good
Friend is chosen instead of Thomas Gardener. It seems their
Interest go's down thereabouts. Sam Jenings complains that a
man can't turn friend of truth now but he is ridicul'd out of it.
I hope the venerable Society will take Mr Bradford's Case into
their consideration, It has cost me ten pounds & more out of
my Pocket to print some Small books to give away, where I could
not stay, that the Church might be served and ye Printer
employ'd without setting forth those that are erroneous, I know
you will not forget ye Revd Mr Innes, who has been so Zealous
for ye Service of ye Church since you put him upon it. I count
him as my Fr. now you are gone, & indeed our Convocation here
had been at a loss for a Foreman had not he supply'd the
Place by his Gravity & Wisdom. I have drawn another Bill
upon Mr Hodges, not knowing when I should have so good
opportunity, besides I have been at more than ordinary Charge
for Horses & Cloaths for I never rec^d any from England since
I came out of it, As for that parcel that my Friend Mr Gilling-

Assembly at
Burlington.

Prints small
Books to
give away.

comends M^r
Innes.

draws a Bill
upon M^r
Hodges.

ham sent by Capt Innifer I can't hear what is become of it, My Horse you know dyed at Burlington & ye Quakers recorded it as a Judgm^t upon me. Ben: Wheat set it down in his Almanack such a day of ye 1st month John Talbot's horse dyed & Barnet Lane haled him into the River. But I was more sorry for the Mare that you were so kind to give me, for she dyed before I came over the Bay in Maryland. I hope y^e

comends all ye Missionary's pticularly Mr Moor.

venerable Society will see good to take you into their number, for it may be of use to them to have one there that has been here. I hope this Letter will come safe to yor hand by Mr Robert Owen Minister of a Church in Maryland who is a very honest Gentleman, And indeed so are all ye Missionary's in General, especially ye English one Mr More, the only Countryman we have amongst us, a man according to my own heart, I'me sorry he's to go so far off as ye Mohocks God knows whether we shall see him again. I had ye same Call and had gone to ye same place, but when I saw so many People of my own Nation and Tongue, I soon resolved by God's grace to seek them in ye first place, and if we could not recover those that were fallen, yet by God's help we may keep them out of ye Pit of Quakers and Hereticks who have denyed ye Faith and are worse than Indians and Heathens who never knew it.

all sensible of ye want of a Suffragan.

As for a Suffragan we are all sensible of ye want we have of one, and pray God send us a Man of peace, for otherwise he will do more harm than Good, as proud, ambitious Covetuous Men use to do, troubling ye State & pplexing the Church, and then they run away and leave all in the Lurch. I saw our hon^d Friend Coll. Nicholson last month at Burlington where he staid a week or Ten days, I was obliged to him much every

Coll Nicholson advises him in a difficult Case.

way prticularly for his Friendly advice in a Case that was difficult to me at that time, but I shall not mention Names because I am resolved by Gods grace to take heed what I say of any man whether good or bad.

Coll. Nicholson took Bills of Mr Bass for the money in hand 70 £ Pensyl^a money and gave it all to ye Churches in these Provinces with Bills of Exchange to make it up 100 £

Coll. Nicholson gives 100£ to ye Churches he has exhibited to ye Churches there about 1000£ besides other Bountys. his Character

Ster: besides what he subscribed to the Churches to be erected at Hopewell, Eliz Town, Amboy and Salem. We have made it appear that he has exhibited to the Churches in these Provinces about 1000 £ besides what he has given to particular psons & ye poor would amount to some hundreds more wch we did not think fit to mention. He is a man of as much prudence, Temperance, Justice & Fortitude as any Governo^r in America without dispagem^t to any & of much more Zeal for the House and Service of God. I have seen 4 of them together at Church in Burlington, but in ye afternoon ye place had been empty had it not been for ye Honble Govr Nicholson, so that I can't but observe ye Example of his piety in the Church is as rare as his Bounty towards it. No wonder then that all that Love ye Church of England are fond of Govr Nicholson who is a true Son or rather a Nursing Father of her in America. I hope you will do him all ye Service you can at home, whereby you will oblige all ye Churches abroad.

Mr Urquhart is well chosen for ye People of Jamaica, and indeed I think none fitter than the Scotch Episcopal to deal with Whigs & fanaticks of all sorts. Had not Hubbart been allowed to preach he had brought them all to ye Church almost by this time, but now they resort most to a Barn that is hard by & will not pay Mr Urquhart what is allow'd by Law tho' my Ld Cornbury has given his orders for it. Mr John Lillingston designs it seems to go for England next year, he seems to be ye fitest pson that America affords for ye Office of a Suffragan & several Persons both of ye Laity & Clergy have wished he were ye man, & if my L^d of London thought fit to authorize him several of ye Clergy both of this Province & of Maryland have said they would pay their Tenths unto him, as my Lord of London's Vicegerent, whereby the Bp of America might have as honorable Provision as some in Europe. Ah Mr Keith, I have wanted you but once, that is ever since you went. I pray God supply yor place with such another, who will pass thro' all Gov^ts serving ye Church, without giving Offence unto the State, I hope Good S^r you will excuse this Long Letter. I had not time to write a short one, therefore p amicitia nostra I desire that you would take all in good part that comes from

> Your most faithful Friend
> and humble Servant
> John Talbot

The Directions for
The Revd Mr George Keith at
Mr Brab Aylmers near ye Royal
Exchange, London.

(marginal notes:) comends Mr Urquhart. Mr Hubbard draws away ye people so that they'l not pay Mr Urquhart comends Mr Lillingston thinks he is ye fittest man for a Suffragan.

(S. P. G. A-Series, II., #XXIII. This letter to Talbot's travelling companion and to one who had achieved great prominence among the Quakers abounds in reference to mutual acquaintances, some of whom cannot be identified; it also reveals the strong feeling which existed between the Anglicans and the Friends. EDWARD HYDE, VISCOUNT CORNBURY, was governor of New York, arriving in 1702 and departing in 1708. FRANCIS BUGG, 1640-1729, wrote *A Brief History of the Rise, Growth, and Progress of Quakerism*, 1697; *The Picture of Quakerism, drawn to the Life*, 1697. *The Pilgrim's Progress from Quakerism to Christianity*, 1698; and other controversial treatises. DANIEL LEEDS, 1652-1720, almanac-maker, surveyor, and author; appointed surveyor-general of West Jersey in 1682; member of Lord Cornbury's Council, 1702-1708; engaged in controversy with Caleb Pusey; a former Quaker, he consorted with Bradford and Keith, and wrote several controversial pamphlets: *News of a Trumpet Sounding in the Wilderness*, 1697; *A Trumpet Sounded out of the Wilderness of America*, 1699; *The Rebuker Rebuked*, 1703; *The Great Mystery of Fox-craft Discovered*, written in conjunction with John Talbot, 1705; *The Second Part of the Mystery of Foxcraft*, 1705. CALEB PUSEY, 1650?-1727, builder and manager of Chester Mills, Penna., and political leader; Quaker controversial writer; member of the

Provincial Assembly and Governor's Council of Pennsylvania; author of *Proteus Ecclesiasticus, or George Keith Varied in Fundamentals; Satan's Harbinger Encountered, His False News of a Trumpet Detected*, 1700; *Daniel Leeds Justly Rebuked for Abusing William Penn and his Foly and Fals-Hoods in His Two Printed Challenges to Caleb Pusey*, 1702; *Remarks on Daniel Leeds Abusive Almanac for* 1703; *George Keith once more brought to the Test and proved a Prevaricator*, 1704?; *The Bomb Search'd and found stuff'd with False Ingredients, being a Just Confutation of an Abusive Printed Half-sheet . . . originally published against the Quakers, by Francis Bugg*, 1705; *Some Remarks upon a late Pamphlet signed part by John Talbot and part by Daniel Leeds, called The Great Mystery of Fox-craft.* 1705? JOHN SHARPE, Church of England clergyman, was chaplain to the British troops in New York, and ministered to various churches in New York and New Jersey. HENRY NICHOLS was the first S. P. G. missionary in Pennsylvania; he was stationed at Chester, 1703-1708. JOHN EVANS was lieutenant governor of Pennsylvania; he was a staunch Anglican, and objectionable to the Quakers. JEDIDIAH ANDREWS, 1674-1746? was a Presbyterian minister in Philadelphia; a house of worship for his use was in process of construction at the time this letter was written. ANDREW RUDMAN, a Swedish clergyman, was appointed by the Archbishop of Upsala to minister to the Swedes on the Delaware, in 1697; he died at the age of forty in 1705. Close fraternal intercourse existed between the Swedish and Anglican ministers in Pennsylvania. EDWARD EATON, a Pennsylvania layman, wrote a letter to GEORGE KEITH, complaining of Rudman's doctrines; this letter is reproduced in *Historical Collections relating to the American Colonial Church, edited by W. S. Perry, II., Pennsylvania*, pp. 26-29. EDMUND MOTT was chaplain to the British forces in New York, 1696-1704. WILLIAM BRADFORD, 1663-1752, was the first printer in Philadelphia; he moved to New York in 1693; orginally a Quaker, was opposed by the Friends when he identified himself with the Church of England adherents. ROBERT OWEN was rector of St. Paul's parish, Calvert county, Md., 1700-1710. THOROUGHGOOD MOOR arrived in New York in 1704, and proceed to Albany as missionary to the Mohawks; owing to the influence of the fur-traders, his labours proved fruitless, and he returned to New York; he next went to Burlington, N. J., where he was scandalised at the conduct of Lord Cornbury and his Lieutenant-Governor, and actually refused to admit the latter to the Lord's Supper; for this he was imprisoned; he contrived to make his escape, and embark for England, but he was lost at sea when the ship foundered. JEREMIAH BASS, New Jersey governor, wrote an account of local conditions, which was published in the *Protestant Episcopal Historical Collections*, 1851. WILLIAM URQUHART was S. P. G. missionary at Jamaica, Long Island, 1704-1709. JOHN HUBBARD, 1677-1705, a Presbyterian minister, claimed the use of the parsonage at Jamaica, Long Island, in which he had dwelt; he was ousted by order of Lord Cornbury, in favour of URQUHART. JOHN LILLINGSTON, rector of St. Paul's parish, Talbot county, Md., was recommended as a suitable suffragan bishop for America).

(7)

Ditto to M[r] Whitfield

Reverend S[r].

I can do no less nor more then return my most humble thanks to the Ven[ble] Society and to yo[r] Self in pticular for all their undeserved favours towards me. Tho' I have not rec[d] y[e] Parcel my Friend sent, nor phaps never shall, yet I can never forget my Obligation is y[e] same to pray God to reward all my

marginal note (left):
has not, nor is likely to receive y[e] parcel sent to him.

helpers and Benefactors both in this life that now is, and in that which is to come. I do believe that God will lengthen out ye Tranquility of the Church and State of England for the sake of those worthys who are so zealous to propagate ye truth of ye Gospel abroad. The 5th of this instant Oct. 12. of us ye Messengers of the Church met here by ye directions of my Lord Cornbury & Govr Nicholson, whose generous Bounty is a constant Fund to ye Churches in N. America, especially where they are not establisht by Law. As is evident by the Scheme wch we have drawn up (with an Appendix) and sent to the ven^ble Society, of all which I intend you a Copy, if ye Ship will give me time, I can't omit to mention our Great Benefactor Govr. Nicholson upon all occasions because in Serving him we serve the Interest of ye Church: I have known him long & do believe and know him to be a man of as much prudence Temperance, Justice & Fortitude as any Govr in North America from N. England to N. Carolina. And for the Church 'tis evident he has done more than they all. Neither is this Flattery in us, nor vanity in him, but some slye Adversarys, that never were contented long with any Government here they have compell'd him, by blazoning his faults and Eclypsing his Noble Acts, wch are more than we can express, however we hope that publick demonstration will pass before private Informations, therefore I shall say no more upon that, But since America has not his like, I pray God She may keep him till England affords a better wch will be hard to do. I know they p^rtend he's alter'd & almost mad, but I'me sure he's not halfe so mad as they that affirm it, Last month I attack't ye great Synagogue of ye Quakers at their yearly meeting in Burlington, we gave them a broad Side wth some of honest Francis Buggs Bombs, but could not get them out to dispute by no means, then I upbraided them wth their Charges, whereas formerly they use to challenge all priests now they could not answer one. Now the case is strangly alter'd, We have seen one defie 1000, and 2 put ten thousand to flight. Then I told them what happen'd the week before, when I was at Hopewell near Delaware falls where I preacht at the house of one Tho: Tyndals a Friend of Mr Keiths, I baptiz'd his ffamily with some more about 12. in all, as we came away a mile or 2. from ye house we found ye Snake in the Grass or rather in the path a great Rattle Snake it was, when I came up with them I found they that went before had bruised his head, so I alighted from my horse and took off his Tail, The Moral I told them was this That G. Keith went before and broke the head of Quakerism and I Talbot came after to cut of his Tail. I pray God give us power to tread on Serpents and Scorpions and over all ye power of ye enemy, that

The Clergy (12 of 'em) meet at N. York.

Character & Comendations of Govr Nicholson.

he attacks the Quakers.

the Quakers are afraid to Dispute.

he baptizes a ffamily of Quakers.

nothing may by any means hurt us nor our noble Benefactors is the hearty Prayer of

(Worthy Sir)

Your most humble

& most obliged Ser^{vt}

N. York Oct 22. 1704

John Talbot

The Directions are

For ye Revd Mr Whitfield

Rector of St Martin's Ludgate

London

(S. P. G. A-Series, II., #XXIV. The rector of St. Martin's, Ludgate, is not to be confounded with the celebrated George Whitefield, who belongs to a subsequent generation).

(8)

Mr Eburne to Mr Talbot

Kingstowne Nov : 12, 1705.

Reverend S^r

<table>
<tr><td>Inhabitants of
Ulster
County de-
sire some
books.</td><td>The Inhabitants of ye County of Ulster do most humbly request the R^t Reverend Father in God Henry Lord Bishop of London as also the Honble Society to furnish them with Six Dozen of Common Prayer Books printed in Dutch, thereby they may the better inform themselves in ye Service of our Church.</td></tr>
</table>

The English Families desire four Doz: of English Common Prayer book for their use & assistance in ye publick Service.

These Inclinations of theirs are well pleasing to me, and may prove beneficial to our Church, And such a Present may provoke their Bounty to an English Minister, if an Encouragment be given from ye Society to continue one in that Place. I leave ye the managm^t of this Affair to your Prudence. ——— Remember my Circumstances when you come to England. I wish you a safe, short, and pleasant Voyage, and I request a few lines from you after you have been with ye Society.

I am

Your affectionate Brother.

Sam: Eburne.

P. S.

Since ye writing of this, ye Inhabitants are about to make Subscriptions for me, I wish all will repair my Habit or Cloathing.

(S. P. G. A-Series, II., #CXIV. SAMUEL EBURNE was the first resident S. P. G. missionary in New England. In 1704, he was sent by Lord Cornbury to Kingston, in order to convert the Dutch inhabitants to the Church of England. He had been minister of Bruton Parish, James City County, Virginia, from 1688 to 1695, and chaplain of the General Assembly at Jamestown; but had resigned in 1695, because of the stand of the vestry in refusing to call a minister for more than a year at a time. His resignation was accepted with resolutions commending his character and work).

(9)

Mr Talbot to ye Society.
May it please ye Rt Reverend & Rt Honble
Society for propagating the Gospel.

After I had travelled with Mr G. Keith thro' 9 or 10 *the Assem-*
Provinces betwixt New England & North Carolina, I took my *bly offer him*
leave of him in Maryland. The Assembly then sitting offered *100£ Sterl*
me 100£. Sterling to go Proselite their Indians but my Call *to go*
was to begin at home, & to teach our own people first whose *Proselite ye*
Language we did not understand, So I returned to Burlington *Indians*
to finsh ye Church wch was so happily begun, There Mr Sharp
came to my Assistance, where I left him to supply that,
Hopewell & Maidenhead, whilst I went to E. Jersey for Amboy,
Eliz: Towne, Woodbridge & Staten Island, This we did by *had an*
turns about half a year till Mr Mott dyed, who was Chaplaine *offer of*
of ye Queen's Fort & Forces at N York, I was offered this *being made*
place also where I should have had Board, Lodging & 130£ p *Chaplain of*
anm paid weekly, But nothing could tempt me from ye Service *ye Fort at*
of ye Society, who were pleased to adopt me into their Service *N York but*
before I had ye Honor to know them, Mr Sharp was glad to *refused it.*
embrace this offer, So I travelled along doing what good I
could, till last Summer I met Mr John Brooks, who brought me
a Letter from my Lord of London & Orders to fix at Burling- *Missionaries*
ton, as I did till November last, There was a General Meeting *Address for*
of ye Missionaries who resolved to Address the Queen for a *a Suffragan*
Suffragan Bishop, that I should Travel with it, and make known *Bp.*
ye Requests of some of the Brethren abroad, whose Case we
had recomended formerly by Letter to ye Venerable Society
but without Success, Twill be four years next June since I associated with Mr Keith. I was allowed 60£ p Anm for 3
yeares, but for ye last I had nothing, neither here or there, I
have no Business here but to Sollicite for a Suffragan, Books
and Ministers for ye propagating the Gospel, God has so blest
my Labours & Travels abroad that I am fully resolved by his
Grace to return, the Sooner the better, having done my Busi- *designs to*
ness that I came about, meanwhile my Living in Gloucester- *return*
shire is given away, but I have no reason to doubt of any Incouragement from this famous Society, who have done more
in four yeares for America then ever was done before. And
your Petr shall ever pray God bless all our Benefactors in
Heaven & Earth, & reward them for ever for all ye Good they
have done to ye Church in General & in pticular to

your most humble Servant
& Obedient Missionary
John Talbot.

London. Mar 14th.

(S. P. G. A-Series, II., #CXLII. This letter is Talbot's official notice to the Society that he has discontinued his tour, and intends settling at Burlington, N. J. JOHN BROOKE, S. P. G. missionary at Elizabeth Town, N. J., was drowned *en route* to England; he had suffered humiliation in company with MOOR. A convention of fourteeen clergymen was held at Burlington, beginning Nov. 2, 1705; the need of a resident bishop was the main subject of discussion; and Talbot made a trip to London, where he presented the views of that gathering.)

(10)

Mr Talbot to the Secretary

Hond Sr

I have received several Letters from my Friends in America who think long for my return which I was forward to do once and agen, but Satan hindred me by raising lyes and Slanders in my way, But I have clear'd my self to all that have heard me, and I hope you will satisfy the Honble Society that I am not the man to whom that dark Character did belong, Mr Keith has known my doctrine & manner of life some years and what I have ventur'd suffer'd and acted for the Gospel of Christ abroad and at home. I desire his Letter may be read to the Honorable Board and that they will be pleas'd to dispatch me the sooner the better for the season is far spent and Ships are going out and if I go at all I wou'd go quickly I know the wants of the poor people in America. They have need of me, or else I shou'd not venture my life to do that abroad which I cou'd do more to my own advantage at home. I shou'd be glad to see somebody sent to North Carolina I hope the Planters Letters is not quite forgot 'Tis a sad thing to live in the Wilderness like the Wild Indians without God in the World.

Pray give my humble duty and Service to all the Members of the Honble Society May God prosper their generous undertakings for the advancement of his glory and the progress of the Gospel wherein I do not rest but labour and travail as a good Soldier of Jesus Christ and Hond Sr

Your humble Servt

John Talbot

London
Apll 16. 1707.

Directions are
To Jno Chamberlayne Esqr &c.

(S. P. G. A—Series, III., #XLV.)

(11)

Mr Talbott to ye Secretary

Reserve at Spithead
23 June 1707.

Hon^d S^r

Wee sailed out of this port on Saturday and in agen being alarm'd by the Dunkirk Squadron which is looking out to Convoy us to France and we having none fit to see them so thought best to tack about, when or where we shall go I know not, nor any body hardly that dos care we have almost 20 passengers on Board, so that there's no room for me at Least No Cabbin and if I will have one I must buy the Boards my self for the Admiralty allow none I am put to extraordinary Charge and trouble so I am obliged to draw a Bill upon the Treas of 15 £ which is now due and it will be well if my Salary bears my travelling Charges if we shou'd stay long here.

The Society have begun a good work and I pray God it may prosper, but I am sure it will not till we obtain the one thing necessary so necessary as a head to the Body Pray give my humble Duty and Service to all the Honble Society. I'me sorry I have none of Mr Keiths Journals please to let us have some of them as soon as may be so I rest

S^r

Your most humble Servt
John Talbot

Capt. Hamilton gives
you his Service.
Directions are
To Jno Chamberlayne Esqr

(S. P. G. A-Series, III., #LXI.).

(12)

Mr Talbot to ye Secretary

Reserve Lisbon
Sepr 4th 1707

Hon^d S^r

Tho' I never had the honor of a Letter from you, yet I think myself obliged to let you know where I am and how I do, we were Ordered by the Prince with the rest of the Fleet to see the rock of Lisbon, we were three weeks in our passage, but not at all in our way for N. England, Therefore we put in here to water, having still a long Voyage before us; I went ashoar to see the City and to refresh my self with some fruits, and a little wine which is all to be gotten here; There was an Embargo put upon Mr Cordiner, Mr Black and the rest of the Missioners on board the Ruby, when they come I hope to hear from you how all our Honble friends of the Society do, mean while I hope they will consider their Condition and allow them wherewith to have a Servant and a Cabbin or else they can neither serve God nor themselves, and will be used more like Camisars than true Prophets. Then how shall Ministers maintain their Characters when ye men are despised? The Ships are under sail, so in all ye hast in ye world I rest

Your most humble Servt

Jn° Talbot

P. S.

This I design to come by Captain Congreve who had ye misfortune to be taken into France after he had lost his arm in the fight. I hope the God whose I trust I am, & whom I desire to serve will preserve us. I hope the Society will employ ye young Student y^t is with Capt Congreve for he is a pretty Modest young Man & will do very well in America

Ans^d 6th Augst 1708

(S. P. G. A-Series, III., #CXI. WILLIAM CORDINER, ex-curate of Billyaghran, was appointed to Shrewsbury, Md., in 1707. He "failed to reach his destination, being carried away into captivity. His case deserves notice as illustrating some of the dangers which Missionaries had to encounter in those days. The Rev. WILLIAM CORDINER, an Irish Clergyman, received his appointment to Shrewsbury in January 1707, with an allowance at the rate of £50 per annum, on condition that he transported himself and family there 'by the first opportunity.' Three months passed before he could find a ship, and when on April 13 he embarked on the *Dover,* man-of-war, at Spithead, it was only for a day—for the *Dover* being ordered on a cruise he landed, and the ship returned disabled. On May 24 he re-embarked on the *Chester,* man-of-war. After being 'sixteen times out at sea'—sometimes fifty and sixty leagues—and driven back by contrary winds or the French, the *Chester* at length left Plymouth in company with five men-of-war and 200 merchantmen in the evening of October 10. At noon on the next day they were engaged by fourteen French men-of-war, and in two hours' time were all taken except the *Royal-Oak* (escaped) and the *Devonshire* (blown up). The *Chester* was on fire several times, and the thirty-seven men on the quarter-deck were all killed and wounded except the captain and two others. The prisoners were searched 'to the very skin' and deprived of all they had. The French sailors, taking compassion on the women and children, gave some things back, which the chief officers then appropriated, even the shoes and stockings of the little children. On October 19 the prisoners were landed at Brest, having suffered from exposure and want of food and clothing. There Mr. Cordiner was offered provision for his mother, wife, and two children if he would betake himself to a convent. On the way to Dinan, which was reached on December 5, they were subjected to ill treatment from the Provost. A great many sick men were 'carried in a very pitiful condition, some . . . being blind with the small-pox and whenever they complained' they were beaten. At Fugiers and at Dinan, Mr. Cordiner ministered to his fellow-prisoners, and encouraged them. An Irish priest (Father Hagan) having stopped his doing so in Dinan Castle, some of the merchantmen procured a room in the town, where service was held every Sunday and on holy days. Several 'who never understood it before' were instructed in the Liturgy and conformed. During their detention at Dinan one of Mr. Cordiner's children and his servant died, and a child was born to him. He was 'several times . . . imprisoned for two or three hours, and daily threatened with close restraint and confinement.' The number of English prisoners, at first 1,000, was increased to 1,700, but some 200 died. The prisoners 'were mightily cheated in their allowance and too much crowded together, and the hospital at Dinan was a place to despatch them out of this world.' When 'the design of the Pretender' was in hand the French abused and beat their prisoners and applauded the Scotch; but when they found 'that he was obliged to return to France . . . they cursed the Scotch bitterly,' saying, 'Scot will be Scot still, always false.' Upon which disappointment the prisoners were sent to England, landing at Waymouth on December 11."—Pascoe: *Two Hundred Years of the S. P. G.*, pp. 31-32. WILLIAM BLACK, S. P. G. missionary in Sussex county, Delaware, 1708-1709. Later he went to Virginia; and was minister of Accomac Parish, Accomac County, from 1711 till after 1724).

(13)

Mr Talbot to ye Secretary

Rhode Island
13 Decr 1707.

Hond Sr

I take all Opportunitys to let you and the Honble Society know where I am and what I do, I went with the two Honest Brethren, Thorowgood Moore and Jno Brooks to Marble Head where they were desired to preach before they departed. but it happened otherwise; so I stayed there a Sunday and preacht twice, they were terribly pleased (as their phrase is) and offered to Subscribe to building a Church and for a Minister, but I resolved to build no more till they be better supplyed which can't be till a Bishop comes over. You see the Missionaries are glad to return faster than they came out, so here's a good work come to nought purely for lack of looking after. I have ventured my life to give a true Account of the present State of poor America, if it was without Success it was not my fault, it wou'd make a Christian's heart bleed to hear the Indians pleading with the Independants of New England, say they, we have been your Neighbours many Years, you never taught us Religion, but as soon as the French came we learnt it of them, and in that we will live and dye, let them look to this that have as much power in their hands but not that Zeale to Stretch them forth to do good. Mr Honyman has a good report of all Christian people here, he has no desire to Change nor they neither, therefore give me leave to recommend to you once more as an honest and able Missioner whom they need not be ashamed to employ in any Part of the Church or the World, I have always said the same thing of him and have no reason to alter my good Opinion of him. pray give my humb duty and Service to the Honble Society I am making the best of my way to Burlington, only as I go I preach the Gospel of

Salvation which is all ye good News I have to tell them, if they
believe that, it is well, let ye world go as it will I remain
Your most hum^{bl} Servant
John Talbot.

Ans^d 6th Augst 1708.

(S. P. G. A-Series, III., #CLVIII.).

(14)

Mr Talbot to Mr Keith
Rhode Island
13. Decr 1707.

Reverend Sir
  I bless God I am got safe over considering the Dangers
of the Sea and the Enemy, I am concern'd for poor Brother
Moore and Brooks who departed hence the last Month in a
Brigantine, I pray God send 'em safe home and here agen in
good time or else I believe all the rest of the Missionaries will
soon follow unless some Overseer be sent to direct and protect them. All friends of the Church ask for you and are glad
to hear of your health and Welfare tho' they can't hope for
the happyness of seeing you, Mr Carr and Mr Brinley and
most of the Church here are dead only your friend Gardiner
lives to do more harm than good Mr Bridge is settled at Nara-
ganset, but wou'd fain change with Mr Honyman here, who
has no mind to it nor the people neither, they say he will do
here just as he did at Boston; I pray when you are with my
Lord of London or any of the Society let them know that M^r
Honyman has a very good Testimony from the best in the
Church hereabouts, that he dos his best to Augment this Church
and propagate the Gospel where it is not; I have always had a
good Character of him from Mr Willokes & Coll Morris therefore you need not fear to commend him to the Society and
that they need not appoint any body else to this Place while
he is here, I understand our friend Jno Barlay is set at Libty
and Mr Willokes came to his house agen, which is all the
good News I have to tell you at present so desiring your
Prayers I remain
Your ever Loving Friend
and Servant
John Talbot

(S. P. G. A-Series, III., #CLXXII. The references not already explained are to mutual acquaintances of the two clergymen.)

(15)

Ditto to Ditto

Westchester
14 Febry 170⅘

Reverend and Dear S^r

I came into this Province before Christmas but the Winter set in so hard that I could go no farther than New York so I came back again and preach't about in several places and dispers't such Books as I had in this and the next Colony Connecticut, Mr *Leslie's five discourses The poor man's help,* and *young man's guide* by Mr Burket. The Independants say if they don't get some Books soon to answer them, they will convert the Country. Mr Muirson is the first y^t read the Common Prayer in that place in Stratford when he set up first the Honble Coll Heathcote came along with him or else I believe their Justices wou'd have put him in prison, Govr Wintrope is dead and was buried at Boston when I was there, and they of Connecticut have chosen Mr Saltonstall preacher at New London to be their Govr he called his Council lately at Milford and shewed them his Letters that he had written home to answer the Quakers' complaint and also to get power to hinder the Progress of the Church in y^t Province, but I hope we shall have as much Toleration as the Quakers have obtain'd there which is all that we expect or desire, Mr Muirson deserves a double Salary for the great pains and prudence that he has shewn in that Matter, The People of several Towns by the way as Norwolk and Fairfield are ready to break open their Meeting Doors to let him in if he wou'd suffer it; they have taken Measures at Stratford to build a Church which never was seen in that Country before I pray God send them an able Minister of the new Test : for they have bin long enough under the old Dispensation, I wish their Case were well known and Considered at home, for I'me sure no man that has any ears or Bowels of Compassion can resist their importunity. I saw Mr Bradford at New York he tells me Mass is set up and read publickly at Philadelphia and several people are turn'd to it amongst which Lionel Brittain the Ch : Warden is one, and his Son another, I thought that Popery wou'd come in amongst friends the Quakers as soon as any way; An Anabaptist Meeting it seems is set up at Burlington and another Independant is come to Elizabeth Town so that for lack of a good Govr we lose our time and the Society their Money and the last State of America will be worse than the first if the rest of the Missionaries go away before any more come; I suppose you have heard of Mr Brook and Mr Moore two of the best hands that were there, are gone and upon what Account ? purely for want of a Bishop to direct and protect them, I pray God help us for we have no body to apply to, and no body cares for our

Souls; Bradford shew'd me a Letter from good Mrs Walker 'tis of an old date almost a year agoe, George turn'd her out of Doors I think Mr Wallace took her in and moved the Court to allow her Maintenance then he took her home and lock't her up, but since it seems God has softened his heart to treat her more gently, I sent your Letters by Mr Hamilton Post Master; I intend to write to her when I go to Jersey which I design next Week & when I hear further I will tell you, mean while I pray God bless you and yours and Prosper your Labours in Word and deed for the faith of Christ Crucifyed, I desire your Prayers and remain

Your Loving Friend
and Servant
John Talbot

P. S.

My love and Service to your

(S. P. G. A-Series, III., #CLXXIII. This letter was written to George Keith. Part of the same is printed in Hawks and Perry: Documentary History of the Church in Connecticut, I., pp. 36-37. WILLIAM BURKITT, 1650-1703, vicar of Dedham in Essex, was the author of *Expository Notes with Practical Observation on the New Testament, 1700-1703.* GEORGE MUIRSON, S. P. G. missionary at Rye, N. Y., 1705-1708, held Church of England services in Connecticut. In his first journeys there, he was accompanied by CALEB HEATHCOTE, 1666-1721, a wealthy gentleman and an ardent lay patron of the Church; HEATHCOTE lived at Scarsdale Manor. FITZ-JOHN WINTHROP, 1638-1707, was governor of Connecticut, 1698-1707. GURDON SALTONSTALL, 1666-1724, minister at New London, was elected governor of Connecticut in 1707; though not a churchman, he was commended for his fair dealings with the Anglicans.)

(16)

Mr Talbot to the Secretary
N: York Janry 10th
170⅞

Honor'd Sir

I got safe here blessed be God at Christmas, but I can't proceed, no Boat can cross the Sound for See; Mr Barclay left me at Boston, he's a man of too much Moderaĉon to take a Winters Journey of 300 miles. I wrote from Rhoad Island Mr Honyman do's as well as he can there, but how can the Gospel be propagated, where no Christian is in Office in the Government, 'tis not so strange as true the Quakers will not fight for the Queen's Government but for their own they fight like Dragons. I came next to Stratford in Connecticut, where I was welcome as cou'd be, I staied one day and preach't twice to the Satisfaction of two or 300 Auditors, I pray God bless them with an able Minister of the Gospel, Mr Muirson has done his part like a Christian Soldier; they sent him several Letters calling lowder than the Man of Macedonia to St Paul *transiens adjuva nos,* I sent them some Books such as I had, tho' I lost almost all mine, I can't tell how nor where, but I hope the Society will send me some more: By the way I saw the Honble Coll Heathcote who is the finest Gentlemen I have seen in America; I wish the report were true that he were appointed Govr it wou'd be the best News next to that of the Gospel that ever came over; methinks 'tis an easy matter for some of the Honble Society to prevail with the Queen, that one of your Honble Members might be a Govr she having promised to be always ready to do her part towards the carrying on so good a Work, which cannot be carryed on without a good Governour in Church and State, now Bishop Heathcote wou'd serve for both the best of any I know if he had but his Commission, we live in hopes and the wicked in fears that their days will be shortened I pray God for His Elect sake they may and moderation in geting of money may take place, the want of that is the root of all Evill, I am to lend Coll Heathecote my travelling Library that he may try his hand with the Stiffnecked Quakers, he (if any body) will perswade them to see, he has the best temper of all if a Man cou'd hit it, to be gentle towards all men, and zealous of all good works;—some Courses must be taken with these Anti Christians, who are worse than the Turks; and if they be let alone will increase to an abominable Desolaĉon I shall say no more but betake myself to my prayers. Arise O Lord Jesu Christ help us and deliver us for thine honour. Since Mr Brooke, Mr Moore and Mr Evans went away there's an Independancy set up again at Elizabeth Town, Anabaptism at Burlington and the Popish Mass at Philadelphia; I thought that the Quakers wou'd be the first to let it in, particularly Mr Penn, for if he has any religion tis that, but thus to tollerate all without controul is the way to have none at all. My duty & Service to the Members of the Honorable Society, if they can do any thing, now is the time, I hope they will consider of them in time so God prosper their good endeavours and these of

S^r

Your most humble Servt

Jno Talbot

I hope Mr Brooke Mr Moore are arrived safe, there was the Wisdom of the Serpent and the innocency of the Dove in those men but neither will protect from evil speaking, &c.

Ans^d 6th Aug^st 1708.

(S. P. G. A-Series, III., #CLXXXVI. THOMAS BARCLAY, S. P. G. missionary at Albany and Schenectady, 1709-1716; worked among the Indians.)

(17-a)

Mr Talbot to the Secretary.
Philadelphia
20th Augst 1708.

Honorable Sir.

I have written several Letters to you from Boston and New York by Brother Brookes and Moore, but I'me afraid they are all lost together, they have been nine Months gon and we saw them not since nor any News of them; I met them at Boston and wou'd perswade them to return but all in vain, they had been so dragoon'd that they had rather be taken into France than into the Fort at New York; I have carryed on ever since at Burlington as well as I cou'd & I thank God wth Success where ever I am, but I can't stay long at any place, because there are so many that want, certainly the present state of that Province is worse than the first we have lost our Labour and the Society their Cost, there being several Churches and no Ministers in all East Jersey to supply them so that they fall away apace to heathenism, Quakerism and Atheism purely for lack of looking after. Mr Moore & Brooke are much lamented being the most pious and industrious Missioners that ever the Honble Society sent over; let the Adversaries say what they will they can prove no evil thing against those men. I have heard all sides and Parties, what can be said pro or con. Mr Honyman is outed, Mr Nichols scouted into Maryland he had come home had I not disswaded him, and I cou'd have hindred all the rest of these Scandals & disorders but that we had no B^p nor hopes of any, you wou'd not hear of it, therefore I said you must hear worse and worse still if ought can be worse than that the Bodies and Souls of men are ruin'd and undone and the Bounty of the Society lost for lack of an Overseer of the poor Church in America, without which the Gospel can't be Planted nor any good work propagated in the World. The Bible you sent to Hopewell I was willing to take to Burlington till more came over because ours is worn out, they that come I hope will bring Books with them, I shall write more particularly by the next opportunity God bless all our friends of the Honorable Society remaining theirs and

Your Humble Servant
Jno Talbot

(S. P. G. A-Series, IV., #LI.)

(17-b)

Ditto to Ditto.

Burlington
24th Augst 1708

Honble Sir.

It is now nine Months ago since I parted with Mr Brooks and Mr Moore at Boston, I sent Letters by them but we are much afraid all are miscarried. I was always glad to see them but much surprized to meet them both there; they told me what hardship they met with from the Govr of N: York and Jersey and how they escaped out of their hands. I was for converting them back agen, telling them the dangers of the Sea and the Enemy but poor Thorowgood said he had rather be taken into ffrance than into the Fort at New York, and if they were sunk in the Sea, they did not doubt but God wou'd receive them since they were persecuted for righteousness that is for Christ's sake and his Gospel and doing their Duty to the best of their knowledge. Truly as it was in the beginning so I find it in the end, all that will live godly in Christ Jesus shall suffer persecution, but somebody must answer for these things at home or abroad; If I cou'd have given them any hopes of a Bp or Suffragan to direct or protect them, I believe they wou'd not have gone; nay, I wou'd have hindred them but alas I had no such hopes myself I came over to be as good as my word rather than on any encouragement to do any good, meanwhile, I am pure from the blood of all men, ye are my witnesses that I pleaded with all my Soul, to send an Overseer of the poor Church but you wou'd not hear, therefore is this evil come upon us. I don't doubt but by God's mercy their Souls are not miscarried, they are in peace where 'ere they be I don't doubt but we Christians in Jersey are most miserable, we have Churches now but no Ministers to open them and if the Gate of Heaven be shut, the Gates of Hell will soon prevail against us. This comes to you in the bosom of Mr Moore's which he gave me at Boston which was the last that I had of him, he's much lamented as indeed they are both, as for Thorowgood I never knew his Fellow of his age, nor ever shall agen I fear, nothing can make this Country amends for their loss but a Good Bp but alas! that is *rara avis in terris* &c I preach't the Gospel at Marble Head where the people offered to subscribe some hundreds of pounds to build a Church but I have resolved to build no more Churches till there are more Ministers to serve the Churches that are built, I preach't at Stratford as I came along in Connecticut Colony where was a Numerous Auditory and Mr Muirson had 40 Communicants there the first time ever the H. Sacrament was rightly administered, and upon the Islands Rhoad Island, Long Island & Staten Island. I preacht till the Winter broke up and then I got to Amboy and Eliza-

beth Town, where had been nobody since Mr Brooke left them
who was an able and diligent Missioner as ever came over; I
got home about our Ladyday, where I was very wellcome to
all the Christian people, but alas, I cou'd not stay I am forced
to turn Itinerant agen for the care of all the Churches from
East to West Jersey is upon me; what is the worst I can't
confirm any nor have not a Deacon to help me; My Clark is
put in prison and was taken from the Church on the Lord's
day upon a Civil Action of Meum & Tuum, I don't know how
soon I may be served so myself, but I bless God I fear no evil
so long as I do none; *Exurgat deus dissipentur inimici* &c I
hear there's another Govr coming from these Provinces, people
are sorry 'tis another Lord for they say there never came a good
one into these Parts, I may say of them as ye Quakers did of
me. Thee comst for money, but I proved them Lyers, for I
have taken no money of them nor yet of others since I came,
I shall say no more in this point but referr all to Mr Moore's
Letter which I hope will have some weight with the Honorable
Society—because they are the last Words of their best Missioner when he was in Prison for the Gospel of Christ and for
a good Conscience: His humble Proposal is that the Honble
Society wou'd use their Interest with the Queen that we might
have men of Morals for Governours, if not of Religion, I say
the same and pray God direct them all for the best so I desire
y^r Prayers for

Sir

Your most Humb Servt

Jno Talbot

(S. P. G. A-Series, IV., #LII. "Thorowgood" designates THOR-
OUGHGOOD MOOR, recently lost at sea in company with JOHN
BROOK.)

(18)

Mr Talbot to the Secretary

Burlington

30th June 1709.

Sir.

I received your long Letter and find *Cartamen est de Lana
Caprina* or your Moderation, which is nothing in the World but
a Name which St Paul never used in all his Epistles nor any
thing like it but one where 'tis wrong translated; it shou'd be,
let your Gentleness be known to all men, which I am for as
much as any body towards Man and beast too, but if you mean
Moderation in Religion, as one said here, I don't care whither
I go to heaven or hell, Good S^r pardon your Servant in this
thing; but let's not differ about words but follow the things
that are for peace, and things whereby we may plant the Gospel
and edify the Church of God. I am very glad to find by the

President's Letter that the Members of the Honorable Society
are convinc't, that a head is necessary to the Body, but if he
don't make hast he will come too late, for here's nothing established but such a Moderation to all that's good, and such a
Tolleration of all that's evil, yea of the most damnable heresies
which by the way is a damnable Toleration, and worse than
the worst persecution that ever was in the World, for that only
destroys Men's bodys but these destroy body and Soul in Hell
for ever, which is damnable with a Vengeance and will make
the last State of Poor America worse than the first, if not
timely prevented: Is it not strange that so many Islands shou'd
be inhabited with Protestants, so many Provinces planted, by
them, so many hundred thousand Souls born and bred up here
in America, but of all the Kings, Princes, & Gov^{rs} all the
Bishops, & Archbishops that have been since the Reformation
they never sent any body here to propagate the Gospel, I say
to propagate it by imparting some spiritual Gift by Ordination
or Confirmation; I thought the Society had set up to supply
these wants and to take off this horrible Scandal from the
Protestant Churches, but truely they wou'd not hear of it till
they had lost their best Missionaries (may lose all the rest for
ought I know before it be legally obtained.)   What is there a
Law against the Gospel? Let it be taken out of the way as
Popish and Antichristian; We can't baptise any body hardly
now for want of Godfathers and Godmothers, for who will be
bound where they are not like to be discharged; I can't get
Children here to be Catechized they are ashamed of any thing
that's good for want of School Masters to teach them better.
Here's one Mr Humphry's come over with my Lord Lovelace,
I suppose not unknown to you by Mr Congreve, he's a pretty
sober Young Man and Graduate of Dublin College; I have got
him 20£ subscribed but that is not enough for one that has a
family;—If the Society please to add so much to it as they
think fit, it will be as good a Work as they can do; Mr Evans
liked him so well that he wou'd have had him for the ffree
School at Philadelphia; but that Wanderer Mr Ross is got in
there I believe by this time, for they wou'd not be quiet till
they got poor Mr Club to resign. I pitty Mr Jenkins's case
and I hope the Society will restore him, for he's young enough
to move pitty and to amend, or if he can't live there let him be
Itinerant in this Province and I will help him what I can; the
Churches in East Jersey are falling to the Ground for lack of
looking after, I can't go there above once or twice a Year to
Administer the Holy Sacraments, that they be not quite Starved.
It had been better not to have put those poor People to the
Charge of building Churches than have no body to supply them,
I can't get so much as a Reader here for any of them and it
were to save their Souls. You that live at home at ease and
Plenty, little do you know what they and we do bear & Suffer

here, and how many thousand Souls are legally lost whilst they at home are legally supplying them, who will answer it to Jesus Christ who will require an Account of us all & that very speedily too; mean while he has Charged all to take care of his flock not by constraint but willingly; not for filthy Lucre but of a ready mind; then they that don't care whither they go to Heaven or Hell will have no reward for that Moderation.

I find in your Books that one Mr Serjt Hooke is willing to give the tenth of his Land to the Church at Hopewell, pray let him send me a Power and I will take care of it and get him a purchaser for the rest. I have got possession of the best house in America for a Bishops Seat; the *A Bp* told me he wou'd contribute towards it and so I hope will others, pray let me know Your Mind in this matter, as soon as may be, for if they slip this opportunity there's not such another to be had. Our Church here dos flourish, God be praised, and the Town too is much more populous than it was; I hope we shall soon be out of Debt, mean while I take nothing of them, there's my Moderation, besides I bless God I have kept the Peace where no body else did or cou'd & that's no Sign of iṁoderaĉon; now I have shewn you my Moderation by my Works, pray shew me Yours that I may learn more how to approve myself as I ought

Your most humb Servt

John Talbot

Pray for God's sake send us
some Books of all sorts especially
Common Prayer Books.

(S. P. G. A-Series, V., #XIX. THOMAS TENISON, 1636-1715, was Archbishop of Canterbury, and President of the S. P. G. from its founding to his death. JOHN HUMPHREY, 1684?-1739, S. P. G. missionary in New York, 1706-1710; Oxford, Pennsylvania, 1711-1713; Chester, 1714-1726. JOHN LORD LOVELACE, Governor of New York, 1708-1709. GEORGE ROSS, 1680?-1754? was S. P. G. missionary at New Castle, Del., 1705-1708; at Chester, 1708-1712; again at New Castle, 1713-1754. THOMAS JENKINS, 1682?-1709, S. P. G. Missionary at Apoquiniminck, Del.)

(19)

Mr Talbot to the Secry.

Burlington
27 Sept 1709.

Sir.

Tho' I have sent you several Letters of late, yet I can't omit so good an opportunity as this by Mr Hamilton of giving my duty and service to the Honble Society: my Comfort is I have always told them the truth both at home and abroad tho' I was not believed till 'twas too late; when I reflect on the Progress of the Gospel (I will not say the Church for we never had it here, nor never shall till there comes over a Propagator to plant and build it up) a Cloud of melancholy thoughts throng'd upon me, for when the Shepherds are smitten the Sheep of the flock must needs be scatter'd abroad. Mr Moore, Mr Brook, Mr Muirson, Mr Rudman, Mr Jenkins, Mr Urquhart all Worthy men dead in less than two Years, and almost all the rest run away, as Black, Crawford, Nichols; Ross is a wandring Star we know not where he will fix, mean while he dos not well to supplant and undermine, let him be confin'd to some place where there's need, and not stay altogether in the Town to do more hurt than good; there's Mr Evans, Mr Ross, and Mr Club all at Philadelphia and none else in all that Province where the Society have sent most; at Chester there's none, at New Castle none, at Appoquininy none, at Dover hundred none, at the Whorekills none, and the People in all these places so abated of their Zeal, that I'm sure it had been much better to have sent none at all, than none to supply the Death & absence of these Men. Here's not one come to supply the loss of these 10 Missionaries and if there dos come any what will they do but find great discouragements, and the last State of their several places worse than the first; wherefore my advice is with humble submission to my Superiors, to keep their money and give us leave to come home, and send no more till they think fit to send a Propagator of the Gospel, for otherwise their planting the Gospel is like the Indians planting Gunpowder which can never take root but is blown away with every wind; Poor Brother Jenkins was baited to Death with Muscatoes & blood thirsty Galknippers which wou'd not let him rest night nor day till he got a fever at Appoquiminy, came to Philadelphia & dyed immediately of a Calenture; My Brother Evans and I buryed him as well as we cou'd; it cost us above 20£ for poor Man he had nothing being out of Quantum wth the Society and his Bills protested. If you please to call to mind, I told the Society when I was there, that those places must be served by Itinerants and that 'tis hardly possible for any body to abide there, that is not born there, till he's Musket proof, those little things are a great plague in some parts and when a Man is persecuted in one place he shou'd have leave to go to another or else he has very hard measure, especially in these parts where our life is a kind of Penance both Winter and Summer and nobody can tell which is the Worst the extream heat or Cold. I hear one Mr Vaughan is arrived at Boston, but is not yet come into this province, he will have enough to do to supply Mr Brook's his Charge at Elizabeth Town, Amboy, Piscataway, who have had none since he left them, but I have done for them may be once in a quarter or some body occasionally passing by that way. But poor Hopewell have built a Church and have had no Minister yet, and he had need be a good one that comes after

Mr Moore; there be many more in England but none so good
as to come over and help us that I can see or hear of. As for
the account of what Indians we have converted, truly I never
saw nor knew any that were Christians indeed, but I know there
are 100. yea thous^{ds} of our white folks that are Turn'd Infidels for want of looking after: Let them that have the Watch
look out and see what they will answer, for he that is higher
than the highest regards, and I have reced nothing from the
People in this Province nor will not till they be out of debt for
the building the Church. I leave honest Mr Hamilton to give
you a farther account of our affairs, & how we do, he has been
one of our Benefactors & given us 10£. I hope when he returns the Society will be so kind as to send us some more
Common Prayer Books wch we very much want here & at
Hopewell, Maidenhead, & every where. I pray God direct &
prosper ye designs of the Sacred Society, that Religion & learning piety and virtue may be establish't amongst us for all gen-
erations so I rest S^r

Yo^r very humb Servt

Jno Talbot

I hope you will put the Society in mind
of what we have often desired a Schoolmaster
for there's none in this town nor in all the
province that is good and without we can't
instruct Children as they ought to be in
ye Catchesim for they will not be brought
to say it in the Church till they have
been taught at School.

(S. P. G. A-Series, V., #42. THOMAS CRAWFORD, a Scotchman, S. P. G. missionary at Dover, Del., 1704-1709; recalled. JOHN
CLUBB, a Welshman; former school-master at Philadelphia; S. P. G.
missionary at Oxford, Pennsylvania, 1709-1711; at Apoquinimink, 1712-
1713; at Radnor and Oxford, 1714-1715; died, Christmas, 1715. ED-
WARD VAUGHAN, S. P. G. missionary at Elizabeth Town, N. J.,
did not assume his duties there till several years after this letter was
written; he died about 1747, having had a very useful ministry. This
letter refers to the death of THOMAS JENKINS, of Apoquinimink,
who "was baited to Death with Muscatoes & blood thirsty Galknippers;"
he died July 30, 1709, and was buried at Trinity Church, Philadelphia.)

(20)

LETTERS FROM THE SOCIETY.

1

Letter from the Secretary to Mr Bartow

29th Aprill 1712

Rever^d S^r

The Ships are now ready to sail and tho' there is not
time Enough to write to you any thing else yet I am directed

to Acquaint you That at ye last Anniversary Meeting of the Society 15th Feb: 1711 An Order was made That Mr Wm Taylor be Secretary of ye Society. and a Standing Order was then made That all Letters for the future be directed in this Form vizt To ye Secretary of the Society for ye Propagation of ye Gospel &c^a to be left at The Lord Arch Bishop of Canterburys Library at St Martins London

I am &c^a

You will please to communicate this to all concerned near you

2

Letter from ye Secretary to Mr Thomas

*(This and the next numbers
3 to 10 inclusive are repe-
titions of the same letter—
to the following :——*

	3	Mr Mackenzie
p. 260	4	Mr Neau
	5	Mr Barclay
p 261	6	Mr Bondet
	7	Mr Hager
	8	Mr Phillips
p 262	9	Mr Talbot.
	10	Mr Vaughan

(S. P. G. A-Series, VII., p. 262, #9, contains the letter to Talbot. Notice is given that William Taylor, Esq., has become secretary of the Society; he succeeded John Chamberlayne. ENEAS MACKENZIE, a Scotchman, was S. P. G. missionary on Staten Island, N. Y., 1705-1722. ELIAS NEAU was in charge of a school for negro youth in New York city from 1704 to 1722. DANIEL BONDET, a French minister driven out of France, was stationed at New Rochelle, N. Y., 1709-1722. JOHN FREDERICK HAEGER was minister to the Palatine refugees in London—Lutherans and Calvinists, whom he accompanied to New York; he was stationed in New York, 1710-1717. FRANCIS PHILIPPS was S. P. G. missionary at Stratford, Conn., at the time of this letter; he proved an unworthy character.)

(21)

Letter from the Secretary to Mr Talbot

Ex   November 6th 1712
Rever^d S^r

Though I cannot now acquaint you with ye receipt of any Letter from you to the Society, Yet I hope that on your Part you will not give me an Opportunity of saying so in my next. For as it is my duty so it shall be my care faithfully to com-

municate to the Society what you shall write and diligently to
Answer your Letters & Correspond with you.
I am directed ....
                (*The rest of the letter
                is the same as the last
                four paragraph of N°. 26.*)
                        I am &c
....

(S. P. G. A-Series, VII., p. 286, #32. This letter evidently forms
one of a series written by the new Secretary soon after taking office.)

(22)

To The Rev^d the Clergy met at New York.

His Excellency our Governour has been pleased to Appoint
the 12th of May for a Meeting of the Clergy of this Province
& New York in Order to justifie what was done att the last
meeting from the Reflections of the Brethren in Pensilvania we
were present at that Meeting of the Bretheren who Asserted
nothing but that Mr Henderson ought not to have been con-
demned as false before he was heard, which we hope will not be
Interpreted a high Reflection, We are Apprehensive That Several Things will be laid before you in order to justifie what
you Asserted in your Letter to Mr Henderson, That Several
Things in his Memorial Were false in fact and beyond the Compass of his knowledge. Should you upon any Representation
whatsoever proceed to Justifie and Maintaine the ffalseness of
his Memorial or any part of it before he himself be heard in a
Meeting of all the Brethren in the 3 Provinces, We protest and
Declare against Such Proceedings as tending to creat ffaction
and Disagreement among our Selves and Injustice to our
Brother, We leave it to his Excellency to Appoint time and
place, providing it be not before Mr Henderson return from
Virginia, We are, dear Brethren Yours &^c.

                        Sic Subb   John Talbot
                                        T. Haliday.
        Burlington.

(S. P. G. A-Series, VIII., p. 271. ROBERT HUNTER, appointed
governor of New York in 1709, was active in religious affairs, but clashed
with certain clergymen, especially WILLIAM VESEY of Trinity
Church, New York. JACOB HENDERSON, a native of Glenavy, Ire-
land, was missionary at Dover and New Castle, Del., 1711-1713; later he
served in Maryland, where he became one of the commissaries of the
Bishop of London; he died Aug. 27, 1751, bequeathing £1000 to the
S. P. G. THOMAS HALIDAY, S. P. G. missionary at Amboy, N. J.,
1711-1713 and 1717-1718; at Elizabeth Town and Hopewell, 1714-1717.)

(23)

Mr Talbot to the Secretary.

Burlington Augt ult. 1713.

S^r

Tho I have not had the ffavour of a Letter from the Hon-
^{rble} Society Since Mr Henderson Arrived in these parts, Yet
I think it my Duty to take all Opportunities of paying all
Dutifull Regards to that Venerable Body, Therefore I could
not faile to Salute them by the hands of my Good Brother Evans
Rector of the Church at Philadelphia, who comes home in the
Service of the Church, which never wanted Patronage so much
as now in all these five Provinces Particularly N: Jersey & N:
York and I may say in Pensilvania too, The Rights of the
Church are invaded and Possest by her Enemies, Affidavits are
procured and dispersed by the worst of men against the best
Missionaries the plate and Books given by the Society and
other Benefactors are violently carried away, and those who
Pretend to be Promotors of the Gospel use all wayes and
meanes amongs, and have perswaded one unworthy Brother
to carry Affidavit ffrom Province to Province ag^t another,
And as I have allways Said wee cannot Expect any better
Treatment till we have a Superior Pastor to Order and Establish the Church, This is the one thing necessary, which I have
been Solliciting these ten Years, I find it all in vain for them
or us to offer to propagate the Gospel or Erect the Church
without Bishop or Deacon, which I humbly Offer to our Superiors at home for the burden is too hard upon us poor Pres-
biters, who labour under all Sorts of Perils and Difficulties
which we are not able to bear any longer; But I need Say no
more by this worthy Brother who has been a faithfull Labourer
here these 13 years and has a Particular Account of the Affaires
of all the Churches, to whom I doe with all Humility referr
the Hon^{rble} Society upon whose Credit they may Safely Depend. So desireing your Prayers and Protection,

I remaine Sr Your humble and faithfull

Servt

John Talbot

(S. P. G. A-Series, VIII., p. 181, #49.)

(24)

May it please yor Excellency

Wee the Clergy of Pensilvania in conjunction wth our
Revd Brother Mr Talbot out of a deep Sense of ye Indefati-
gable pains and vast Charge Yo^r Excellency has been at to
Erect and Settle the Church upon this whole Continent and the

Incouragement you have always given to our Function doe
wth Hearts full of gratitude rejoyce at yo[r] Excellency's Safe
Arrival into these parts and the Honours her Majesty has been
pleas'd to conferr upon you; if a Steady Adhering to the constitution in Church and State are Principles only to be relyed
on this continent can justly approve of her Majestie's choice,
and the Deserved Title yo[r] Excellency had to her Favour.

Wee are Blessed in the Administration of our most gracious
Soveraign who has always prov'd herSelf a Nurseing Mother
to the Church and was never wanting in handing over to us
in these Remote parts of her Dominions the best Evidences
of her Inclination and readiness to promote the growth and
Settlement of the Infant church Planted here but Since matters could not as yet be brought to bear so as to procure for
us Governours to Exercise Church Discipline and propagate a
Succession of Pastors We Humbly apply to yo[r] Excellency to
represent to your royal Mistress the great disadvantage the
Church Labours under for want of those Spiritual Persons,
and to use Yo[r] Intrest to remove soe great a grievance. Wee
doubt not but your Excellency is truely Disposed to promote
Soe Laudable a work And that Application made by one Soe
much Distinguished by many Instances of Royall ffavour will
have it's just Effect and weight at home.

Wee wish Yo[r] Ex-
cellency all health and happiness and Remain

Hon[ble] S[r]

Philadelphia
November y[e] 18:1713

Will[m] Vesey Rector
N: York
Nov:23: of Trinity Church
1713
In the City of New
York

Yo[r] most Obedient and
hum[ble] Serv[ts] John Talbot
Rector of the Church of Burlington Francis Philipps Rector of the Church at Philadelphia John Humphreys Rector of y[e] Church at Oxford
Geo: Ross Rector of y[e]
Church at Chester Jacob Henderson Rector of the Church
at New Castle

Endorsed From y[e] Rev[d] M[r] Talbot &c
N[o] (7)
(7)

(S. P. G. B-Series, I., #152, p. 545.)

(25)

The Secretary to Mr Talbot

18th Decr 1713.

Rev^d S^r

Your with Mr Evans's joynt Letter of 4th Decr last was received and Communicated to the Society, who had Answered the Contents thereof to the Govern^r before they rec^d the Same. I hope you have had mine of the 29th of April & 16th November 1712. The last by Genl Nicholson, No Letter from your Self Singly hath Since come to my hands, And therefore you will not Expect I should Say any thing in Answer. I am directed to Acquaint you That the Society have rec^d Some information wch Seem to impeach the Conduct and Behaviour of Mr Haliday their Missionary at Amboy, They were not willing to come to any Resolutions concerning him untill they had receive the Opinion and Report of Genl Nicholson who was desired when in the Plantations to Enquire &^c of the Society's Affairs there, but at the Same time comanded me to desire You to Acquaint them whether Mr Haliday be now upon his Cure, if he hath been Absent from the Same and for what time, and likewise of his Character and Behaviour In this matter you will be faithfull and Sincere, least otherwise the Society be led to make Such Order as may Seem contrary to their good purposes And pious Designe I have Nothing more to add than to Acquaint you the Society have lately made Some Standing Orders, a Copy of which I here Send you vizt ———— As before to M^r. Bartow, N°. 7.

(S. P. G. A-Series, VIII., p. 327, #18. JOHN BARTOW, S. P. G. missionary in Westchester County, N. Y., 1702-1725.)

(26)

Letter from several Ministers
to Genl Nicholson.

Enclosed in his of the 11th May 1714

May it please Your Excellency

S^r

The Almighty good and Mercifull God has been graciously pleased to give wonderfull Success to the Pious and Charitable Undertaking of that Religious Society of men, whom his Wisdom was pleased to raise up and make use of as instruments in his hands for effecting the great and glorious work the Salvation of Men. Accordingly we see many fair Edifices raised for the true and Orthodox Worship of God, and several large Congregations as yet destitute of that convenience supported in Conformity to our pure and Apostolick Church, by the labours of the Missionaries, so that we may justly entertain hopes that the Kingdom of Satan draws nigh to a Period, and that his long and uncontroled Reign will soon give place to that Divinely glorious ffaith which the Prince of Peace has promised that the Gates of Hell shall not prevail against: it is known however that the subtle Malicious Fiend the Enemy of God and Religion, the Inveterate Enemy of Man has never been wanting in his Attempts by particular Instruments which he knows where to find and how to choose, to disturb the Peace of the Church and to Obstruct ye progress of the Gospel; Accordingly late years present to our view some disorders in which its sufficiently evident the evil Spirit has acted a great part. Not to go higher than the barbarous and execrable usage of the Revd Mr Prichard at New York who had his Throat cutt by his and the Churches Enemies & then was brought in by the Verdict of a Jury as Felo de se. The persecution of the Revd Mr Vesey ye present worthy Rector of the above named Church calls for a particular Notice and we Implore Your Excellency in his behalf that he may be protected from such outrages as were lately committed and from worse treatment farther designed and lately threatned against him even a barbarous design of Sacryficing him as it was villanously expressed. Your Excellency knows better than we can tell you, the dismal consequence of such abuses offered to ye Ministers of Religion and as you have the Power, so we are well Assured You have the Will to Screen us from Violence.

Mr Poyers Case deserves the like Regard Your Ex^{cy} knows how Presbiterian Violence has been countenanced against the Church and himself the Rector of it, and the bleeding wounds of both loudly call to You to apply the healing Balsam to them.

The later Indignities offered to one of our Number the Revd Mr Philipps both at New York and since his Removal to the Church of Philadelphia, have been we must say extreemly brutish and this Affair we likewise most humbly refer to your Excellencys Inspection; for his prudent and good Conduct among us wholly giving the lie even to the smallest faults laid to his charge engage us to recommend him to your Excellencys favour and Protection.

But oh! we want Words to represent to Your Excellency the Horror and Indignation we and all good men conceive at ye Execrable Villany lately perpetrated at New York by presumptuous Miscreants who impudently and sacrilegiously broke into the house of God, and most irreligiously prophaned and defiled the Holy Books and Vestments wth Ordue in defiance of God and Religion; a wofull instance how far the Rage and

Malice of certain Persons, who dissent from and are irreconcileable Enemys to the Established Church Constitution wou'd transport them, were they not curb'd and restrain'd by the Supreme Civil Authority at home from outrages they have a hearty good will to commit, and we need not tell your Excellency to what these things are owing here.

To Mention no more of those Ungratefull Matters, we think it our Duty lastly to Complain to your Ex^llcy of an Affair which we belive will be a very great obstruction to the progress of the Gospel in the Governm^t of the Jerseys viz. an Act of Assembly lately passed at Burlington, entituling the Quakers & a part in the Legislature with an Indulgence to them of the Affirmation tho regected at home for the Manifold Injuries & wrongs done by it, This pernicious Act was long aim'd at but ineffectually by reason of the Interposition of Some honest Gentlemen members of the Church of England but these being by the restless Malice of a party by indirect Means viz. by accusing them most falsely of being Disturbers of the peace of the province, procur'd to be remov'd frome the Council, at this time no friend of the Church being in the way this Act pass'd without opposition.

These and a great number of affronts offered to the Church of Christ and the Injurious treatm^t of us the Ministers of it, put us under a necessity of crying aloud for Succour and protection, & we have reason to bless God that Y^r Excellency is now upon the Spot invested with power to Examine where the Cause of all this liyes.

We have cause to fear that if a Speedy Stop be not put to those grivances the fruit of our Labours here will be destroy'd and the pious aims of the Ven^ble Society for promoting Religion and Piety will be render'd frustrate The onely remedy we can See for preventing of these Calamities is the Speedy Sending a Bishop into these parts to protect us & Stand in the Gap against any Person who may Encourage or countenance any Lawless designs against the Church, S^r the house at Burlington bought in the Name of the Ven^ble Society for his habitation, is Compleatly repair'd for his Reception According to their Order, we most pray for Such a Person & the Affairs of the Church Languish for want of him & if Notwithstanding all this we are not Soe happy as to have one Sent to us, we are likely to run into Independency and Confution Manifold have been the representations of this Nature, which we thought it our Duty from time to time to offer to the prudent Consideration of pious & Ven^ble persons, whome we believed Immediately concerned in providing for our Relief God knows not without great Cause, but with great Grief we Speak it, all hitherto ineffectuall—S^r we are a considerable Body & Should not be left destitute of a head, the Cause is the greatest of all causes, the Glory of God and the good of

Souls which our holy Church Engages herSelf to promote;
it is owing to the alone Mercy of the great & good God that
it has flourish'd as we now See it, but as it is Surrounded with
Enemys, Attacked frome many Quarters by Violent & restless enjines of Satan we are not without reason and fear that
the last State may be worse then the first, unless Speedy Succour be Administred to our Distresses—

To you then S^r we have recourse in this our Exigency
and humbly intreat Your Excellency who have upon all Occasions demonstrated YourSelf to be a worthy Son friend and
patron to this best of Churches, & its Ministers, to transmit
this our Complaint with which we make bold to trouble your
Excellency, together with Your Sentiments upon the Matter to
the Venerable Society & all other Noble Patriots, who have
Sincerely at heart the Cause of God & Religion & we Shall
acknowledge this in all humility, as the greatest Obligation you
can lay upon us to be for Ever

> May it please your Excellency
> Your Excellencys
> Most Obliged and
> Most humble Servants

> John Talbot Rector
> of the Church of Burlington

> Andrew Sandel Minister
> at Wicaco near
> Philadelphia

> Francis Phillips Minister
> of Christs Church in
> Philadelphia

> John Humphreys Minis-
> ter of the Church at
> Oxford near Philadelphia

(S. P. G. A-Series, IX., p. 208, #10. THOMAS PRITCHARD
was inducted into the Church of Rye, N. Y., by order of Lord Cornbury; the dissenters resisted his incumbency. WILLIAM VESEY was
subjected to considerable embarrassment because of the opposition of
GOVERNOR ROBERT HUNTER. THOMAS POYER, S. P. G. missionary at Jamaica, Long Island, 1710-1731, suffered shipwreck in his
journey to America; his ministry was rendered difficult by the opposition of the dissenters, who sought to gain possession of his parish
by legal means. On the night of Feb. 13, 1713, Trinity Church, New
York city, was broken into and shockingly desecrated; vestments were
torn to rags, service books scattered about, windows smashed, and
outrages of various sorts committed. It was felt by the signers of this
letter that the presence of a resident Bishop would afford the Church
a protection which it did not otherwise enjoy. ANDREW SANDEL,
Swedish minister at Wicaco near Philadelphia, was friendly to the Church
of England.)

(27)

Mr Talbot to the Secretary

Burlington Octor 28 1714

Sr

I sent a Letter by Mr Evans wherein I desired leave of the Honble Society to come home I have been long enough in these Parts to see Iniquity established by Law and that by some of your own Members, and what good can Your Missionaries do. I have been sick a long time this fall with a Burning Feaver wch made me so weak that I could Scarce Speak, I could not preach nor read prayers, so the service of ceased. In all this Province of West New Jersey there never was any Minister of Christs Church settled but myself, I have built 3 Churches since I came here, but have nobody to help them nor myself neither. We have had a very hard time this year, I have buried more than in ten before and many Christian People dyed that had no body to visit them when sick nor bury them when dead—Let them that have the watch look out, tis they must give Acct, I am clear of the blood of all men abroad and at home, and so I hope to keep myself The Society were once upon a good Resolution to send Deacons to be School-masters, if they had done so to Burlington to Bristol to Hope-well they might have kept the Church doors Open, they could read the Prayers and Homilies Baptize and Catechise they could Visit the sick and bury ye dead but now they must bury one another; they have no where to go but to Quakers Meetings which are as bad as Indians there's nothing but Pawawing and Conjuring to raise a Devil they cannot lay again and now this Wickedness is Establisht by Law what should we do here any Longer. They do declare in presence of God Almighty They don't swear Call him to witness all they say is no more than Yea and Nay.

The Church at New Bristol over against Burlington was opened about St James Day and so called St James's Church by the Revd Mr Philips who preacht the first Sermon, The Church was full of People from all parts who were Liberal Con-tributors to it, I went now and then to preach there on Sundays in the Afternoon before I was sick but since that I have not been able, so the Church has been shutt up almost ever since it was Opened, The Church at Hopewell has been built this ten or twelve years and never had a Minister settled there yet, tho' they have sent several Petitions and Addresses to the Society, but I understand since that Hopewell Maidenhead &c were kept under the Thumb for Cotton Mather and the rest of the New England Drs to send their Emissarys; and those Hirelings have often come there, and as oft run away, because they were hirelings and cared for no souls but themselves.

As for the Church at New Bristol it was first begun by the Zealous Thorowgood Moore of pyous Memory, and when he was taken by this same Cursed Faction thats now Rampant I was unwilling any of his good Works should fall to the Ground so I crost the Water at my own Cost to serve those poor People who lived in Darkness and the Shadow of death in the Midst of Heathenism Atheism and Quakerism, but it pleased God by our preaching the word in season and out of season some came to believe and were baptized they and their Children, and two of the Chief People there Mr John Rowland and Mr Anthony Burton were willing to undertake to build a church which since they have done and I beleive they will Endow it too if they get a Minister before they dye, I gave them five pounds and a Pulpit of Black Walnut which cost as much more to encourage them, I promised to lay their Case before the pious Society that they make take some care of them, that they be not a Reproach to the Heathenish Quakers, who are too Apt to reflect upon us, Where is your Priest Where your Minister and wheres your Church it may serve us for a Meeting house &c Pudet hac Opprobria nobis dici potuisse et non potuisse repelli.

But the History of the Church at Burlington &c has been so much better done by Coll Jeremiah Bass Esqr Secretary of this Province and transmitted home by the hands of the Honble Genl Nicholson, that I need say no more at Present but desire the Prayers & blessing of the Venerable Society for

their most humble and

faithfull Missioner and Servt

John Talbot

(S. P. G. A-Series, IX., p. 167, #40. COTTON MATHER, 1663-1728, distinguished New England divine; active in propagating Independency in the colonies.)

(28)

To Mr Talbot.

17th Decr 1714

Rev^d S^r

Yours of ye 31st of August 1713 has been rec^d and communicated to the Society I have also rec^d from Genl Nicholson some papers relating to the State of the Church in the Jerseys which have been before the Committee who Agreed to lay ye same before the Society, but for that Genl Nicholson is now dayly expected they have not as yet been consider'^{d} by them after his Arrival I hope in a short time to acquaint you with ye Resolution of the Society thereon. I am &c

(S. P. G. A-Series, IX., p. 252, #18.)

(29)

To the Revd Mr Talbot

7 April 1715

Rev^d S^r

Since my last to You of the 17th of Decem^r I rec^d Yours of the 28 of October last which has been communicated to the Society, the Contents thereof are indeed very Affecting. I have in Command only to inform You that the Society comply with your desire of coming hither if You think fit. They receive Affectionately and in Good Part what You propose therein and therefore have Agreed that the Bearer the Revd Mr Walker be sent with a Salary of 60£ p Annum your Assistant at Burlington and to supply the Cures of New Bristol and Hopewell and in case you leave Burlington that he succeed You there with the like Care of Bristol and Hopewell till further Order from the Society. Sr Mr Walker is well recommended to the Society, and I hope will prove very acceptable to You, and be an Instrument of doing much Good among those he shall have under his Care.

I am &c^a

W T

(S. P. G. A-Series, X., pp. 268-269. ROBERT WALKER, S. P. G. missionary at Burlington, New Bristol, and Hopewell, 1715-1718.)

(30)

To the Revd Mr Talbot.

23^d August 1715

Rev^d S^r

I wrote to You of the 7th of April in answer to yours of the 28 of October last which will come by the Revd Mr Walker, but because possibly this may come to your hands before his Arrival, I have inclosed a Copy thereof. I am order'd to acquaint You that at a Meeting of the Society the first of July last the Right Reverend the Lord Bp of London laid before them an Extract of a Letter communicated to him by the Lord Commissioners of Trade and Plantations which was sent to them from Brigadier Hunter Governor of New York containing a complaint against You wth Respect to your Behaviour in those Parts, the Society consider'd the same and thereupon Orderd a Copy of the said Extract should be sent to You, that You may have an Opportunity of Giving your Answer to that Charge, a Copy of which Extract is likewise here Inclosed. I have nothing more in Charge to Communicate to You at present.

I am &c^a

W T.

(S. P. G. A-Series, X., p. 271. This letter was prompted by GOVER-NOR ROBERT HUNTER'S letter to the Board of Trade, April 9, 1715, in which he said: "Mr Talbot has Incorporated the Jacobites in ye Jersies under ye name of a Church in order to Sanctifie his Sedition & Insolence to ye Governm^t, if ye Society take not more care for ye future y^n has been taken hitherto in ye Choice of their Missionaries, instead of Establishing Religion they^{ll} destroy all Governm^t & good manners"— S. P. G. A-Series, XI., p. 301.)

(31)

Mr Talbot in a Letter to the L^d Bp of London Dat^d ye 18 Octr 1715
    writes thus
        The Society's House at Burlington is put to ill uses, I desire an order under the Seal of the Society, that I or some other Person may live in it and take Care of it.——

(S. P. G. A-Series, XI., p. 281.)

(32)

Mr Ellis to the Secretary
S^r
        By the letter I have sent, I should think my Self troblesom to you, but as you give me an Account of none this great while, I am amazed to hear it & under a great apprehension what is become of y^m, I am very sorry y^t ye Honble Society should Judge to hard of me, but still if their is none Arr^d I cant blame y^m, tho' my Self is Innocent of ye charge as the within Certificate will testifie, & I hope will in great measure Satisfie ye best of Society and reconcile y^m again to their unwearied Ser^t who for a small Salary is both ready & willing to do & observe their Command, this & ye Certificate herein Inclosed, I humbly beg you to Communicate to ye Honble Society together wth my Duty I rem with my humble Service to you,
                                                        S^r
                                            Your most obliged &
                                            most hum^{ble} Servt
                                            Rowland Ellis.
Burlington
Nov: 29th 1715

The Certificate in behalfe of Mr Ellis
        These are to Certifie y^t ye Gentleman Mr Rowland Ellis whom ye Honble Society &c. made Choice of & sent as School-master for this Town, hath behaved himself Piously and Soberly, & hath been & still is Circumspect and Carefull in his Calling, with Constant Attendance on the Business Committed to his Care notwthstanding ye Abuses & oppositions he met with, since his being here

(S. P. G. A-Series, XI., pp. 327-328. ROWLAND ELLIS was school-master at Burlington, N. J.)

(33)

Mr Talbot to the Secretary

S^r

ffirst I am bound to render thanks to the Right Rev^d & Right Honble Society for sending honest Mr Walker to my Assistance. I hope he'd Answer the Good Character given of him on all hands, I have offer'd him my house at Burlington & all my Intrest is at his Service

Next I am Obliged to ye Society for giving me leave to Answer for my Self touching ye Reflections Cast upon me by Brigadier Hunter, To be an Accuser is bad, To be a false Accuser is worse, but a false Accuser of the Brethren is literally ye Divil, I make no difference, for I call God to witness I know no Soul in ye Church of Burlington, nor in any other Church y^t I have plant^d, but is well affect^d to ye Protestant Ch: of England and pres^t Governm^t in the House of Hannover therefore he y^t accused us all for Jacobites has the greater Sin, I can Compare it to nothing more or less y^n Doeg ye Edomite who Stab'd ye Priests Character & then Cut all their Throats, or Haman ye Agagite who Slanderd all ye Jews as Jacobites who did not observe the Kings Laws, So they were appointed as Sheep to ye Slaughter, but God deliver^d them & so I hope he^{ll} do us from ye hand of ye Enemy, The Honble Coll^{el} Bass our Chief Ch. Warden as diligent & faithfull Servt of ye Church & Crown as any, has been bely^d out of his Secretarys office & fin'd & Confin'd in the Common Goal for nothing but defending ye Royall Law of King George agst an Idol of ye Heathenism Quakers. Mr Alex^r Griffiths Dyed heart broken, being falsely Accused & Abused, as a disaffected Person to ye Governm^t, he Dyed at Amboy, Poor Mr Ellis ye Schoolmaster is very much Discouraged in his buisness by a Quaker Schoolmaster being set up in Opposition to his Lycence, he has made his Complaints oft, not without Cause, but all without Effect, he's a very Sober, honest young Gentleman & deserves better Encouragm^t.

I wish ye Society would take some better care of Burlington House, as for Govr Hunter he does not Come here once in 3 Years, & as soon as he gets his Money Spends it all at New York, So y^t we have only ye burthen not ye benefit of Govern^t Therefore we have the Greater need of a Chorepiscopus a Rural Bishop or Suffragan, to Impart some Spiritual Gift, without which there never was or can be any being or well being of a Church.

This is the Burden of all our Lamentations & so it will

be till its Answer'd the Sooner ye better cum bono Deo, So
Desiring prayres of ye Sacred Society I remain

Your humble Obliged Servt
and Obedient Missionary

John Talbot

Burlington 10^b 1st
1715

(S. P. G. A-Series, XI., pp. 328-329.)

(34)

Mr Talbot to the Secretary

S^r

I suppose you have heard by this time the sad news of
honest Dr Clubbs Death sad indeed to us, to his Poor Wife &
Child, and to the whole Church in this Province he Dyed ab^t
Xtmas last, being worn out in mind body & Estate, with travels
at home and abroad between 2 Churches Oxford and Radnor
30 Miles distant from one another wch have now none to help
them, God help ye Poor hes the only overseer, else we might
perish in our affliction for all any else, I can doe no less, nor
more, than Commend the Widdow Isabella Clubb to ye bounty
of ye Society Tho' they are not a Society of Charity, yet I hope
they are not without, we should take Care of our own Widdows
&c or else we have denyed the faith & are worse y^n the Mohocks,
for what they take in hunting they share with ye Widdow &
Children all one as when ye ffather was alive, so God bless you
all

Your most humble
ffaithfull & obedient

Servt
J^{no} Talbot

Philad^a April   14
1716

(S. P. G. A-Series, XI., pp. 296-297.   DAVID HUMPHREYS,
1689-1740, became Secretary of the S. P. G. in 1716; he published a
valuable *Historical Account of the Incorporated Society* . . . in 1730.)

(35)

. To Mr Talbot

23^d April 1716

Rev^d S^r

Your Last to the Society bears date ye 28th of Oct^r
1714 wch is now near Eighteen Months Agoe if you Consult
the Standing ——————— orders of the Society you^{ll} find
it is your duty to write every 6 Months and to give an Acco^t of

the State of your Parish &c. ———————— Since you have reced any Letter from the secretary ——————— Made known to you You are desired to put the Schoolmaster in mind of observing the rules & orders of the society and particularly that he Send ——————— Teaching I am ——————— have been in their Service and do find that there was further due to you a X^{t}Mass 1£ 17^s 6^d after the rate of 10£ P Ann I am directed to put you in mind of Observing all the rules and orders of the Society of wch Mr Barlow Will Inform you & particularly y^t you Send ——————— teaching I am

(S. P. G. A-Series, XI., p. 370.)

(36)

To Mss^{rs} Walker, Talbot, Vaughan, Haliday Poyer, Mackenzie, Bartow, Bridge, Thomas, & Bondet.
Rev^d S^r
     The Society have Ordered me to Acquaint you and the rest of your Bretheren ye Clergy with their resolution that at your Next Meeting pursuant to a Standing order of the Society vizt Order 12 page 22^d you would After inquiry Made inform the Society if any of your Brethren are disaffected to the Government of his Majesty King George and if there be any Such that you would Specifie the Matters of fact upon which Charge of Such disaffection are Grounded and that before it is transmitted hither you would Cause A Coppy of Such Accusation to be delivered to the persons Accused that if they have any thing to Offer in defence of themselves they May have a Speedy Opportunity of Tranmitt^g it to the Society. The Society have wrote to the Severall Governors of ye plantations to the Same effect as you will observe by ye inclos'd W^{ch} is a Coppy of y^t Letter——

(S. P. G. A-Series, XI., p. 373. Insinuations having been made regarding the loyalty of the clergy to the Crown, a letter was transmitted, calling on them to declare their allegiance.)

(37)

To Mr Clubb, Humphreys, Ross, Walker, Talbot, Mackenzie, Poyer, Bartow, Bridge, Thomas, Bondet, Lucas, Honyman, Shaw, Urmstone, LeJau, Maule, Taylor, Hassell, Bull & Jones.

June 11th 1716
Rev^d S^r
     The Society for the propagation of ye Gospel in fforreign parts have Made lately two New Orders relateing to the Mis-

sionaries Which I take this Opportunity of Acquainting you
with the first is Concerning the Manner of your Corresponding
with the Secretary Which they have ordered should be in the
following Method vizt That each the Missionaries take a receipt of the Master of the Ship (if it Can be obtained) for
every Letter ye Send to the Society Mentioning the day &
year When they delivered the Same and that they keep a Coppy
of all Letters and papers transmitted to the Society And Send
Duplicates by the Next Conveyance and therewith a Coppy of
ye receit of their Originall Letter and if the place of their residence be not a Seaport they Send Such Letter to one of their
Brethren who resides at Such Seaport desireing him to forward
the Same by the first opportunity takeing ye like receit and
that they Give An acco^t of the time the Ships Name by which
they receive any Letter from the Society

The other new order of the Society is That the Mission-
aries Should transmitt to ye Society a very Just and particular
Acco^t of what allow-ances they have by Act of Assembly and
Also what Voluntary Contributions they receive from their par-
ishes, and further in What manner the allowances by Ac^{ts} of
Assembly or the Voluntary Contributions are paid Whether in
Money or in the Commodities of the Countrey

I am &c

(S. P. G. A-Series, XI., p. 376. HENRY LUCAS, S. P. G. mis-
sionary at Newbury, Mass., died Aug. 23, 1720. WILLIAM SHAW,
S. P. G. missionary at Marblehead, Mass., 1715-1717. JOHN URM-
STONE, ex-curate of Eastham, Essex; S. P. G. missionary in North
Carolina, 1709-1720; afterwards fell into disrepute, and was employed in
Maryland; accused Talbot of disloyalty to the Establishment, and reported rumours regarding his episcopal consecration; said to have been
burned to death in North Carolina, 1732. FRANCIS LeJAU, 1665?-1717,
S. P. G. missionary at Goose Creek, S. C.; active in work among
the negroes and Indians. ROBERT MAULE, 1680?-1717; S. P. G.
missionary, St. John's parish, S. C., 1707-1717; bequeathed £750 to the
S. P. G. EBENEZER TAYLOR, S. P. G. missionary in the Caro-
linas, 1711-1719. THOMAS HASELL, minister at Charleston, S. C.,
1705-1708; rector of St. Thomas's parish, S. C., 1709-1743. WILLIAM
TREDWELL BULL, minister of St. Paul's parish, S. C., 1712-1723;
Commissary of the Bishop of London, 1716-1723. GILBERT JONES,
minister of Christ Church, S. C., 1713-1721.)

(38)

To Mess^r Talbot & Vesey

July 16th 1721

Rev^d S^r

The Society have reced a Letter from Mr Bass dated
6th of October 1715 adviseing that he hath Made An Adittion
of Some Land to Burlington house which lay vacant and Un-
survey'd contiguous to it & which he Says Would have prov'd
Very prejudiciall if they had been Taken Up by Any other
person The Society desire that you together with the rever'd

Mr Talbot will Inquire in What Manner the Said Lands are Setled and endeavour to get a Conveyance of them to the Society in the Same Manner as Burlington house was Convey'd I am &c ———

(S. P. G. A-Series, XI., p. 377.)

(39)

M^r. Talbot to the Secretary

S^r

I have not had ye favour of a Letter tho' I have sent sev^ll since Mr Walker Arriv'd I have put him into ye Church at Burlington & into a house which out of my Poverty, I have prepar'd for ye Service of ye Church for ever, & for ye Use of ye Missionaries for ye time being fro ye Honble Society, if I dye in Y^r Service and be not forc'd to Sell it again for pure Necessarys.

I hear y^t one of my bills was ord^d to lye by for ½ Year, I wish I had known ye reason of it y^t I might have Answer'd by ye bearer, ye Honble Coll: Coxe who comes here with another Gentleman of ye Vestry of ye Ch: of Burlington to Clear y^t Church fro ye Slanders y^t Coll: Hunter has raised ag^st us, only because we were Xtians and Could not Serve God & Mammon Xt: and Belial &c.

I don't know any thing y^t I have done Contrary to my Duty either in Church or State, But if it be Resolved, y^t no Englishman Shall be in Mission or Commission, Apud Americanos I dont know what we have done y^t we should all give place to Scotch, Irish, but I am Content to Suffer with good Company, ferie quam Sortem Patiunter omnes nemo remsit, I suffer all things for ye Elects sake, The Poor Church of God here in ye Wilderness, Thers none to Guide her among all ye Sons y^t she has brought forth, nor is their any y^t takes her by ye hand of all the Sons y^t she has brought up, When ye Ap^tles Heard y^t Samaria had recd ye Word of God; Imediatly they sent out 2 of ye Cheif, Peter & John to lay their hands on them & pray y^t they might receive the holy Ghost, they did not stay for a Secular design of Salary, & when the Ap^tles heard y^t ye Word of God was preach'd at Antioch presently they sent out Paul & Barnabas that they should goe as far as Antioch to Confirm ye Disciples, & so ye Churches were Establisht in ye faith & Increased in number daily, & when Paul did but Dream y^t a man of Macedonia call'd him, he set Saile all so fast, & went over himself to help y^m, but we have been here these 20 Year Calling till our Hearts Ake, & y^y own tis ye Call & Cause of God, & yet y^y have not heard or have not Answ^d and y^ts all one, I must say this if ye Honble Society dont do more in a short time than they have in a long, they will I fear loose their Hon^r & their Charact^r to, I don't pretend to prophesy but you know how they said the Kingdom of God shall be taken from y^m & given to a Nation y^t will bring forth ye fruits of it, God give us all ye Grace to doe the things y^t belong to our Peace So God bless you all

& Yours

Jno: Talbot

You may Imagine what you please of Y^r Irish Missionaries, but I am sure we have lost Mr Brook & Thorogood Moor, 2 English men y^t were worth all ye Teagues y^t ever came over.

(S. P. G. A-Series, XI., pp. 334-335.)

(40)

Pensilvania Letters
to the Society
Mr Talbot to the Secretary

Philada Xbris 5th 1716

S^r

Yo^{rs} received with the 2 Orders of the Honable Society. The first I doubt is hardly feezable, Masters of Vessels do not use to give a receipt unless they get by it it is well if a poor Mission^r can get the runing of a Lre by a passenger however I shall do my Endeavour to comply with this and all Other Orders of the Hona^{ble} Society in omnibus Licitis et Honestis 2dly: I have Served all the Churches at times in this province and the next, but have had little for here. Hopewell—Bristol—Oxford—Radnar and all these Churches together are destitute of Ministers, who if they had any would willingly do their endeavours to Assist then tho' they be not able wholly to Maintaine them I received 12 £ in these 12 Month from some good people of Philada but the Vestry that Mr Phillips Left will do nothing. The Queens bounty is gon and the King's is not, were it not for some few perquisites nobody could live here, I had formerly 20 £ P Ann subscribed by the Vestry at Burlington, Honable Coll: Cox was one (never I suppose at home) he paid me P 5 £ P Ann. but now the Case is altered and the Quakers being Chief here and there. It cannot be Expected they should do any thing for Gospel of Christ, which they Call beastly wear, dust death and serpents Meat &c.

Indeed formerly in pious times when and where they have been Christian Govern^{rs} they always promoted the Gospel, as Virginia and Mary Land, there the Churches of Christ are pretty well settled and served blessed be God and the people preserved from the Infection of Quakerism This Hon^r is due to the Honable Coll^{ll} Nicholson who has done More for the propagating the Gospel of Christ and his Church in this wast howling Wilderness, than all the Govern^rs that Ever to these Dominions I doubt not but God Almighty will reward his good works in heaven, for this world is not worthy The Noble Lord Cornbury now Earl of Clarendon is not to be forgotten on this Occasion for he took a great deal of Pains to settle the Church in the province of N: York Lovey Island Staten Island and so he would have done at N: Jersey if he had stayed I cannot think but Honable Society had done Much more if they have found one honest Man to bring Gospell Orders over to us, no doubt as they have freely received, they would freely give, but there's a Nolo Episcopari Only for poor America but she shall have her Gospel day even as others, but we shall never see it unless we make more hast than we have don.

I would not be further Tedious to yor hon^rs at this time but for the Importunate Widdow Mrs Clubb.

I was with Poor B^r John when dyed, he left not Money enough to bury him his widdow has Administred and paid his debts, I received the Society's Books to the Library here, there they Are till further Orders, I am very sorry and ashamed to hear that her bill of 15 £ pound is not paid. The Money was due yor Missioner while he Lived and when he dyed, The society Ordered One half a year's Salary to be paid to Any Missioners relict, but I am not now pleading for Bounty and Charity but for Justice Tis a reproach to the Honable Society that this Poor Widdow should be put to it, sell her bed and Curtains Over her head in this Could weather as she has don to pay this Money again to Dr Saml Monkton, I cannot think but Honable Body will Consider her when they hear the Case they Cannot plead Poverty, for we know That Coll^n Coddringtons Estate at Barbzadoes would supply more than All the Missioners and Americans. If there had been a Good Overseer, and how can any thing do well in Church or State without him. God help all those to Right that suffer wrong where shall we Expect it, if not from a society that Sett up for propagating the Gospell which is the Rule of all Righteousness, Let not the Ungodly Quakers tryumph and say agen that the Society instead of Propagating, they did but Scandalize the Gospel.

Pudet hac Opprobria nobis et dici potuisse et non potuisse repelli.

Iniquity does abound and the Love of many waxes Cold and Charity dys at home how can She go abroad, Let them look out that have, they watch and what will they Answer, when they are reproved for not doing their first works, people will be forced to turn Papists here in a little time to be of som Religion, the Presbyterians are very busye in sowing Tears and Preaching their damnable Doctrine of Predestination and Reprobation they Cause some to despair and Others to turn Quakers.

They Ordain their Pretended Elders in all places and if their Orders be good why may not we do the same, if it Please the Society to favour us with an Answer to this last point it will be a great Satisfaction to all Christian People. Especially to yor Most Obedient humble and Obliged Servant.

John Talbot

I have enclosed a Catalogue of the Book that you may know if there be all if not I may know what they are and I shall make it my business to them Out for Tho' the Honable Society gave no books to the Library at Burlington yet I am Concerned to see every Church and every body have their Right as far as I can go.

(S. P. G. A-Series, XII., p. 177. LOVEY ISLAND probably means "Long Island;" the A-Series consists of copies, and the scribes doubtless made many errors. EDWARD HYDE, THIRD EARL OF CLARENDON, 1661-1724, was a patron of the S. P. G. CHRISTO-PHER CODRINGTON, 1668-1710, Chief Governor of the Leeward Islands, bequeathed his estate to the S. P. G. for the founding of a college in the Barbados.)

(41)

Mr Talbot to the Secretary

Burlington 7^{ber} 17th 1717

S^r

I received an order from the Society to look after some Lands belonging to the house at Bur: together with Mr Vessey but he is not yet come this way so I shall say Nothing to that point at present because it is but an Acre or 2 and that is Safe enough. the Quakers would have got that as they have all the rest of the Meadow Lands belonging to the Bps house and divided them amongst themselves. I never saw such a Cheat since I come to America Coll Cox's Ladey is Come home and they can give the best Acc^t of it that we have I was sent for Down to Sallem where I never was before upon an Extraordinary Occasion the sheriff was Murdered there and 3 or 4 persons were concerned in it, but the man that did the fact would not Confess till a Minister came to him then he was very penitent Confess all the Matter how the Devil and a Quaker put him upon it. he did declare first and last that the Devil Appeared to him personally Clapt him on the shoulder and told him ffriend go on with thy design Never fear they Escape I preacht upon Repentance towards God and faith towards our Lord Jesus Christ of the Resurrection of the Dead & Eternal Judgem^t to a 1000 people. More they were so well Affected that they said if they had a Minister they would N'ere go to the Quakers Meeting any more so I leave it to the Pious Consideration of the Honable Society whither we shall propagate the Kingdom of Christ or let the Kingdom of the Devil take place I bought a piece of Land to build a Church but how shall they hear without a preacher and how shall preach Except they be sent if the Society please to be Informed further of these things I shall refer all to Coll¹ Coxs who is very Capable to give an Acco^t of Our Affairs and how we do in this Most Miserable County in the world y^t belongs to the Governm^t of Christians. My heart is full and I could say much. but God help us against the Enemy for vain is the help of Man so I desire yor prayers for yor Most humble and faithful Labourer

John Talbot

(S. P. G. A-Series, XII., p. 390.)

(42)

Mr Talbot to the Secretary
Burlington May 3rd 1718

S^r

I used to write to you now and then, tho' I seldom have the favour of answer. or not to the point all yor Missioners here abouts are going to Maryland hie for the sake of themselves their wives and Children for my part I cannot desert the poor flock that I have gathered nor will I if I have Neither Money Credit nor Tobacco But if I had known as Much as I do now that the Society were not able for their parts to send Bps priests nor Deacon no Techures nor Catechist no hinter nor holderforth I would never put the good people in these parts to the Charge and trouble of Building Churches (Nay Now they Must be Stalls or Stables for Quakers horses when they come to Markett or Meeting) as I see before, but some people will not believe till tis too late. Dr Evans himself is gon to Maryland, for he says No body will serve the Church for Nought as I do for My part I cannot blame the people in these parts for they do what they Are Able & no body can desire More Rich or poor for those that do them any good
My Duty to the honoble Society I am

Yo^r Most humble Servant
John Talbot

(S. P. G. A-Series, XIII., p. 374.)

(43)

The Deposition relating to Mr Halliday by Mr Vaughan
& Talbott

New Jersey
Middlesex &s

Memorandum That on the fourth day of Septr 1718—upon the Complaint of George Willcocks of Perth Amboy that the revered Mr Thomas Halliday being at his house the day before in Company with the Rev^d Mr John Talbot & Mr Edwd Vaughan he the Said Mr Halliday Asked for more Drink which he the said George Shewed his unwillingness to give insinuating that it might do more hurt then good to Mr Halliday After some hours Conversation Mr Halliday Address'd this Discourse to Said George and told him that if he Should Say any thing of him he would resent it the Said George Answered he, was proof against Anything he would Say he replied that if he was against his tongue he Should not Against his hands the said George desired he would be pleased to go home upon which Mr Halliday Cross'd ye room & took up a flint quart decanter and struck forcibly at Said George who endeavoured to fend off the blows & with the force thereof he Struck it against ye wall wch pieces thereof wounded & bruis'd Said Georges face in Sev^ll places & further that he the Said Mr Halliday used his endeavour to beat the Said George untill he was prevented by the interposition of y^m ye S^d Messrs Talbot & Vaugh^n who forced him out of ye house & y^t he struck or bruised Mrs. Willcox w^n y^y were a putting him out

                                        Jno Talbot
                                        Ed Vaughan

         Sworn before me ye day
& year above written Wm Eier Just

    (S. P. G. A-Series, XIII., p. 421.)

    (This letter refers to the altercation between THOMAS HALIDAY and GEORGE WILLOCKS—not "Willcocks." This WILLOCKS was probably the same individual referred to in the 14th Letter. He was a wealthy settler and prominent in the early history of Perth Amboy; he left considerable property to St. Peter's Church there. In W. Northey Jones's *History of St. Peter's Church in Perth Amboy,* there is a detailed account of this quarrel, pp. 40-42).

                        (44)

    Mr Talbot to the Secretary
                                    Amboy 7^ber 5th 1718
S^r

    The Honble Society refered it to me formerly to give a Character of Mr Tho: Haliday, but I having nothing to say in his favour, and being very loath to give an ill report of a Bro^r of the Order, I let all sleep in hopes of Amendm^t But all hopes of that being gon he growing worse and worse every day in principle and practice, It shall be no longer my ffault that he is Continued in the Mission a hindrance to the Gospel, a Scandal to the Church and a dishonour to the Society. It is a sad Case indeed when he that should be a preacher of righteousness, is himself a practisner of Iniquity a Glutton a drunkard a Railer a striker &c. The last time

I was in his Company (which shall be the last of all) we were friendly entertained by one of his parisho^{nrs} in this place, and when he had Liquor more then enough he was more like a drunken Indian wild for more but being denyed he took up a Quart decanter and broke it in above 100 pieces Over the Gen^{t}mans head who gave him no provocation by word, or, deed the blood ran down his Eyes and Nose and had not I and Bro^r Vaughan Interposed with all our Might I doubt not but he had Committed Murder. Next day he was had before the Mayor when he Owned the Matter of fact he was Ordered to find Baile for his good behaviour which he could not that night, so the Next Morning he ran away from the Sherrif If he comes not Agen, They will all forgive him, But if he returns they have Ordered the Church wardens to Lock the Church, Doors had there been any Overseer of the poor Church in these parts this Mad Man had not been Continued halfe so long in the Sacred Service of the Honble Society however I am Sure he would not have been Ordered agen for this Church at Amboy where he was once before turned out for his Misdemeanours, and, has had such Malice in his heart ever since as if he designed to Murder some body, for I never saw or heard of a more barbarous action of Assault and battery since Cain rose up against his Bro^r Abel and Slew him. Upon the whole if you would know my private Opinion of Mr Haliday saving his Charecter I take him to be the worst of Men. He has been oft threatened with the Commissary Mr Vesey at New York but he set at Naught all Councel and dispised all reproof saying he can do nothing but represent or report and I can do that as well as he It is a sad thing when people's Souls are Committed to such hands as are not fit to be entrusted with Camels I need say no more but refer yor Hon^{rs} to the Report of the Church Wardens and Bro^r Vaughan who saw and heard the Matter. Let Mr Haliday say what he pleases, tis a case admitts of No Vindication Now all these Churches are like to be destitute Woodbridge Amboy ffreehold &c. It will be half a year before we can hear and Another halfe before we can Expect Any Redress. I am very sorry for the Occasion of this Report but I could do no less for the truth sake, so Right Honble Lords and Gentlemen I desire yor benedictioned prayers and Remaine

Yo^r Hono^{r}s
Most Obedient Servt
and ffaithfull Missioner
John Talbot

(S. P. G. A-Series, XIII., pp. 352-354.)

(45)

Mr Talbot and Mr Vaughan to the Secretary
Amboy the 1st of October 1718.

To The Right Reverend Father in God John Lord Bishop of London and to The Honourable Society for the Propagating the Gospell In forreign Parts.

The Address of the Missionaries of The Province of New Jersey Humbly Sheweth

That as it Appertaineth to the Disciplin of the Church, that Inquiry be made of Evill Ministers and that they be Accused by those that have knowledge of their Offences, so it is with A View to this so Necessary A part of our Duty In which the Glory of God and the Good of Souls is Nearly concerned That we Humbly Crave leave to inform yor Lordship and yor Honble Body, that Mr Thomas Haliday of Amboy in New Jersey Missionary, has been all along and is now so far from Adorning his sacred function with Morall Virtues and Christian Graces that on the contrary he has taken A great deal of pains to deface his Life and Conversation through the whole Course of his Ministry and Mission by the practice of severall Irregular Actions; Such we take to be his Quarreling and fighting with his Land-Lord, while he lived in Elizabeth Town on the Evening of the day of Our Lord's Nativity after he had in the Morning of that festivall, administred the Blessed Sacrament of the Lords Supper to his then Congregation. In the said Towne, Such May be Accounted his throwing of a Cup of scalding hot Coffee into the face of one, and a tankard of Cold Syder into the Bossom of an other Gen^{t}woman of Our Neighbourhood without any weighty provocation of a Peice with Part of his Conduct, May be Reckoned his Abuseing stricking and Grieveously wounding Mr Willocks at his Own house at Amboy with a' Large fflint bottle or Quart decanter, Any Other Cause, reason or provocation that we heare of but what is Mentioned and Contained in Deposition (Lately taken and Transmitted to yor Lordship and Hon^{r}s) to which we refer you for a further Testimonie of his Misbehaviour to which we very believe he was Excited by the Influence of his Passion inflamed meerely with the help of Wine or some Other Spirituous Liquors to the use of which he is so much Adicted and Accustomed, that he hath by his intemporance grievous Scandall and Great Offence to the Churches of God in this part of the world, and hath raised strong Prejudices not only against his Profession but against person, so that he is now utterly incapable of advanceing the true interest of religion, while all man kind look upon him as A Mercurial Post that directs the way to Others and never stirs or walks it selfe in it. The case being so, We leave it to yor Lordship and Hon^{r}s to

Consider In yor Great Pietie and wisdom, whether it be not More Equall and Just to Cutt him off that troubles the Church from his Mission, and to substitute in his stead and Place a Sober Pious and Examplarie Divine, In Compliance with the Earnest Request of the People of Amboy, then the Gospell by his continuance among them, should be reproached, It's Progress and Improvement hindred more and More, an Occasion should be given to Our Adversaries to speak Evill of Christ and his Church, and Men of all sects, sizes and denomination, should be dettered and kept back from inbracing and recieving the truth as it is in the Lord Jesus. We pray God to direct you In all yor Pious Consultations, And are with Great Respect.

May it Please yor Lordships and
Hono^{r}s
Most Devoted Obedient
and Humble Servant
John Talbot
Edward Vaughan

(S. P. G. A-Series, XIII., pp. 388-391.)

(46)

The humble Petition of John Talbot
To the Right Rev^d & R^t Honble the Society
for the propagation of the Gospel in
Foreign parts.

Sheweth

That his Grace ye late Arch Bp of Canterbury having by codicil to his last Will bearing date 2^d Decemb 1715, bequeathed 1000£ towards ye Settlem^t of Bpps in America & (untill such lawfull employment) directed that the Interest thereof should be apply'd to the benefit of such Missionarys being Englishmen of the province of Canterbury as have taken true pains in ye respective places comitted by ye s^d Society to their Care in ye fforeign plantations, & have been by unavoidable accidents, Sickness or other infirmities of body or old age disabled from ye performance of their Duty & forced to return to England.

That y^r Petitioner having been in ye Service of this Honble Society as their Missionary in the foreign plantations near 18 years (for his Service dureing that time he refers to certificates under ye hands of the Several Neighbouring Clergy & others) & having been by Sickness old Age & other unavoidable Accidents disabled from ye performance of his duty in ye s^d places & forced to return to England.

He therefore humbly prays (as he conceives himself intitled to ye Intrest of the s^d Legacy being also an Englishman

& of the Diocess of Norwich & province of Canterbury) that this Honble Society will be pleased to Certifie ye same under their Seal or otherwise, to ye R^t Honble the Lord Chancellour or other proper persons, in order for his being paid ye s^d Intrest.

And y^r Petitioner shall ever pray &c^a

(S. P. G. A-Series, XIV., pp. 44-45.)

(47)

The State & Condition of Burlington house in new Jersey in America purchased by Coll' hunter by order of ye Society for the propagation of ye Gospel in fforeign parts for ye Residence of a Bishop humbly offered to the s^d Society by John Talbot Missionary to Burlington aforesaid.

All the Meadow Lands belonging to this house are parcell'd out & Sold to Several people of ye Town by him that Married Mr Tathams Widow, & if there be any other Lands belonging thereto they are claimed by the Quakers, the Coach house & Stable are fallen down & ye timbers are Stolen away & all the other out houses are fallen except one & the Bakehouse Stands a tiptoe & will fall if speedy Care be not taken to prevent it every Sunday ye rabble goe & rob ye orchard & garden,—having broke ye fences & pul'd down the Gates they also get into ye house leave open ye doors & so it remains from one Week to the other, The windows of ye house are very much broken ye house being reported to be haunted no single person will live in it, & unless some ffamily be placed there to take Care of ye house and the lands they will be lost for want of looking after & unless some allowance be made to ye person none will be prevail'd on to live in it, if Coll hunter has not employ'd some person to See where ye Lands lay & take them up in ye name of the Society he has not acted like a friend to that hon^{ble} body the original writeings wch are in Coll Depuisters hands the s^d Jno Talbot is humbly of opinion may be deposited either in the hands of ye Churchwardens for ye time being, or in ye Library there & an Authentick Copy under the Seal of ye Jerseys transmitted to the Society.

(S. P. G. A-Series, XIV., p. 34.)

(48)

Certificate in behalfe of Mr Talbot Sealed by the Society.

To all People to whom these p^rsents shall come.

The Society for the Propagation of the Gospel in fforeign parts sendeth greeting.

Whereas his Grace D^r. late Arch Bp of Canterbury did by a Codicil to his last Will & Testament bearing
date 2^d Decemb^r 1715 bequeath 1000 £ towards ye settlem^t
of Bishops in America & until such Lawful appointm^t of
Bps as afores^d did direct that the Intrest thereof should be
apply'd to the benefit of such Missionaries being Englishmen
& of the province of Canterbury as have taken true pains in
the respective places comitted by the s^d Society of their Care
in the foreign Plantations & have ben by unavoidable accidents, Sickness or other Infirmities of the body or old age
disabled from ye performance of their Duties in the s^d places
& forced to return to England—
    These are therefore to Certifye that the Revd John Tal-
bot formerly Rector of Frethorn in the County & Diocess of
Gloucester & province of Canterbury hath been in the Service
of the s^d Society for the propagation of the Gospel in foreign
Parts as their Missionary in the foreign plantations near
18 years dureing wch time he hath taken true pains in the
discharge of his holy Function in the Several places Comitted
to his Care by the s^d Society (And by his zeal & exemplary
Life & Conversation hath done great Service to ye Church
in America) in consideration hereof, The s^d Society do
recomend him as a person qualified to receive the Interest of the
Thousand pounds above mentioned he having been (as they
Credibly informed & believe) by Sickness infirmities of Body
contracted in the Service of the Church Age & other unavoidable Accidents disabled from ye performance of his duty
in the said places & forced to return to England, In Witness
whereof the s^d Society have hereunto caused to be affixed
their Comon Seale the 17 day of ffebry Ano Dni 1720 & in
the 7th Yeare of the Reigne of his Majesty King George &c^a

(S. P. G. A-Series, XIV., p. 55.)

(49)

Church Wardens and Vestry in behalf of M^r. Talbot

New Jersey 1720
To the Right Revd and Right honble The Society for the
propagation of the Gospell in Forreigne parts—
    We should justly accuse o^rselves of ye highest ingrati-
tude did we not take this opportunity by o^r worthy pastor the
Revd Mr John Talbot to return You o^r hearty thanks for
the inexpressable benefit that we have received by the Mission
of him amongst us; A true and unfeigned Zeal for the Glory
of God & ye good of his Church hath during his time with us
influenced the whole of his life & conversacon & his exemplary piety hath as much adorned (wth grief we may say)

ye unguarded lives of some y^t hath been Missionaries amongst us hath scandalized ye Gospell of o^r blessed Lord & Saviour Jesus C^t Our constant prayers will be for his speedy & safe return, & y^t You would consumate ye favour already bestowd by ye appointing him again to a people than to whom nothing can be more acceptable unless ye arrival of one of ye true Apostolick and Episcopal Order y^t hereby infidellity & immorality may be Curbed & Scandalous offend^{rs} reproved Holy Orders to such as may be qualified without ye Vast Expence of going to England Conferred, o^r Youth confirmed etc^a wch good Work cannot be justly expected to be expedited by any so much as a Society whose concern is ye propogation of ye Gospel amongst Us. to wch this would be ye greatest Stepp & wthout wch all other measures are almost ineffectual: we beg pardon for y^s o^r presumption & leave to Subscribe o^{r}selves: R^t Rev^d and R^t honble Y^r most humble & very much Obliged Sons & Servants.

Peur Bard	Rowland Ellis				
Abr: Heulings	Johnathan Lovett	Vestry	Joh Bass		Church
Jno Allen	Thos Hunloke	Men	Geor: Willis		Wardens
Jos: White	Mich^l Pyier		William Budell		

Certificate in behalf of the Revd Mr Talbott

We whose Names are underwritten do hereby certife y^t ye Revd Mr Jno Talbot has for severall Years been conversant amongst us and during ye time he has spent in the service of the Church in America his fidellity and zeal in ye discharge of his holy function & his uprightness of conversation has been so very eminent & conspicuous y^t he has allong preserved the fairest Character so we cannot but recommend him to ye highest Esteem & love of all y^t sincerely love ye Inter^t of ye Gospell of C^t given under o^r hands ye 29th of March 1720.

Robt^t Walker Minister of Hopewell &c^a New Jersey
William Vesey Rector of Trinity Church New York
Robert Jenney Chaplain to ye Fort at New York
Thomas Haliday Minister of Amboy New Jersey
Edward Vaughan Minister at Elizth Town New Jersey
Rowland Ellis School M^r at Burlington New Jersey
Evan Evans Minister at Philadelphia Pensilvania
Jno Humphreys Minister at Chester Pensilvania
Jno Vicary minister of ye same place 24 June 1720.
Andrew Salden Minister of Wicaco near Philadelphia
George Ross Minister of Newcastle Pensilvania
Eneas Mackenzie Minister of Staten Island New York
Thomas Poyer Minister of Jamaica Long Island, N. York
John Thomas Minister of Hampstead long D^o New D^o
Elias Neau Catechist at New York ———

(S. P. G. A-Series, XIV., pp. 151-152. ROBERT JENNEY served various charges in New York, particularly Hempsted, where he ministered from 1725 to 1742; he became rector of Christ Church, Philadelphia, 1742-1762, and was Commissary of the Bishop of London. JOHN VICARY, who had been appointed to the rectorship of Christ Church, Philadelphia, by the Bishop of London, presented his license to the vestry, Sept. 4, 1719, and immediately entered upon his charge; failing health soon compelled him to seek the aid of the neighboring clergy; in 1722, he ceased to officiate, dying soon afterwards. ANDREW SALDEN is probably meant for "Andrew Sandel".)

(50)

Certificate in behalf of Mr Rowl^d Ellis   1720

These are to Certifie that Rowland Eliss Schoolmaster appoint'd by ye Society for the Town of Burlington has Ever since he came here behaved and to ye Uttmost of his power and Ability has performed the business committed to his charge with care dilligence & unwearied Constancy notwithstanding the many disapointm^{ts}. he hath mett with amidst A Crooked and perverse people. In Testimony whereof I have hereunto Set my hand this 23 June 1720.

Jno Talbott Rec^r

(S. P. G. A-Series, XIV., p. 148.)

(51)

Copy of the Order for Mr Talbots receiving the Interest of ye late A. Bp Tenisons 1000 £.

Sabti 30 die Junij Año Octave regni Regis
Georij Inter Georgiu ffage etc (?) Quer
Edwardu Tenison Doctor Divina et Ux et al.

Defts

Upon the humble Petition of John Talbott Clerk this day preferred to the R^t Honble the L^d high Chancellor of great Britain thereby setting forth that Dr Thomas Tennison lat A. Bp of Canterbury did by Codicill to his Will bequeath 1000 £ towards Setlem^t of Bpps in America & untill such Lawful Appointm^t of Bishops did direct that ye Interest should be applyed to the benefit of such Missionarys being Englishmen of the province of Canterbury as have taken true pains in ye respective places comitted by the Society to their Care in the foreign Plantations & have been by unavoidable Accidents Sickness or other Infirmitys of ye body or old Age disabled from ye performance of their Dutys in ye s^d places & forced to return to Engl^d and that upon the hearing of this Cause it was amongst other things ordered that ye s^d 1000 lb. should be placed out at Interest on such Governm^t or other Security as Mr Bennet to whom ye Accompt of the Testors psonal Estate was directed to be taken should Approve of & the Interest thereof is to be applyed according to the directions of the Testors will till one month after ye appointm^t and consecration of two such Bps & that the s^d John Talbot was formerly Rector of ffreethorn in the County & Diocess of Glouc^r & province of Canterbury hath been in the Service of the s^d Society for ye propagaĉon of the Gospel in foreign parts as their Missionary in ye foreign plantaĉons near 18 years during wch time he hath taken true paines in discharge of his Holy ffunction in the Several places committed to his Care by the s^d Society & by his zeal and exemplary life & conversation hath done great Service to the Church in America & therefore is qualified to receive the Interest of the s^d 1000 £ as by the Certificate of the s^d Corporation under their Coṁon Seal hereunto annexed may appear & that their having no Bpps been yet appointed in America & the s^d John Talbott being ye only Miss^{ry} that is an Englishman & of the province of Canterbury been so long & behaved himself so well in ye s^d Service as by the s^d Certificate appears the s^d John Talbot by the direction of ye s^d Society applyed himself to the s^d Mr Bennett for the s^d Interest who apprehends he canot pay the Same without the direction of this Court & thereupon ye s^d John Talbott on ye 22^d of April 1721, apply'd himself to your Lordp that the s^d Mr Bennett might pay such Interest as was then due to him wch was ordered accordingly and that the s^d Mr Bennett pursuant to the s^d order did pay unto the s^d Mr John Talbot all the Interest then reced & the s^d John Talbott hath applyed to the s^d Mr Bennett for what Interest has been reced Since, who app^rhends he canot pay the same without your Lordps further directions. Therefore & in as much as there is no other person intituted to receive any part of the s^d Interest It is prayed that the s^d Mr Bennett may be ordered to pay such Interest as is now due & that shall from time to time become due to the s^d John Talbott or as he shall appoint which is ordered Accordingly whereof notice is forthwith to be given.

p Ricu Price
Deput Reg^r

(S. P. G. A-Series, XVI., pp. 48-51.)

(52)

Mr Talbot to the Secretary

Burlington Nov: 27.

S^r

I and Mr Skinner arived Safe in 6 Weeks at Philad^a never better Weather nor so good a passage as the Capt' said (who was a Quaker) they & the Sailors Used to say they had no

good luck when yᵉ Priests were on board but now they are both prettily Convinced & finely converted to say no more all Sorts & Conditions of Men Women & Children wer glad to see us return for they had given me over. I was Yesterday at New Bristol in pensilvania to call yᵉ people to Church but they had almost lost the way it was so overgrown with Bushes they cou'd hardly find the Church having had nothing to do there for 2 year & a half Since I came away the Church there has Suffer'd very much, but yᵉ Bps house here at yᵉ point is in yᵉ worst Condition of all, 'tis made nothing but a bawdy house a Sheeps Coat & playhouse the boys have broke the Windows from top to bottom they brake the doors Steal the Leads & Iron Bars they pul down the pales & cut yᵉ Cedar posts they Steal the ffruit & Brake the Trees 'tis in vain to repair it any more, unless some ffamily be put in to guard it, I thank I have a house of my own just by the Church & I wou'd not live in yᵉ point house if they wou'd give it me, but I am loath to See it fall down as yᵉ Coach house & Stables are already & what will they do for yᵉ Meadows they will be lost if not claimed Speedily the Witnesses will be dead that know where the Land lyes, if the Society think fit to send any orders abᵗ these things I hope they will come before it is too late. I thought my duty to lay these things before the honorable Body & I hope You will lead it to the Committee & Society, that something may be done before the whole house drops through, this is the last time of asking so I crave your Prayers & remain Your most humble
Servᵗ   J. Talbot

P. S.

The Society had never bought this house for some Gentleman or other such as Col. Cox wou'd have done very wel with it, but since they have bought & can't Sell it again for yᵉ Worth they had better make a ffree School or a College its very wel contrived for that purpose Several of Mʳ Skinners Schollars at Philadᵃ are fit for the Academy but heres no place to send them to, they can't afford to send their Children to Europe for Education, Sailing is now to' dangerous troublesom & chargeable something of a College must be had here the Sooner the better.

J. T———

(S. P. G. A-Series, XVI., pp. 214-216. WILLIAM SKINNER, 1687?-1758, catechist at Philadelphia; afterwards missionary at Perth Amboy, N. J.)

(53)

Burlington 14ᵗʰ Sep 1723

These are to Certifie to Rᵗ Revᵈ and Right Honble the Society that Rowland Ellis whom they sent as a School Master

for this Town of Burlington Continues in his Vocation with Diligent Attendance is very Circumspect and of a Sober Conversation I beg leave to Subscribe my Self
                    Yo^r most Obedient
                    humble serv^t
                                    John Talbott

(S. P. G. A-Series, XVII., p. 237.)

(54)

Mr Talbot to the Secretary.
                            Burlington 20th Sepr 1723
Revd Sir.

I have more work to do now than I had before and I have no Assistant they have both gone & have left me and the Church in the Lurch I have 15 Miles to Travell from the Capes of Delaware to the Hills & Mountains in East Jersey and none to help me but Mr Lidenius a Swedes Minister and he is going away I have been this Month at Trenton at Hopewell and am well preaching and Baptizeing 19 persons in one day I visited several persons that were Sick who had been Quakers & were come off their Errors wth Mr Geo: Keith they were near 80 Years of Age and had not reced the H Sacrament of the Lords Supper in all their Lives but were loth to dye wthout the benefitt and Comfort of it so I was feign to come back again to Burlington to get the Elements; then Returned to the Mountains & did Administer to their great Satisfaction They are preparing to build a Church in the Spring but when they will have a Minister I cannot tell, but tis a Solemn thing (as they say in New England) for the lost Sheep to go astray in the Wilderness, to be among Wolves is Worse, but for Sheep to be without a Shepherd is the most Deplorable Case of all, mean while it's some Comfort to See the Bps house at Burlington in Repair again it is as well finisht and furnisht as ever I saw it the Gover^r of New York is coming to Reside here for a Month or Two we have got an honest Church man as we Suppose to live there keep it in good order, now tis so by Care and Ord^r of Col: Cox if the acc^t comes not by this Ship Old Annise it will by the next this fall in Captn Richmond I have set up one Mr Searle a Schoolmaster to read prayers and preach on Sundays at Springfield I lent him some Sermons of Dr Tillotsons & Beveridges severall Quakers came to hear him and are much taken wth him they say they never thought the priests had so much good Doctrine, I'm sure he is a much better Clerk than M^r H————n saving his Orders therefore I commend him to the Society for their encouragem^t and hope they will count him worthy to be an half pay Officer in their Service I pray God

bless all our Benefactours and prosper all the Labours of All
their honest Missioners especially

Yo[r] most faithfull
and Obedient serv[t]
John Talbot.

(S. P. G. A-Series, XVII., p. 237. ABRAHAM LIDENIUS,
Swedish minister; frequent references to him are found in Dr. Clay's
Annals of the Swedes. JOHN TILLOTSON, 1630-1694, published
numerous sermons during his lifetime.)

(55)

M[r] Talbot to the Secretary.

Philadelphia 9th Decem[r] 1723

Rev[d] S[r]

This place is my hard quarters. I was taken very ill in
the church last Sunday at Burlington with Cholera Morbus
so that was forc[t] to leave the church. After I read the Psalms
I could go no further. After I had laid by some days I came
down to Philadelphia to consult the Doctor and, thank God, I
have had my health very well. When I can get any help I send
them to Burlington and go myself some times, but 'tis a thousand
pities this place should be destitute. Here are much people and
tho' they are poor, they ought not to be lost for lack of looking
after. They are well rid of wth _____
_____at last, he was wors than_____
_____ and would not go away till he was starved out. Here's
nothing but a little paper coin current, neither money, credit
nor Tobacco. The best of the people had left the church so
they would muster nothing but they would give him some what
to go away so they got rid of him at last. Col[l] Coxe and M[r]
Trent have done their parts towards the Society's house Burlington. They have put it all in good order both within and
without. The Gardens, Orchard and pasture are fenced all
round and, what is more than ever was done, they have got an
honest man (as we suppose), to live there as Adam did in Paradise to dress it and keep it so 'tis fit now for any Governor in
Church or State. M[r] Burnet has been there this quarter almost,
& he says 'tis more pleasant than Salisbury in England. Therefore I am not fallen out with my first love, Dear Bur: but I have
some pity of poor Philadelphia. Because she has none to help
her, there is more need there at present. I can do most good
till some body else comes so I commend myself and service to
the Hon'ble Society & desiring their prayers I rest their &
Your humble Servant,
Jo: Talbot.

P. S. I have enclosed a Memoran[m] from the Collector here
about the Royal bounty & I desire that it may be laid before the
board that they may see and know where it sticks. The School-

master here one Mr Walter Jones was going away but I persuaded him to stay another half year till we hear further about that business.

(S. P. G. A-Series, XVII., p. 250. This letter appears in Perry: *Historical Collections relating to the American Colonial Church*, Vol. II., Pennsylvania, pp. 133-134. Talbot refers to the enforcing resignation of JOHN URMSTONE. WILLIAM BURNET, Governor of New York, 1720-1728.)

(56)

Mr Talbot to the Secretary.
Rev^d S^r
I have been here altogether this last half Year I preach once on Sunday morn & Catechize or homilize in ye afternoon, I read the prayers of the Church in the Church decently according to the order of Morning and Evening prayer daily through't the Year & that is more than is done in any Church that I know apud Americanos I bought a house & two or three Lots of Land adjoyning to ye Church Yard & Since I came over last I have settled by Deed upon St Marys Church at Burlington a parsonage & Glebe, tho' there was neither Church house nor Glebe before I came I hope there will be one now for ever, I design to send the Society some Acc^t of the particulars of this in my next & this is more then anybody has done before that I know of my own proper Cost & Charge So that I have been a good husband to do this of my poverty ffor I have no Salary from ye people I had formerly 20£ p ann when there was money, but now here's neither money Credit nor Tobacco nothing but a little paper Coin that is nothing but Sorry Raggs & we can hardly get them to pay the Clark 10£ that is allowed him by the Year. Wee are amongst a Set of people called Quakers who have deny'd the ffaith & are worse than Infidels they Serve no God but Mamon & their own Bellys, & it's ag^st their Conscience to let ye priest have any thing either by Law or Gospel. I have comonly the Sacram^t administred once a Month & at the great ffeasts two or 3 daies together ye number of Communicants is uncertain sometime 20. 30 40 or 50 psons.
     There's no parochial Library Yet, for I never had any from ye Society, but I design to leave mine and Mr Thoro good Moore when I dye to that Use meanwhile we want Comon prayer Books very much. If it please the honble Society instead of 5£ in small tracts to let y^t money be laid out in Comon prayer Books they wou'd be of Great use to the people in all parts who can't get them here for love or money, Those small tracts were but of small Use, for they laid up & did no Good & not being bound they soon perish in ye using for it cost more to bind books here then to buy it in Brittain, I shall say but one thing more at p^rsent wch I omitted when I was in England

for my money was Short or else I wou'd have got some Bells wch we want here very much, I dont mean a Ring of Bells in a Steeple for Idle fellows to make a Vain Jangling but one in Church that the people may know when to come together to Worship God. I pray for you all as I hope You do, for,

Your most humble Servt

John Talbot

Burlington in New Jersey
7^{bris} 7th 1724

(S. P. G. A-Series, XVIII., p. 184.)

(57)

Burlington July 8th
1725

Revnd S^r

Yours Reced March ult. That I am out of Quantum wth the Society & also a Bill protested since that payable to Mr Graham of 30 £ value Reced I heard nothing of this before our Lady last past, Therefor I have Drawn a Bill for 3 Quarters Salary, for so Long I was actually in y^r Service, at my proper cost & charg in propagating the Gospel, & this is as much due to me as any I have Reced from them S^r I desire the favour of y^r selfe to Lay the Case before the Honble Board, & wⁿ they Consider the thing as it is, They will please to pay this Bill to my worthy ffriend Mr Tho : Tovey ffor I never Knew any Board Discard ye officers but they paid em for the time being in their Service & Knew nothing of thir will & pleasure to the Contrary, I remaine

Your most humble &
oblidgd Servt

John Talbot

To the Revnd Mr David Humphys

Addressed

(S. P. G. B-Series, I., #94, p. 347.)

(58)

EXTRACT FROM LETTER OF THE REV. CHRISTOPHER WILKIN-SON, ST. PAUL'S PARISH, QUEEN ANNE COUNTY, MARY-LAND, TO THE BISHOP OF LONDON, SEPT. 14, 1724.

May it please your Lords^p

Since my last of ye 9th of September I have rec^d an account y^t there are now two non-juring Bishops ye one Mr Talbott, an old Missionary in ye Jerseys; the other Dr Welton, at Philadelphia in Pensilvania. The Clergy of this Shore, being well affected to his present Maj^{ty} King George, will have no regard to 'em shud they come down hither. I am also informed y^t ye Commissarys office in this Province worth Six hundred pds p^r an, bestowed by his Maj^{ty} on my Ld Baltimore during pleasure, may be obtain'd for ye Support of a Bishop. I find y^t Dr Bray in his Bibliotheca Parochiales p: 128 declares y^t for ye Support of a Suffragan Govern^r Nicholson at ye request of ye Assembly had Setled a competent maintenance; wch I'm told, was by ye Commissarys office. But this does not appear by his Book; nor can I inform my Self here how it was to be raised; Dr Bray (who is yet living) can no doubt inform your Lords^p more fully in y^t matter; but I thought fit to acquaint your Lords^p of it.

 I am
  May it please Your Lords^p
   Your Lords^{ps} most dutyfull & most obedient Servt
        Chris: Wilkinson
Sep: 14th 1724.

(Fulham MSS., Virginia, Box I., #140. CHRISTOPHER WIL-KINSON, became incumbent of St. Paul's parish, Queen Anne's county, Maryland, in 1713; in 1716, he was appointed Commissary of the Bishop of London for the Eastern Shore of Maryland; he died April 15, 1729.)

(59)

Fulham MSS. Pennsylvania
          Burlington 8^{ber}
             21
             —
            1715

My Lord
 We had the honor of your Lordships Lett^{rs} on Saturday last wch were delivered according to order, to the Govr & Mr Philips they both promised obedience but neither intend^d to p^{r}form, I waited on the Govr on Sunday morning wth Mr Trent the Chiefeman in the church so we went to the Church warden & I demanded the Church in y^r Lordships name, & I would see who hinders me. He s^d he would not, when the Govr & he came together they agreed that Philips should not Preach so I went to Church peacably & quietly & brought the people back agen, to the Great Joy of that City. But the Govr went away to the Sweeds Ch: wch he understands as much as I do Arabick.
 I have written to the Rest of the Bre. & given them a Copy of y^r Ldships orders to serve till Dr Evans comes, Mr Jenny has been Gon to N. York 2 or 3 months ago.
 I'me very Glad to hear that B^r Vesey is arrived safe at Boston wth the Kings Lettr for his Salary, ffor the Govr had put in such a Mayor as s^d he shoud never have it, he told me so himselfe. God help us for Gov^t here apud Americanos

officially y^r Out Lying Members I don't know one of 'em Good.
I'me sorry I shoud be accused of sedition in my old age, after
I have traivld more then anybody to keep the peace in Ch:
and State. My Ld. Please to ask Mr Secretary Hall & he will
tell you that I was a Williamite from the Beging. Let 'em consult the Admiralty Office & they will find I took all the oaths
that were necessary to Qualifye me for the service wch I have
p^{r}formd faithfully abroad & at home. As soon as I have time
I will call the Ch: together to answer for themfs & me too to y^e
Illustrious Society for propagating the Gospel &c. meanwhile
the Ld Rebuke that evil Spirit Lying & Slander that is gone out
agst the Church, here & there they spare none, I suffer Like
my Ld & M^r between 2, at Philad^a & N. York, but God has been
my succour & I doubt not but he will still Deliver me from the
snare of the Hunter. The people of Philad^a said If ye L^{ds} Lett^{rs}
had been directed to the Govr they had been stifled, but I hope I
shall be always Zealous to approve my Selfe.

My Lord
Your Ldships most
obedient Son & humble
Ser^t
John Talbot.

P: S: Mr Philips gives out that he will come home &
Clear Selfe, I wish he could, but I believe he designs for the
West Indies where the worst Priest ye best Clerk.

To
The R^t Revnd ffather in God
John Lord Bishop of
London
at Somerset house
Pensylvania
Mr Talbot

15
Rec'd Jan: 17 —
16

about Philips
dated Oct. 21

(Fulham MSS., Pennsylvania, #74.)

INDEX TO THE PROPER NAMES IDENTIFIED IN THE NOTES ON THE TALBOT CORRESPONDENCE.

BOOK THREE

—

EXCERPTS
FROM THE
JOURNAL OF GEORGE KEITH

EXCERPTS FROM THE JOURNAL OF GEORGE KEITH

GEORGE KEITH—AN INTRODUCTION.

GEORGE KEITH, who introduced John Talbot to the service of the Society for the Propagation of the Gospel in Foreign Parts, was born in Aberdeen, Scotland, about the year 1639, and was educated at the University of his native city. Originally connected with the Kirk of Scotland, he joined the Quakers soon after taking the degree of Master of Arts. He engaged in controversy with noteworthy skill, and he was the means of making a number of converts to the Society of Friends. In his zeal to promote the cause, he not only took part in disputes in the British Isles, but journeyed to Holland with certain eminent Quakers in order to visit and encourage the brethren settled there. In 1682, he settled in East Jersey; for awhile, he held the office of Surveyor-General. Seven years later, he removed to Philadelphia, where he was employed in superintending the education of the children of some wealthy families. In 1690, he travelled as a Quaker preacher into New England. (This date has been disputed.)

Returning to Philadelphia, he proposed some changes in the discipline of the Society; and, when his suggestions did not meet with ready response, he succeeded in drawing off a large number of people with him. The members of this secession called themselves "Christian Quakers" or "Friends", but by others they were known as "Keithians". In 1694, Keith appealed to the yearly meeting of the Society in London, against the exscinding act of the Pennsylvania Quakers; and appeared in person to defend his cause. It is said that on that occasion he showed so much passion that it became apparent that reconciliation was hopeless. He was denounced as an apostate, and his rejection was finally confirmed. From that time, he denounced the Quakers in general with great severity.

He formally joined the Church of England in 1700, and was ordained by the Bishop of London. Having criticised the Church prior to taking this step, he did not escape the imputation of inconsistency; indeed, some person published a selection from his printed works, entitled "Mr. George Keith's Account of a National Church and Clergy, humbly presented to the Bishop of London." Keith, however, was regarded as a valuable acquisition by the bishops; and he was chosen as the first missionary to America by the S. P. G. He left England, April 24th, 1702, on an inspection tour of the colonies; it was his task to visit the British settlements, study their religious needs, and report his findings to the Society. On the journey he was associated with Governor Dudley, of Massachusetts, and Governor Morris, of New Jersey; the Reverend John Talbot, chaplain of the vessel, decided to accompany him in his mission. Landing in Boston in June, the missionaries (Keith and Talbot) lingered for a few days, and then began their travels. The tour extended from the Piscataqua River to North Carolina, and covered a distance of more than eight hundred miles. Keith's labours were most abundant in Pennsylvania and New York; he showed an earnest desire to convert the Quakers, but he found them little disposed to listen to him. In 1704, he returned to England; but Talbot remained in America.

Keith was a prolific and forceful writer. An ardent controversialist, he was uncompromising and frequently severe. The journal of his American tour was published in 1706, after he had become Vicar of Edburton in Sussex. There he remained until his death in 1716.

Robert Proud, a member of the Society of Friends, characterises George Keith in the following language:

> "He was a man of quick, natural parts, and considerable literary abilities; acute in argument, and very ready and able in logical disputations and nice distinctions, on theological subjects; but said to be of a brittle temper, and overbearing disposition of mind; not sufficiently tempered and qualified with that Christian disposition and charity, which give command over the human passions,—the distinguishing characteristic of true Christianity; of which he himself had not only made high profession, but also, in his younger years, as appears by his writing, had a good understanding."

A contemporary account of Keith appears in Bishop Burnet's *History of His Own Times:*

> "The Quakers have had a great breach made among them by one George Keith, a Scotchman, with whom I had my education at Aberdeen; he had been thirty-six years among them; he was esteemed the most learned man that ever was in that sect; he was well versed both in the Oriental tongues, in Philosophy, and Mathematics. After he had been above thirty years in high esteem among them, he was sent to Pennsylvania to have the chief direction of the education of their youth. In those parts, he said he first discovered that which had been always denied to him, or so disguised that he did not suspect it; but being far out of reach, and in a place where they were masters, they spoke out their mind

plainer, and it appeared to him that they were Deists, and that they turned the whole doctrine of the Christian Religion into allegories; chiefly those which relate to the death and resurrection of Christ, and the reconciliation of sinners to God by virtue of his Cross; he, being a true Christian, set himself with great zeal against this, upon which they grew weary of him, and sent him back to England. At his return, he set himself to read many of their books, and then he discovered the mystery which was so hid from him that he had not observed it. Upon this, he opened a new meeting, and, by a printed summons, he called the whole party to come and see the proof that he had to offer, to convince them of their errors. Few Quakers came to his meetings, but great multitudes of other people flocked about him; he brought the Quakers' books with him, and read such passages out of them as convinced his hearers that he had not charged them falsely; he continued these meetings, being still in outward appearance a Quaker, for some years, till, having prevailed as far as he saw any probability of success, he laid aside their exterior, and was reconciled to the Church, and is now in Holy Orders among us, and likely to do good service in undeceiving and reclaiming some of those misled enthusiasts."

This paragraph of Bishop Burnet was answered by Alexander Arscott, a writer of note among the Friends; and it was avowed that Keith, on his death-bed, expressed his regrets at forsaking the Quakers.

"The Bishop has told us, after a long detail of his performances, that he is now (in the year 1700) in Holy Orders amongst us, and likely to do good service in undeceiving and reclaiming some of those misled enthusiasts. But what if it should appear, after all, that he deeply repented of what he had done? I shall relate what has come to my knowledge, and leave the reader to judge of the truth of it. The fact, as related, is this—that one Richard Hayler, of Sussex, made a visit to George Keith on his death-bed, which visit was kindly taken by him; and, among other things that passed, George Keith expressed himself in these words: 'I wish I had died when I was a Quaker, for then I am sure it would have been well with my soul.' This I have from a person now living, of unquestioned reputation, who had it from the widow of the said Richard Hayler, and her sister, both since deceased, but persons of unblemished characters."

(The Keith bibliography is extensive. The facts related above all occur in the article on Keith, in *Sprague's Annals of the American Episcopal Pulpit,* with the exception of a couple of dates, which have been altered, and the usual abridgement.—E. L. P.)

The Excerpts from Keith's Journal.

(Page 50) *October* 1. From the Ferry by *New-York,* we came to *Reedhook* on *Long-Island,* where we waited for a fair Passage, and next Day we got over to *Staten-Island,* and from *Staten-Island* to *Amboy* in *East-Jersey.*

October 3. Sunday. I preached at *Amboy* in *East-Jersey;* the Auditory was small: My Text was *Tit.* 2:11, 12.[1] But such as were there, were well affected; some of them, of my former Acquaintance, and others who had been formerly *Quakers* but were come over to the Church, particularly *Miles Foster,* and *John Barclay* (Brother to *Robert Barclay,* who published the Apology for the Quakers) the Place has very few In-/ (Page 51) habitants. We were several Days kindly entertained by *Miles Forster* (sic) at his House there.

October 10, 1702. Sunday. We went to the Meeting of the Quakers at *Toponemes,* in Freehold in *East-Jersey,* who used to keep a separate Meeting from the other Quakers, for their gross Errors; and joined with me and my Friends in the Separation, about the Year 1692; and it happened to be their Yearly Meeting, where diverse came from *West-Jersey* and *Pensilvania:* One of their Preachers pray'd and preached before I began. After he had done, I used some of the Church Collects I had by heart, in Prayer; and after that, I preached on *Heb.* 5:9[2]. There was a considerably Auditory of diverse sorts; some of the Church, and some Presbyterians, besides the Quakers; they heard me without any Interruption, and the Meeting ended peaceably. Their two Speakers lodged in the same House with me that Evening, at the House of *Thomas Boels,* formerly a Quaker, but is now of the Church. I had some free Discourse with them about several weighty things: I told them, so far as they used their Gifts to instruct the Ignorant, and reclaim them from the vile Errors of Quakerism, they were to be commended; but that they

NOTE. *The original edition of the journal of George Keith (1639?-1716) has been followed in every particular; the errata will appear in the footnotes. The title and pagination are as follows:* A JOURNAL OF TRAVELS FROM NEW-HAMPSHIRE TO CARATUCK, ON THE CONTINENT OF NORTH-AMERICA. BY GEORGE KEITH, A. M. LATE MISSIONARY FROM THE SOCIETY FOR THE PROPAGATION OF THE GOSPEL IN FOREIGN PARTS; AND NOW RECTOR OF EDBURTON IN SUSSEX, LONDON, PRINTED BY JOSEPH DOWNING FOR BRAB. AYLMER AT THE THREE-PIGEONS OVER-AGAINST THE ROYAL-EXCHANGE IN CORNHILL, 1706. *(21 cm.; pp. 92.) The errata of the 1706 edition will alone be used.*

[1]*Titus 2:11, 12.* "*For the grace of God that bringeth salvation hath appeared to all men, teaching us that, denying ungodliness and worldly lusts, we should live soberly, righteously, and godly, in this present world.*"
[2]*Hebrews 5:9.* "*And being made perfect, he became the author of eternal salvation unto all them that obey him.*"

had taken upon them to Administer Baptism and the Lord's Supper to any, they were greatly to be blamed, having no due external Call, or Ordination, so to do.

October 11. Monday. We met again the next Day, and had the like Auditory: Their other Speaker pray'd and preached, and after that, I pray'd, using the same Collects as the Day before, and preached on 1 *Thes.* 5:19[3] without any Interruption, and the Meeting peaceably ended. I could blame nothing in the Matter of their second Spaker, nor in the former, except where he said in his Discourse, *That they who were in Christ, need not fear Hell.* I endeavoured to clear the Matter in my Dis-/ (Page 52) course, by distinguishing betwixt an Absolute Fear of Hell, such as the Wicked ought to have, and a Conditional Fear, which Good Men, even such who are in Christ, ought to have; and about this he and I had some private Discourse also betwixt us, but he was dissatisfied, and would not own, *That any who were in Christ, ought to have any Fear of Hell,* so much as Conditional.

October 17. Sunday. I preached at *Midleton* in *East-Jersey,* where, before Sermon, Mr. *Talbot* read the Church Prayers, and I preached on Mat. 28:19, 20.[4] One main part of my Sermon being to prove Infant-Baptism to be included in the Apostles Commission, as well as that of Adult Persons, there being several of the Auditory who were Anabaptists, who heard me civilly, without any Interruption; but most of the Auditory were Church People, or well affected to the Church.

October 24. Sunday. 1702. I preached at *Shrewsbury* in *East-Jersey* at a House near the Quakers Meeting-house, and it happened that it was the Time of the Quakers Yearly Meeting at *Shrewsbury:* My Text was 2 *Pet.* 2:1, 2.[5] The Church Prayers being read before Sermon, we had a great Congregation, generally well affected to the Church, and diverse of them were of the Church, and that Day I sent some Lines in Writing to the Quakers at their Yearly Meeting; which Mr. *Talbot* did read to them in their Meeting, wherein I desired them to give me a Meeting with them some Day of that Week, before their Meetings were concluded; in which Meeting, I offered to detect great Errors in their Authors Books, and they should have

---

[3] *I Thessalonians 5:19. "Quench not the Spirit."*

[4] *St. Matthew 28:19, 20. "Go ye therefore, and teach all nations, baptizing them in the name of the Father, and of the Son, and of the Holy Ghost: teaching them to observe all things whatsoever I have commanded you: and lo, I am with you alway, even unto the end of the world."*

[5] *II. St. Peter 2:12. "But these, as natural brute beasts made to be taken and destroyed, speak evil of the things that they understand not; and shall utterly perish in their own corruption."*

full Liberty to answer what they had to say in their Vindication. But they altogether refused my Proposition; and several Papers pass'd betwixt us: In some of their Papers, they used gross Reflections on the Church of *England,* as much as on me. We con-/ (Page 53) tinued our Meetings three days, as the Quakers did theirs. And the second Day of our Meeting at the same House, where we had formerly met, I detected the Quakers Errors out of their printed Books, particularly out of the Folio Book of *Edw. Burroughs* Works, collected and published by the Quakers after his Death, and did read the Quotations to the Auditory, laying the Pages open before such as were willing to read them, for their better Satisfaction, as some did read them.

Some of the Quotations were such as follow.

Page 126. *Their* (i. e. the Ministers) *Prophecy and Preaching would soon be ended, if they had not the Scripture to preach their Imaginations upon.*

Pag. 273. *Quakers Sufferings greater and more unjust than the Sufferings of Christ and the Apostles.*

Pag. 19. *He denies a written Word: . . . No other Word* (saith he) *do I own but Christ.*

Pag. 402. *He will revoke if any can prove, that the Scriptures call themselves the Word.*

Pag. 484. *The Spirit of God, the only standing Rule to walk by, not the Scriptures.*

Pag. 292. *The Flesh of Christ's Body Infinite.*

Pag. 515. *God and the Spirit, not Persons, but Infinite Beings.*

Pag. 698. *They* (i. e. the Quakers) *are One with the Father in Nature.*

Pag. 432. *All that Christians practise is become Idolatry.*

Pag. 27. *That which sinned could not be saved, &c.*

October 26, 1702. Tuesday. I preached again at *Shrewsbury* on *Mat.* 7:13.[6] In all these Meetings at *Shrewsbury, Midletoun* (sic), and *Toponemes,* or where-ever else, on *Nethersinks,* Mr. *Lewis Moris,* and diverse others of best Note in that Country, frequented the Congregations and Places where we preach-/ (Page 54) ed, and did kindly entertain us at their Houses, where we lodged as we traveled too and again; particularly Mr. *Moris,* Mr. *Innes,* Mr. *Johnston,* Mr. *Boels,* and Mr. *Read;* Mr. *Innes* being in Priest's Orders, has oft preached among them, and by Preaching, and Conferences frequently with Quakers and other sorts of People, as also by his pious Con-

---

[6]*St. Matthew 7:13.* *"Enter ye in at the strait gate: for wide is the gate, and broad is the way, that leadeth to destruction, and many there be which go in thereat."*

versation, has done much Good among them, and been very instrumental to draw them off from their Errors, and bring them over to the Church.

October 29. 1702. We arrived at *Burlington in West-Jersey.*

November 1. Sunday. We preached in the Town-House at *Burlington* (the Church not being then built) and we had a great Auditory of diverse sorts, some of the Church, and some of the late Converts from Quakerism. Mr. *Talbot* preached before Noon, and I in the Afternoon. My Text was, *John* 17:3[7] Col. *Hamilton,* then Governor of *West-Jersey,* was present both Forenoon and Afternoon, and at his Invitation we dined with him.

November 3. At *Burlington* I detected the Quakers Errors out of their great Authors, *George Fox* his great Mystery, and *Edward Burroughs* Folio Book, and others, having given the Quakers Preachers Notice two Days before, to come and defend their Principles and Authors; but none of them would appear in the Cause.

November 5. We arrived at *Philadelphia,* and were kindly received by the two Ministers there, and the Church People, and especially by the late Converts from Quakerism, who were become zealous Members of the Church.

November 8. Sunday. I preached in the Church of *Philadelphia,* at the Minister's Request, on *2 Pet.* 3:15, 16[8] in the Afternoon. Mr. *Talbot* preached there in the Forenoon. And again I preached another Sermon, on the same, that Evening, after six a Clock (it being usual once a Month to preach an Evening-Sermon in that town). We had a very great Auditory, so that the Church could/ (Page 55) not contain them, but many stayed without and heard.

That Week a Meeting of the Clergy being appointed to meet together at *New-York,* by general Consent, we accordingly did meet, being Seven, in number; at our Meeting we drew up an Account of the State of the Church in these *American* Parts of *Pennsylvania, West* and *East-Jersey,* and *New-York* Province; a Copy whereof we sent to the Honourable Society at *London, for the Propagation of the Gospel in Foreign Parts.* Colonel *Nicolson,* Governour of *Virginia,* to encourage us to meet, was so generous to bear our Charges, (I mean of all of us that lived not at *New-York*) besides his other great and generous Benefactions to the Building and Adorning many

[7]*St. John 17:3.* *"And this is life eternal, that they might know thee the only true God, and Jesus Christ, whom thou hast sent."*

[8]*II. St. Peter 3:15, 16.* *"And account that the long suffering of our Lord is salvation; even as our beloved brother Paul also according to the wisdom given unto him hath written unto you; as also in all his epistles, speaking in them of these things; in which are some things hard to be understood, which they that are unlearned and unstable wrest, as they do also the other Scriptures, unto their own destruction."*

Churches lately built in these Parts, whereof a particular Account has been given to the Honourable Society.

November 15. 1702. I preached at New-York on Revel. 3:20,[9] being Sacrament-Day.

November 22. Sunday. I preached again at *New-York,* on Rom. 6:17, 18[10] in the Forenoon, and Mr. *Talbot* in the Afternoon. My Lord *Cornbury,* Governour of *New-York* and the *Jerseys,* was very kind to us, and at his Invitation, we did eat at his Table both *Sundays* and other Times.

November 26. Thursday. I preached at *Hampsted* on *Long-Island* on *Acts* 26:18.[11]

November 29. 1702. I Preached again at *Hampsted,* on *Heb.* 8:10, 11, 12.

Sunday, *December* 3. 1702. I visited again the Quakers Meeting at *Flushing* on *Long-Island,* having obtained a Letter from my Lord *Cornbury,* to Two Justices of Peace to go along with me, to see that the Quakers should not interrupt me, as they had formerly done: But notwithstanding the Two Justices that came along with me, to signifie my Lord *Cornbury's* Mind, by his Letter to them, which was read to them in their Meeting by Mr. *Talbot,* they used the like interruption as formerly, and/ (Page 56) took no notice of my Lord *Cornbury's* Letter, more than if it had been from any private Person. They renewed their former accusation against me, that I had broke the Act of Toleration; I replyed, I had not broke it, for I did not interrupt any of them; they answer, I interrupted their silent Worship; I said, I know no Clause in *that Act,* that forbid the interruption of their silent Worship. I brought the Printed Act of Toleration with me to their Meeting, and Mr. *Talbot* did Read several Passages out of it to them, to shew that they had neither qualified their Meeting-Houses, nor their Preachers, as the Act required. But nothwithstanding they objected the Act of Toleration against me; when I objected it against them, they said, that Act did not extend to *America;* Behold their Partiality! We stayed and heard three of their Speakers one after another, though it was very grievous to us to hear so much nonsense, and perversion of Scripture, uttered by them; and all this upon pretence of being moved by the Spirit of God. Their chief

[9]*Revelation 3:20.* "*Behold, I stand at the door, and knock; if any man hear my voice, and open the door, I will come in to him, and will sup with him, and he with me.*"

[10]*Romans 6:17, 18.* "*But God be thanked, that ye were the servants of sin, but ye have obeyed from the heart that form of doctrine which was delivered you. Being then made free from sin, ye became the servants of righteousness.*"

[11]*Acts 26:18.* "*To open their eyes, and to turn them from darkness to light, and from the power of Satan unto God, that they may receive forgiveness of sins, and inheritance among them which are sanctified by faith that is in me.*"

Speaker, who is a most ignorant Person, said, *Balak had sent Balaam to Curse the People of God:* His Sense and perverse Application of that historical Passage of Scripture, is easie to understand without Commentary.   After they had done, they generally went away, Speakers and others; but many, who were not Quakers, stayed, and heard me resume and detect the gross Perversions and Misapplications of the Scriptures, which they had made.   And after this, I detected out of a Book of *George Whitehead,* called *The Divinity of Christ,* his vile Error concerning Christ, both with respect to his Godhead and Manhood, and I did read the Passages out of his Book in the Hearing of the Auditory.   In his said Book, he blames his Opponent, *Thomas Vincent,* for affirming,/ (Page 57) that the Son proceeded from the Father by an eternal Act of Generation, and chargeth it with Confusion and Nonsense.   Also in the same Book he brings many Places of Scripture, all which he grosly perverts, to prove that Christ suffered as God.   And in the Appendix to his Book, he blames his Opponent, *Tho. Dawson,*[12] for saying, *Christ, as Man, had a created Soul and Body;* and from his so saying, doth infer, by way of Quary, Doth not this render him a Fourth Person?   And *George Fox* in his Preface to that Book, most ignorantly and perversely argues against the Three Persons in the Godhead, inferring, by way of Quary, (their common way of Disputing) Doth not this render them Four Persons? Just as *John Whiting,* a late Author among them, in his Book called, *Judas and the Chief Priests,* doth ridicule that Passage in the Litany of the Church of *England, O Holy Blessed and Glorious Trinity, Three Persons and One God;* inferring from that this there should be Four Persons; for that Three and One are Four: Whereas in the Act of Toleration, there is an express Clause that excludes all such from the Benefit of the Act, *That either in their Speaking or Writing, deny the Holy Trinity, as taught and professed in the Church of* England: And yet these very Persons that thus revile and ridicule the Doctrine of the *Holy Trinity as taught in the Church of* England, are mighty Pleaders for their Liberty by the Act of Toleration; as if not only their Meetings and Preachings were Tolerated, but Authorized by the Act.

December 6. 1702. I Preached at Oysterbay in the Town-House, on Rom. 10:7, 8, 9.[13]   And we were kindly entertained at the House of Mr. *Edward White* above mentioned.

[12]*Thomas Danson, Errata (1706 ed.): "p. 57, 1, 6, for Dawson r. Danson."*
[13]*Romans 10:7, 8, 9.   "Or, Who shall descend into the deep? (that is, to bring up Christ again from the dead.) But what saith it? The word is nigh thee, even in thy mouth, and in thy heart: that is, the word of faith, which we preach; that if thou shalt confess with thy mouth the Lord Jesus, and shalt believe in thine heart that God hath raised him from the dead, thou shalt be saved."*

December 13. I preached at *Staten-Island* in the Town-House, on *Titus* 2:11, 12.[14]

December 20. 1702. I preached at Dr. *Johnston's* at *Nethersinks,* on *Rev.* 22:14.[15]

(Page 58) *December* 25. Friday, *being* Christmas day. I preached at the House of Mr. *Morris,* on Luke 2:10,11.[16] And after Sermon, diverse of the Auditory received with us the Holy Sacrament; both Mr. Morris and his Wife, and diverse others. Mr. *Talbot* did administer it.

Decemb. 27. Sunday. 1702. I preached in *Shrewsbury* Town, near the Quaker Meeting-House, at a Planter's House, and had a considerable Auditory of Church People lately converted from Quakerism, with diverse others of the Church of best Note in that Part of the Country. My text was *Heb.* 8:10, 11.[17]

January 1. Friday. I preached at the House of Mr. *Thomas Boels* at *Freehold* in *East Jersey:* My text was *Isaiah* 59:20, 21.[18] Before Sermon, after the Church Prayers, I baptized all his Children; two Sons and three Daughters. He was formerly a Quaker, but is now come over to the Church; also a Son of *Samuel Dennis,* a late Convert from Quakerism.

January 3. Sunday. 1702. I preached again at his House, on the same Text, and before Sermon, Mr. *Talbot* baptized two Persons belonging to the Family of *John Read,* formerly a Quaker, but was lately come over to the Church with all his Children; one Son and two Daughters. His two Daughters were baptized by Mr. *Talbot, October* 24. 1702. As also the same Day were baptized *William Leads* and his Sister *Mary Leads,* late Converts from Quakerism to the Church:

[14]*Titus 2:11, 12.* "*For the grace of God that bringeth salvation hath appeared to all men, teaching us that, denying ungodliness and worldly lusts, we should live soberly, righteously, and godly, in this present world.*"

[15]*Revelation 22:14.* "*Blessed are they that do his commandments, that they may have right to the tree of life, and may enter in through the gates into the city.*"

[16]*St. Luke 2:10, 11.* "*And the angel said unto them, Fear not: for, behold, I bring you good tidings of great joy, which shall be to all people. For unto you is born this day in the city of David a Saviour, which is Christ the Lord.*"

[17]*Hebrews 8:10, 11.* "*For this is the covenant that I will make with the house of Israel after those days, saith the Lord; I will put my laws into their mind, and write them in their hearts; and I will be to them a God; and they shall be to me a people: and they shall not teach every man his neighbour, and every man his brother, saying, Know the Lord; for all shall know me, from the least to the greatest.*"

[18]*Isaiah 59:20, 21.* "*And the Redeemer shall come to Zion, and unto them that turn from transgression in Jacob, saith the Lord. As for me, this is my covenant with them, saith the Lord; My Spirit that is upon thee, and my words which I have put in thy mouth, shall not depart out of thy mouth, nor out of the mouth of thy seed, nor out of the mouth of thy seed's seed, saith the Lord, from henceforth and for ever.*"

And some Days before, at the House of *John Read,* Mr. *Talbot* baptized the Wife of *Alexander Neaper* and his three Children. Both he and his Wife had been Quakers, but were come over to the Church.

January 4. 1702. I came to the House of *Robert Ray* in *Freehold* in *East-Jersey,* accompanied with *Thomas Boels,* and lodged at his House that Night. At his and his Wife's Desire, I baptized all his Children; some Boys and some/ (Page 59) Girles, in number Five: they both had been Quakers. His Wife is come over to the Church, but he was not then come thoroughly off from Quakerism.

January 10. Sunday. I preached at *Burlington* at the House of Mr. *Revel,* on Mat. 6:33.[19]. And I baptized a Man's Child who was a Church-man, where I had a large Auditory.

(Page 62, line 10) *February* 21. Sunday. 1702. I preached at *Burlington* in *West-Jersey,* on Rom. 10:7, 8, 9[20] and *Feb.* 22 I baptized the Wife of Mr. *Rob. Wheeler* and his three Children, and five others; in all 9 Persons. He and his Wife had been Quakers, but are come over to the Church. He did most kindly and hospitably entertain us at his House, *gratis,* the several times that we travelled to and fro in those Parts: And the like kind and free Entertainment he gives to all Ministers of the Church that travel that way.

(Page 73, next to last line) *August* 22. Sunday. I preached at the New Church at *Burlington,* on 2 *Sam.* 23:3, 4.[21] My Lord *Cornbury* was present and/ (Page 74) many Gentlemen who accompanied him, both from *New-York,* and the two *Jerseys,* having had his Commission to be Governour of *West* and *East-Jersey,* Read at the Town-House there, some Days before. It was the first Sermon that was Preached in that Church.

August 29. Sunday. I preached again at the Church in *Burlington,* on *Jam.* 1:22.[22]

[19]*St. Matthew 6:33.* *"But seek ye first the kingdom of God, and his righteousness; and all these things shall be added unto you."*

[20]*Romans 10:7, 8, 9.* *"Or, Who shall descend into the deep? (that is, to bring up Christ again from the dead.) But what saith it? The word is nigh thee, even in thy mouth, and in thy heart: that is, the word of faith, which we preach: that if thou shalt confess with thy mouth the Lord Jesus, and shalt believe in thine heart that God hath raised him from the dead, thou shalt be saved."*

[21]*II. Samuel 23:3, 4.* *"The God of Israel said, the Rock of Israel spake to me, He that ruleth over men must be just, ruling in the fear of God. And he shall be as the light of the morning, when the sun riseth, even a morning without clouds; as the tender grass springing out of the earth by clear shining after rain."*

[22]*St. James 1:22.* *"But be ye doers of the word, and not hearers only, deceiving your own selves."*

Sept. 5. Sunday. I preached at *Philadelphia,* on *Acts* 2:41, 42[23] being Sacrament Day.

Sept. 12. Sunday. I preached at the Church in *Burlington,* a Second Sermon, on *Jam.* 1:22.[24] Mr. *Talbot* preached that Day at *Chester* in *Pensilvania.*

Sept. 15. I preached at *Will. Hewlins* in *West-Jersey,* on *Tit.* 2:11.[25]

Sept. 19. Sunday. I preached at *Philadelphia* in the Afternoon, on *Mat.* 16:6.[26]

Sept. 21. Tuesday. I preached at *Philadelphia,* on *Jude* 3.[27] This Week being the time of the Quakers yearly Meeting in *Philadelphia,* the Minister of *Philadelphia,* the Reverend Mr. *Evans,* with the consent of the Vestry, having agreed together with us, to have both Prayers and Sermons at the Church in *Philadelphia,* all the Days that the Quakers had their Meetings in that Week, which use to continue three Days; there happens commonly in that Week to be a great concourse of People at *Philadelphia,* not only Quakers, but also of many others, as at some great Fair.

Sept. 21. Tuesday. Mr. *Talbot* went to the Quakers Meeting at *Philadelphia,* that met at the New Meeting-House, called, the *Banck-Meeting,* about 9 of the Clock in the Forenoon, and began to read a Paper to them which I had Writ, containing some Observations on the Attestation, taken and Signed by some of the most noted Quakers in *West-Jersey,* in order to their being made Members of the Council in the Province of *West* and *East-Jersey.*/ (Page 75) The Quakers were so rude, that they pushed him on the Breast, and drove him by violence from the threshold of the Door, where he stood; yet he continued Reading, till he had finished it; but by the Tumult that the Quakers raised he was little heard. After which, I went in to their Meeting-House, and stood up on a Bench to Read it in their hearing within doors, but I had scarce read three Lines, till a Quaker, whose Name I spare, pulled it out of my Hand with great violence, and some of them overturned the Bench I stood upon, but I had no hurt, Praised be God; for as I was falling, some that were not Quakers

---

[23]*Acts 2:41, 42.* "*Then they that gladly received his word were baptized: and the same day there was added unto them about three thousand souls. And they continued steadfastly in the apostles' doctrine and fellowship, and in breaking of bread, and in prayers.*"

[24] *See note (22).*

[25]*Titus 2:11.* "*For the grace of God that bringeth salvation hath appeared to all men.*"

[26]*St. Matthew 16:6.* "*Then Jesus said unto them, Take heed and beware of the leaven of the Phariseees and of the Sadducees.*"

[27]*St. Jude 3.* "*Beloved, when I gave all diligence to write unto you of the common salvation, it was needful for me to write unto you, and exhort you that ye should earnestly contend for the faith which was once delivered unto the saints.*"

supported me with their shoulders till my Feet gently touched the Ground; another Person that was no Quaker, pulling the said Paper out of the Quakers hand, it was torn in two pieces betwixt them; but by the order of a Justice of Peace, who was no Quaker, the Quaker returned to me that torn piece of the Paper which he had kept. Of this Rude and Disorderly Carriage of the Quakers at the same Place, the said Day, diverse Persons of Good Credit gave an Affidavit before a Justice of Peace at *Philadelphia*. I need not here recite the Contents of my Observations on these Quakers Attestation, for the like Observations have been made by another hand, and published in Print lately, in these *American* parts, and perhaps may be Reprinted at *London* ere long.

Sept. 26. Sunday. I preached in *Burlington* Church, a third Sermon, on *Jam.* 1:22[28] in the Forenoon, and Mr. *Talbot* in the Afternoon.

October 3. Sunday. I preached in *Burlington* Church, on *Heb.* 8:10, 11, 12[29] both Forenoon, and Afternoon, and read the Prayers before Sermon.

(Page 76) *October* 10. Sunday. 1703. I preached at *Toponemes* in *Freehold* in *East-Jersey,* on *Acts* 2:41, 42[30] and had a considerable Auditory, diverse of them late Converts from Quakerism to the Church. Mr. *Innesse* above mentioned did read the Prayers. Mr. *Talbot* staid to preach in several places in *Pensilvania,* and *West-Jersey,* for some time.

October 17. Sunday. I preached at *Shrewsbury* near the Quakers Meeting there, on *Psal.* 103:17, 18,[31]

October 24. Sunday. I preached again there, on *Heb.* 8:10, 11.[32] And Mr. *Innesse* Baptized two Men and a Child.

[28]*St James 1:22.* "*But be ye doers of the word, and not hearers only, deceiving your own selves.*"

[29]*Hebrews 8:10, 11, 12.* "*For this is the covenant that I will make with the house of Israel after those days, saith the Lord; I will put my laws into their mind, and write them in their hearts: and I will be to them a God, and they shall be to me a people: and they shall not teach every man his neighbor, and every man his brother, saying, Know the Lord: for all shall know me, from the least to the greatest. For I will be merciful to their unrighteousness, and their sins and their iniquities will I remember no more.*"

[30]*Acts 2:41, 42.* "*Then they that gladly received his word were baptized: and the same day there were added unto them about three thousand souls. And they continued steadfastly in the apostles' doctrine and fellowship, and in breaking of bread, and in prayers.*"

[31]*Psalm 103:17, 18.* "*But the mercy of the Lord is from everlasting to everlasting upon them that fear him, and his righteousness unto children's children; to such as keep his covenant, and to those that remember his commandments to do them.*"

[32]*Hebrews 8:10, 11.* "*For this is the covenant that I will make with the house of Israel after those days, saith the Lord; I will put my laws into their mind, and write them in their hearts: and I will be to them a God, and they shall be to me a people: and they shall not teach every man his neighbor, and every man his brother, saying, Know the Lord: for all shall know me, from the least to the greatest.*"

October 31. Sunday. I preached at *Amboy* in *East-Jersey,* on *Titus* 2:11, 12, 13, 14.[33]

November 3. I preached at *And. Craig's* in the *Township* of *Elizabeth Town,* on 2 *Pet.* 1:5[34] and Baptized his Four Children.

November 4. I Baptized the Children of *Andrew Hanson.*[35] Eight in Number; He and his Wife are come over from Quakerism to the Church. And *November* 3. I Baptized seven Children of a Widow-Woman there.

(Page 78, line 7) *December* 12. Sunday. I preached at *Amboy,* at my Lord *Cornbury's* Lodging, where he was present, and many with him. My Text was *John* 12:35, 36.[36]

December 19. Sunday. I preached at the House of Col. *Tomsley*[37] in *Elizabeth-Town,* both Forenoon and Afternoon, on 1 *Pet.* 2:9.[38] Many of that Town having been formerly a sort of Independents, are become well affected to the Church of *England,* and desire to have a Minister of the Church of *England* sent to them: There I baptized a Child of Mr. *Shakmaple.*

December 25. Christmas-day. I preached at *Amboy* in *East-Jersey,* on 1 *Tim.* 3:16.[39]

(a) *December* 26. Sunday. Mr. Talbot preached there on *Psal.* 125 and baptized a Young Man, called *John Brown,* who had a Quaker Education, and a Young Woman.

December 21. 1703. I preached at Capt. *Bishops* by *Ravai-River* in *East-Jersey,* on *Jude* 20[40] and baptized a Child of *Robert Wright.*

December 29. Wednesday. I preached at the Independents Meeting-House in *Woodbridge,* at the Desire of Mr. *Shepherd,* and some

---

[33]*Titus 2:11, 12, 13, 14.* *"For the grace of God that bringeth salvation hath appeared to all men, teaching us that, denying ungodliness and worldly lusts, we should live soberly, righteously, and godly, in this present world; looking for that blessed hope, and the glorious appearing of the great God and our Saviour Jesus Christ; who gave himself for us, that he might redeem us from all iniquity, and purify unto himself a peculiar people, zealous of good works."*

[34]*II. St. Peter 1:5.* *"And besides this, giving all diligence, add to your faith virtue; and to virtue, knowledge."*

[35]*Andrew Hemton.* Errata (1706 ed.): "*p. 76, 1, 16, for Henson r. Hemton.*"

[36]*St. John 12:35, 36.* *"Then Jesus said unto them, Yet a little while is the light with you. Walk while you have the light, lest darkness come upon you: for he that walketh in darkness knoweth not whither he goeth. While ye have light, believe in the light, that ye may be the children of light."*

[37]*Col. Tounsly.* Errata (1706 ed.): "*p. 78, 1. 10, for Tomsley, r. Tounsly.*"

[38]*I. St. Peter 2:9.* *"But ye are a chosen generation, a royal priesthood, a holy nation, a peculiar people; that ye should shew forth the praises of him who hath called you out of darkness into his marvelous light."*

[39]*I. St. Timothy 3:16.* *"And without controversy great is the mystery of godliness: God was manifested in the flesh, justified in the Spirit, seen of angels, preached unto the Gentiles, believed on in the world, received up into glory."*

[40]*St. Jude 20.* *"But ye, beloved, building up yourselves on your most holy faith, praying in the Holy Ghost."*

others there, on 1 *Tim.* 3:16.⁴¹ After Sermon Mr. *Shepherd* kindly entertained us at his House.

December 30. Thursday. I preached at *Piscataway* in *East Jersey,* on *Rom.* 10:6, 7, 8, 9.⁴²

January 2. Sunday. I preached at *Amboy* on *Heb.* 8:10, 11.⁴³

(b) *January* 9. Sunday. (b) I preached at the House of Dr. *Johnston* on *Nethersinks,* on *Psal.* 119. v. 113⁴⁴ and had a considerable Auditory.

January 16. Sunday. I preached at Mr. *Morris* House at the Falls of *Shrewsbury* in *East-Jersey,* on 2 *Cor.* 5:17.⁴⁵

(Page 79) *January* 23. Sunday. I preached again at Mr. *Morris* House on 2 *Pet.* 1:5.⁴⁶

(c) *January* 30. Sunday. (c) I preached at the House of Mr. *Thomas Boles* in *Freehold* in *East-Jersey,* on 1 *Cor.* 15:58.⁴⁷

February 6. Sunday. I preached at the House of Mr. *John Read* in *Freehold* in *East-Jersey,* on *Psal.* 119:96.⁴⁸

February 13. Sunday. I preached at *Burlington* Church in *West-Jersey,* on 1 *Cor.* 15:58.⁴⁹

(Page 80, line 4) During the most part of Winter, in the Year 1703, Mr. *Talbot,* by my free Consent, did travel in diverse other Parts in *Pensilvania, West* and *East-Jersey,* Preaching and Baptizing many in those Parts where I was not with him. For the greater Service of God and his Church, we did oft travel separately, (being still one in Heart and Affection) and I had very good Friends that

---

⁴¹*See note (39).*

⁴²*Romans 10:6, 7, 8, 9. "But the righteousness which is of faith speaketh on this wise, Say not in thine heart, Who shall ascend into heaven? (that is, to bring Christ down from above:) Or, Who shall descend into the deep? (that is, to bring up Christ again from the dead.) But what saith it? The word is nigh thee, even in thy mouth, and in thy heart: that is, the word of faith, which we preach; that if thou shalt confess with thy mouth the Lord Jesus, and shalt believe in thine heart that God hath raised him from the dead thou shalt be saved."*

⁴³*Hebrews 8:10, 11. "For this is the covenant that I will make with the house of Israel after those days, saith the Lord; I will put my laws into their minds, and write them in their hearts: and I will be to them a God, and they shall be to me a people: and they shall not teach every man his neighbor, and every man his brother, saying, Know the Lord: for all shall know me, from the least to the greatest."*

⁴⁴*Psalm 119:113. "I have vain thoughts: but thy law do I love."*

⁴⁵*II. Corinthians 5:17. "Therefore if any man be in Christ, he is a new creature: old things are passed away; behold, all things are become new."*

⁴⁶*II. St. Peter 1:5. "And besides this, giving all diligence, add to your faith virtue; and to virtue, knowledge."*

⁴⁷*I. Corinthians 15:58. "Therefore, my beloved brethren, be ye steadfast, unmoveable, always abounding in the work of the Lord, forasmuch as ye know that your labour is not in vain in the Lord."*

⁴⁸*Psalm 119:96. "I have seen an end of all perfection: but thy commandment is exceeeding broad."*

⁴⁹*See note (47).*

travelled with me in his Absence, to accompany me from place to place, in all those places where I travelled.

(Page 82, line 8) Thus I have given an entire Journal of my two Years Missionary Travel and Service, on the Continent of *North-American,* betwixt *Piscataway-River* in *New-England,* and *Coretuck* in *North-Carolina;* of extent in Length about Eight Hundred Miles; within which Bounds are Ten distinct Colonies and Governments, all under the Crown of *England,* viz. *Piscataway, Boston, Rhod-Island, Connecticut, New-York, East and West-Jersey, Pensilvania, Maryland, Virginia,* and *North-Carolina.*

I travelled twice over most of those Governments and Colonies, and I preached oft in many of them, particularly in *Pensilvania, West* and *East-Jersey,* and *New-York* Provinces, where we continued longest, and found the greatest Occasion for our Service.

As concerning the Success of me, and my Fellow-Labourer Mr. *John Talbot's* Ministry, in the Places where we travelled, I shall not say much; yet it is necessary that something be said, to the Glory of God alone, to whom it belongs, and to the Encouragement of others, who may hereafter be imployed in the like Service.

In all the places where we travelled and preached, we found the People generally well affected to the Doctrine that we preached among them, and they did generally join with us decently in the Liturgy, and Publick Prayers, and Administration of the Holy Sacraments, after the Usage of the Church of *England,* as we had Occasion to use them.

(Page 83) And where Ministers were wanting, (as they were wanting in many Places) the People earnestly desired us to present their Request to the *Honourable Society,* to send Ministers unto them, which accordingly I have done: and in answer to their Request, the Society has sent to such Places as seemed most to want, a considerable Number of Missionaries.

Beside the general Success we had, (praised be God for it) both in our Preaching, and much and frequent Conference with People of diverse Perswasions, many of which had been wholly Strangers to the Way of the Church of *England;* who, after they had observed it in the Publick Prayers, and reading the Lessons out of the Holy Scripture of the Old and New Testament, and the Manner of the Administration of Baptism, and the Lord's Supper, were greatly affected with it, and some of which declared their great Satisfaction and the Esteem they had of the Solemn and edifying manner of our Worship and Administration, far above whatever they could observe in other Ways of Worship known to them.

To many, our Ministry was as the Sowing the Seed and Planting, who, probably, never so much as heard one orthodox Sermon preached to them, before we came and preached among them, who received the Word with Joy; and of whom we have good Hope, that they will be as the good Ground, *That bringeth forth Fruit, some Thirty, some Sixty, and some an Hundred Fold.* And to many others it was a Watering to what had been formerly Sown and Planted among them; some of the good Fruit whereof we did observe, to the Glory of God, and our great Comfort, while we were with them, even such Fruits of true Piety and good Lives, and sober and righteous Living, as prove the Trees to be good from which they did proceed.

(Page 84) Many or most of those who had borne the Name of *Separatist Quakers* (for their leaving the Meetings of the Quakers, because of Opposition to the great Fundamentals of the Christian Faith, and had embraced the Doctrine they heard preached by us, concerning the Way of Salvation by Faith in Jesus Christ, both God and Man, as he outwardly came in the Flesh, died for our Sins, and rose again, &c. about the Years 1691 and 1692, and had set up distinct Meetings,) we found had joined with the Church of *England* Congregation at *Philadelphia,* before our Arrival, when we came among them; they received us with great Joy and Satisfaction to hear us preach what tended to their farther Confirmation in the Christian Faith, and in Communion with the Church of *England.* And they expressed the great Benefit they had received by my several Epistles I wrote to them from *London,* about the Years 1698 and 1699, to answer the Scruples and Objections some of them had made to me in some of their Letters, against joining with the Church of *England,* which they told me, gave them great Satisfaction, by the Blessing of God, to join with the Church, and with which they joined soon after. And the like Service my Epistles did to others of their Friends, in *East* and *West-Jersey,* and other Parts of that Country, to whom they had imparted them, at my Desire.

The Reverend Mr. *Evan Evans,* the Minister of the Church of *England* Congregation at *Philadelphia,* informed me, that (beside the considerable Number of Converts to the Church from Quakerism, that the former Minister, the Reverend Mr. *Claiton* had baptized) by his Account, since he was Minister there, he had baptized of Men, Women, and Children, in *Pensilvania* and *West-Jersey,* of *English* and *Welsh,* about Five hundred; many, or most of them, having been Quakers, and the Chil-/ (Page 85) dren of Quakers, and Quakerly affected; and beside these, many who had left Quakerism, and had joined to the

Church, had been baptized in Infancy, not having been born of Quaker Parents.

Since our Arrival into those *American Parts,* by the Blessing of God upon our Labours among them, in *Pensilvania, West* and *East-Jersey,* and *New-York* Province, there have been, by modest Computation, at least two hundred Persons baptized of Quakers, and their Children, and Servants, and of such who were Quakerly affected, by Mr. *Talbot,* and Mr. *Evans,* and by me, and some by the Reverend Mr. *Vesey,* Minister of *New-York,* in that Town. And beside these, many who had been baptized in Infancy, have come off from Quakerism and joined to the Church in these Countries, since we travelled and preached among them, and had much Conference with diverse of them in private from House to House. Diverse also of Dissenters formerly disaffected to the Church, who were not Quakers, are become well affected to the Church, and her Publick way of Worship, and Administration of the holy Sacraments, as well as to the Truth of Her Doctrine, since our Labouring among them, both in *East* and *West-Jersey,* and else where; so that, God be Praised, almost in all these Countries where we Travelled and Laboured, in some of which there was little to be observed but Quakerism, or Heathenism, which are much one (and if we may believe some of the Quakers great Authors, they are altogether one, Viz. the Religion of the Quakers, and of such Heathens, who were obedient to the Light within them, but without all Faith and Knowledge of Christ, as he came in the Flesh.) I say, in all these Countries almost, by the Blessing of God on our Labours, there are good Materials prepared for the Building of Churches, of Liv-/ (Page 86) ing Stones, as soon as, by the good Providence of God, Ministers shall be sent among them, who have the discretion and due qualifications requisite to Build with them. The Truth of which some of the late Missionaries have found, to their great Comfort, who, as soon as they Arrived into these Parts, unto which they were sent, did find a People prepared to receive them; so that what others had sown before them, they have Reaped, and I hope will more abundantly Reap.

In *Pensilvania,* where there was but one Church of *England* Congregation settled, to-wit, at *Philadelphia* (and even that but of few Years standing) at our Arrival there; there are now, Blessed be God, Five Church of *England* Congregations supplied with Ministers, and who have convenient Churches, where the People assemble constantly every Lord's Day to the Prayers and Sermons, and where the Holy Sacraments are duly Administered, according to the Church of *England.* The places in *Pensilvania,* where these Churches are set up, are, the first, *Philadelphia,* the second *Chester* or *Upland,* the third *Franckfort* alias *Oxford,* the fourth *New-Castle,* the fifth *Apoquimene.*

At *Philadelphia,* they have Prayers in the Church, not only on the Lord's Days, and other holy Days, but all *Wednesdays* and *Fridays* weekly, and the Sacrament of the Lord's Supper administered Monthly, and the Number of the Communicants considerable. The Church is commonly well filled with People every Lord's Day, and when they are fully assembled, both of the Town and Country that belong to that Congregation, they may well be reckoned, by modest Computation, to amount to Five Hundred Persons of Hearers. But sometimes there are many more; and generally the Converts from Quakerism, are good Examples, both/ (Page 87) for frequenting the Church Prayers, and frequent partaking of the Lord's-Supper, with zeal and devotion, and also of sober and virtuous Living in their daily conversation, to the frustrating the lying Prophecies and Expectations of the Quaker Preachers especially, who used to Prophecy, that whoever left the Profession of Quakers, after that should be good for nothing, but as unsavoury Salt, to be trod under foot of Men. But to God's Praise be it said, they may be generally compared with the best Quakers for their Morals, and far to exceed many of them in that respect; and which greatly casts the Ballance, *that the Morals* of those converted from Quakerism, both in *England* and *America,* or any where else, are Built on the Foundation of the Prophets and Apostles, *Jesus Christ being the head corner Stone,* which the Quaker Morals (no more than the Heathens) are not Built upon.

At *Burlington* in *West-Jersey,* Twenty Miles distant from Philadelphia, on the other side of *Delaware-River,* there is now a settled Congregation, with a fixed Minister, to-wit, the Reverend Mr. *John Talbot,* my Fellow Labourer, where there is a large Congregation, and a considerable Number of Communicants, many of them having been formerly Quakers, and Quakerly affected, or such as were of no particular denomination. And such of them as had not been Baptized in Infancy, have received Baptism, partly by Mr. *Evans,* and partly by Mr. *Talbot,* and some of them by me. Mr. *Talbot* has Baptized most of them who have been Baptized, since our Arrival among them, and particularly all the Children, both Males and Females, of *William Budd,* who formerly was a Quaker-Preacher, but is come over from Quakerism, to the Church, with diverse others of the Neighbourhood,/ (Page 88) in the Country about the Town of *Burlington,* who come usually to the Church at *Burlington* on the Lord's-Day; some of them, Six, Eight, and some of them Ten, or Twelve Miles, and some of them more.

In some other Places they are Building Churches, both in *West* and *East-Jersey*.

The place at *Franckfort in Pensilvania,* where the Congregation assembles on the Lord's-Day, is called, *Trinity Chappel,* it was formerly a Quaker Meeting-House, Built, or fitted by Quakers, but some time ago has been given to the Church, by such who had the Right to it; Some Land adjoining was given by a Person well affected to the Church, for the use of the Minister, who should reside there, for a House, Garden, and small Orchard.

I can say little to any Success we had in *America,* amongst the other sort of Quakers, though, as the above-written Journal showeth, I Laboured much among them, in true Love, and good Will; but they being misled, and prejudiced by their Leaders, seemed too generally to reject my Labour of Love; however, I am not without hope, that the Seed that God had enabled me to Sow among them, will in some of them, in due time, take Root downward, and bear Fruit upward, though little of it doth yet appear.

There are now Thirteen Ministers in the Northern Parts of *America,* all placed within these two Years last past, and generally Supported and Maintained by the *Honourable Society for the Propagation of the Gospel in Foreign Parts.*

In all the Places where we travelled, the Governours of all the several Provinces, did very kindly treat us, and give us all possible Countenance and Encouragement that we could desire or expect.

BOOK FOUR

BIBLIOGRAPHY

BIBLIOGRAPHY.

I. WRITTEN BY TALBOT.

TALBOT, JOHN (1645-1727), AND DANIEL LEEDS (1652-1720).

The great mistery of Fox-craft discovered, and the Quaker plainness & sincerity demonstrated; first, to their great apostle George Fox; secondly, in their late subscribing the oath or act of abjuration. Introduced with two letter (*sic*) written by George Fox to Coll. Lewis Morris, deceased, exactly spell'd and pointed as in the originals, which are now to be seen in the Library at Burlington in New Jersey, and will be proved (by the likeness of the hand, &c.) to be the handwriting of the Quaker's learned Fox, is denied. To which is added, a Postscript, with some remarks on the Quakers Almanack for this year 1705. (N. Y.: Printed by William Bradford, 1705). pp. 16.

> This title is not in the Library of Congress. John Talbot, in his letter to George Keith, October 20th, 1704 (S. P. G., A-Series, II., #XXIII.), refers to the controversy with the Quakers, and to the part played by Daniel Leeds, 1652-1720, in the writing of pamphlets pertinent thereto.

II. BOOKS ABOUT TALBOT.

A. Sources.

ARCHIVES OF THE STATE OF NEW JERSEY. FIRST SERIES.

Documents relating to the colonial history of the state of New Jersey, edited by William A. Whitehead, Corresponding Secretary of the New Jersey Historical Society; Author of East Jersey Under the Proprietary Governments; Contributions to the Early History of Perth Amboy and the Surrounding Country; Editor of the Papers of Lewis Morris, and of an Analytical Index to the Colonial Documents of New Jersey, etc., etc. Volume IV. Administrations of Governor Robert Hunter and President Lewis Morris. 1709-1720. Newark, N. J.: Daily Advertiser Printing House, 1882. 8½ in., pp. xv., 464.

> See Index under Talbot.

COLLECTIONS OF THE PROTESTANT EPISCOPAL HISTORICAL SOCIETY.

Collections of the Protestant Episcopal Historical Society, for the year 1851. Published by order of the executive committee of the Society. New York: Stanford & Swords, publishers. 1851. 23¼ cm., pp. xliii., 187.

> The first 98 pages are devoted to Talbot material. The Keith journal of travels from New-Hampshire to Caratuck is reprinted.

KEITH, GEORGE (1639?-1716).

A journal of travels from New-Hampshire to Caratuck, On the Continent of North America. By George Keith, A. M. Late Missionary from the Society for the Propagation of the Gospel in Foreign Parts; and now Rector of Edburton in Sussex. London, Printed by Joseph Downing for Brab. Aylmer at the Three-Pigeons over-against the Royal-Exchange in Cornhill, 1706. 21 cm., pp. 92.

PERRY, WILLIAM STEVENS (1832-1898), editor.

Historical collections relating to the American Colonial Church edited by William Stevens Perry, D. D. Volume II.—Pennsylvania. Printed for the subscribers. MDCCCLXXI. (Two hundred and fifty Copies Printed. No. .... The Church Press, Hartford, Conn.) 4to.; pp. xxi., 607.

> See Index under Talbot; also pages 515-518 of the Notes. Some of the correspondence relating to the alleged consecration of Talbot and Welton is reprinted.

PERRY, WILLIAM STEVENS (1832-1898), editor.

Papers relating to the History of the Church in Maryland, A. D. 1694-1775. Edited by William Stevens Perry, D. D., LL. D. Privately printed. 1878. 4to.; pp. xii., 370.

> See Index under Talbot; the letters of Urmstone and Henderson throw light on the question of the consecration of Talbot and Welton to the episcopate.

SOCIETY FOR THE PROPAGATION OF THE GOSPEL IN FOREIGN PARTS.

Contemporaneous publications.

(1) Account of the Society . . . 1704.

(2) Annual sermons: 1702 et seq.

(3) Account of the Society . . . 1706.

(4) A collection of papers, printed by order of the Society . . 1706.

> The annual sermons, printed almost every year, contain valuable appendices regarding the work of individual missionaries and their several fields. Complete sets of the S. P. G. sermons and abstracts are in the John Carter Brown Library, the General Theological Seminary, and certain other American libraries; most of them are to be found in the New York Public Library.

B. General.

ALUMNI CANTABRIGIENSES.

Alumni Cantabrigienses; a biographical list of all known students, graduates and holders of office at the University of Cambridge from the earliest times to 1900. Compiled by John Venn . . . , and J. A. Venn . . . . .Part I.: From the earliest times to 1751. Vol. IV: Saal-Zuinglius. With an appendix containing additional information relative to previous volumes. Cambridge: At the University Press, 1927. 4 vols.

> John Talbot, p. 197. Very brief biographical sketch.

ANDERSON, JAMES STUART MURRAY (1800-1869).

The history of the Church of England, in the colonies and foreign dependencies of the British empire. By the Rev. James S. M. Anderson, M. A. chaplain in ordinary to the Queen, chaplain to the Queen Dowager, perpetual curate of St. George's Chapel, Brighton, and preacher of Lincoln's Inn. Vol. I. London: Francis & John Rivington; and Robert Folthrop & Co., Brighton. 1845. 8vo.; pp. xxviii., 482, 2 p. 1.

Vol. II. London: Francis & John Rivington, and Robert Folthrop, Brighton. 1848. 8vo.; pp. xvi., 769, 2 p. 1.

The history of the Church of England, in the colonies and foreign dependencies of the British empire. By the Rev. James S. M. Anderson, M. A. chaplain in ordinary to the Queen, preacher of Lincoln's Inn, and rector of Tormarton, Gloucestershire. Vol. III. London: Rivingtons, Waterloo Place. 1856. 8vo.; pp. xxiv., 807, 3 p. 1.

> Second edition: 1856.

BLOMEFIELD, FRANCIS.

An essay towards a topographical history of the county of Norfolk, containing a description of the towns, villages, and hamlets, with the foundations of monasteries, churches, chapel, chanteries, and other religious buildings . . . By Francis Blomefield. . . . Vol. I. . . . . Printed at Fersfield, 1739. 5 vols.

> See Index under Talbot.

BROXAP, HENRY (1865-   ).

The later non-jurors. By Henry Broxap, M. A. Cambridge, at the University Press. 1924. 23cm.; pp. xxiii., 360; 2 facsimiles.

> Reviews the Brett manuscript, which throws light on the alleged consecration of Talbot to the episcopate.

BURLESON, HUGH LATIMER (1865-1933), editor.

How our church came to our Country, a Series of Illustrated Papers, edited by Hugh L. Burleson, Milwaukee: Morehouse Publishing Company, 1920. Pp. 280.

"Beginnings in New Jersey;" pp. 49ff.

COLEMAN, LEIGHTON (1837-1907).

The Church in America. By Leighton Coleman, S. T. D., LL. D., Bishop of Delaware, U. S. A. With Map. New York: James Pott and Co. Astor Place. (1895.) 19 cm., pp. 391.

See Index under Talbot.

CROSS, ARTHUR LYON (1873-).

The Anglican Episcopate and the American colonies by Arthur Lyon Cross, Ph. D. instructor in history in the University of Michigan / sometime assistant in American history in Harvard University. New York / Longmans, Green, and Co. London and Bombay. 1902. 8vo.; pp. ix., 368, (1).

See Index under Talbot.

CROSS, ARTHUR LYON (1873-).

Schemes for Episcopal control in the colonies. American Historical Association, Annual Report, I. (1896), pp. 233-241.

Touches briefly on Talbot.

DEWEY, EDWARD H.

John Talbot.

Article in The Dictionary of American Biography, Vol. XVIII., pp. 278-280. Charles Scribner's Sons, New York. 1936.

EVANS, HUGH DAVEY (1792-1868).

An essay on the Episcopate of the Protestant Episcopal Church in U. S. A. Philadelphia: Herman Hooker, 1855.

This is cited by Edward H. Dewey in The Dictionary of American Biography. Copy in the New York Public Library and the Cathedral Library.

FULTON, JOHN (1834-1907).

The non-juring Bishops in America.

Monograph No. V. in William Stevens Perry: The History of the American Episcopal Church, post cit., Vol. I., pp. 541-560.

HAWKINS, ERNEST (1802-1868).

Historical notices of the missions of the Church of England in the North American colonies, previous to the independence of the United States: chiefly from the MS. documents of the Society for the Propagation of the Gospel in Foreign Parts. By Ernest Hawkins, B. D. Fellow of Exeter College, Prebendary of St. Paul's, and Secretary to the Society for the Propagation of the Gospel. "She stretcheth out her branches unto the sea, and her boughs unto the river."—Ps. LXXX. 11. London: B. Fellowes, Ludgate street. 1845. 8vo.; pp. xix., 447, 1 p. 1.

> See Index under Talbot.

HAWKS, FRANCIS LISTER (1798-1866).

Contributions to the Ecclesiastical History of the United States. By Francis L. Hawks, D. D., Rector of St. Thomas's Church, New York. Volume II. Maryland. New York: John S. Taylor, Theological and Sunday-School Bookseller, Brick Church Chapel, 1839. Sub-title: "A Narrative of Events connected with the Rise and Progress of the Protestant Episcopal Church in Maryland."

> Bears on the question of Talbot's consecration to the episcopate.

HILLS, GEORGE MORGAN (1825-1890).

History of the Church in Burlington, New Jersey; comprising the facts and incidents of nearly two hundred years, from original contemporaneous sources. By the Rev. George Morgan Hills, D. D., rector of St. Mary's Parish, and dean of the convocation of Burlington. Trenton, N. J.: William S. Sharp, printer. 1876. 8vo.; pp. 739.

> Second edition: 1885. pp. 831.
> Deals extensively with Talbot. The author is convinced that Talbot was consecrated bishop.

HILLS, GEORGE MORGAN (1825-1890).

John Talbot, the first bishop in North America.

> Pennsylvania Magazine of History and Biography, III., No. 1, pp. 32-55 (1879).
> This also appears in monograph form under the title: "The first bishop in North America. A monograph read before the Historical Society of Pennsylvania, 1878." By G. M. Hills. Philadelphia, 1879. pp. 28.

HILLS, GEORGE MORGAN (1825-1890).

The transfer of the Church in America from colonial dependence to the freedom of the republic. A sermon preached at the opening of the ninety-third annual convention of the diocese of New Jersey, in

St. Michael's Church, Trenton, May 30th, A. C. 1876. By the Rev.
George Morgan Hills . . . Printed by a vote of the convention. Trenton, N. J.: W. S. Sharp, steam-power book and job printer, 1876.
pp. 20.

Devoted largely to Talbot's work in New Jersey.

HUMPHREYS, DAVID (1689-1740).

An historical account of the Incorporated Society for the Propagation of the Gospel in Foreign Parts. Containing their Foundation,
Proceedings, and the Success of their Missionaries in the British Colonies, to the Year 1728. By David Humphreys, D. D., Secretary to
the Honourable Society. London, Printed by Joseph Downing, in
Bartholomew-Close, near West-Smithfield. MDCCXXX. 8vo.;
pp. 356.

An invaluable early narrative of the S. P. G. and the work of the
colonial missionaries.

JONES, WILLIAM NORTHEY (1866-   ).

The history of St. Peter's Church in Perth Amboy / New Jersey /
the oldest congregation of the church in the state of New Jersey /
from its organization in 1698 to the year of our Lord 1923 and the
celebration of the 225th anniversary of the parish / also a genealogy of
the families buried in the churchyard / By the Rev. W. Northey Jones,
M. A. rector of St. Peter's Church / Perth Amboy (1924). 23¾ cm.,
pp. 519; illus.

Contains several allusions to Talbot and his contemporaries.

LATHBURY, THOMAS (1798-1865).

A History of the Nonjurors: their controversies and writings; with
remarks on some of the rubrics in the Book of Common Prayer. By
Thomas Lathbury, M. A., author of "A History of the Convocation,"
"A History of the English Episcopacy from 1640 to 1662," etc., etc.
London: William Pickering, 1845. 8vo.; pp. x., (4), 530.

This book was cited by George Morgan Hills in substantiating the fact
of Talbot's consecration as bishop.

MANROSS, WILLIAM WILSON (1905-   ).

A history of the American Episcopal Church, by the Reverend
William Wilson Manross, fellow and tutor of the General Theological
Seminary. New York / Milwaukee: Morehouse Publishing Com-
pany. 1935. 20 cm.; pp. xvi., 404.

See Index under Talbot.

McConnell, Samuel David (1845-   ).

History of the American Episcopal Church from the planting of the colonies to the end of the Civil War. By S. D. McConnell, D. D., Rector of St. Stephen's Church, Philadelphia. Sixth edition. New York: Thomas Whittaker, 2 and 3 Bible House. 20 cm.; pp. xiv., 392, 11 p. 1.

> First edition: 1890.
> See Index under Talbot.

Overton, John Henry (1835-1903).

The Nonjurors. Their lives, principles, and writings. By J. H. Overton, D. D., rector of Gumley, and canon of Lincoln. New York: Thomas Whittaker, 1903. 22 cm.; pp. vi., 503.

> See pages 348-350. Talbot and Welton are listed among the bishops.

Pascoe, Charles Frederick (1854-   ).

Two Hundred Years of the S. P. G.: an historical account of the Society for the Propagation of the Gospel in Foreign Parts, 1701-1900. (Based on a digest of the Society's records.) By C. F. Pascoe, assistant secretary of the Society.

> "God is working His purpose out, as year succeeds to year:
> God is working His purpose out, and the time is drawing near—
> Nearer and nearer draws the time, the time that shall surely be,
> When the earth shall be filled with the glory of God, as the waters cover
>   the sea.
>
> All we can do is nothing worth, unless God blesses the deed,
> Vainly we hope for the harvest, till God gives life to the seed;
> Yet nearer and nearer draws the time, the time that shall surely be,
> When the earth shall be filled with the glory of God, as the waters cover
>   the sea." A. C. Ainger.
>
> "Lift up now thine eyes, and look . . . northward and southward, and east-
>   ward and westward. . . . Arise, walk through the land." Gen. xiii. 14-17.

Vol. I. London: Published at the Society's Office, 19 Delahy street, Westminster, S. W. 1901. (All rights reserved.) 4to.; pp. xli., (1) 500n.; illus.

Vol. II. 4to.; pp. (1), 501-1429; illus.

> An invaluable digest of the records of the S. P. G. and a key to the work accomplished by individual missionaries.

Perry, William Stevens (1832-1898).

The history of the American Episcopal Church 1587-1783 by William Stevens Perry, D. D., LL. D. Bishop of Iowa. In two volumes. Vol. I / The planting and growth of the American colonial Church

1587-1783. Projected by Clarence F. Jewett. Boston / James R. Osgood and Company 1885. 27 cm., pp. xx., 665.

> For Talbot material, see Chapters IX., XII., XIII.; Monograph V.; pp. 599-603. The Index is in Vol. II.

SCHUYLER, HAMILTON (1862-1933).

The Church in New Jersey.

> American Church Monthly, XXXI., pp. 133-144 (1932). Two pages devoted to Keith and Talbot.

SPRAGUE, WILLIAM BUELL (1795-1876).

Annals of the American Episcopal Pulpit; or commemorative notices of distinguished clergymen of the Episcopal Church in the United States, from the early settlement of the country to the close of the year eighteen hundred and fifty-five with an historical introduction. By William B. Sprague, D. D. New York: Robert Carter & Brothers, 530 Broadway. 1859. 23 cm., pp. xxi., 822.

> Keith and Talbot, pp. 25-33.

STILES, EZRA (1727-1795).

Extracts from the itineraries and other miscellanies of Ezra Stiles, D. D., LL. D., 1755-1794 with a selection from his correspondence / Edited under the authority of the corporation of Yale University by Franklin Bowditch Dexter, Litt. D. New Haven, Connecticut / Yale University Press MDCCCCXVI. 25 cm., pp. vi., (1), 620; illus.

STILES, EZRA (1727-1795).

Letters & papers of Ezra Stiles president of Yale College 1778-1795 presented to Yale University Library by Mrs. Edward S. Harkness / Edited by Isabel M. Calder / New Haven / Yale University Library / 1933. 27 cm., pp. x., 123; front., illus.

STILES, EZRA (1727-1795).

The Literary Diary of Ezra Stiles, D. D., LL. D. president of Yale College / Edited under the authority of the corporation of Yale University by Franklin Bowdith Dexter, M. A.

Volume I / January 1, 1769-March 13, 1776.

New York / Charles Scribner's Sons 1901. 25 cm., pp. 665; illus.

Volume II / March 14, 1776-December 31, 1781. 25 cm., pp. 573; illus.

Volume III / January 1, 1782-May 6, 1795. 25 cm., pp. (1), 648; illus.

TANNER, EDWIN PLATT (1874-   ).

The province of New Jersey 1664-1738 by Edwin P. Tanner, A. M. Sometimes Fellow in American History, Columbia University / Instructor in History in Syracuse University / Submitted in partial fulfilment of the requirements for the degree of doctor of philosophy in the Faculty of Political Science / Columbia University 1908. 23 cm., pp. xvi., 712.

> Studies in history, economics and public law, edited by the faculty of political science of Columbia University, Vol. XXX. See Index under Talbot.

TIFFANY, CHARLES COMFORT (1829-1908).

(American Church History) A history of the Protestant Episcopal Church in the United States of America by Charles C. Tiffany, D. D. archdeacon of New York. New York / Charles Scribner's Sons 1916. 20 cm., pp. xxiv., 593.

> Copyright, 1895, by The Christian Literature Company.
> Chapter VII.: The colonial Church in New Jersey.

WHITE, WILLIAM (1748-1836).

Memoirs of the Protestant Episcopal Church in the United States of America containing 1. A narrative of the organization and of the early measures of the Church / II. Additional statements and remarks / III. An appendix of original papers / by the Right Rev. William White, D. D. Edited with Notes and a Sketch of the Origin and Progress of the Colonial Church by the Rev. B. F. DeCosta. New York: E. P. Dutton & Company, 713 Broadway, 1880. 23¼ cm., pp. lvi., 474; front.

> See preliminary section; "Origin and progress of the colonial Church," for Talbot material.

III. MANUSCRIPT SOURCES.

A. Correspondence of John Talbot.

(NOTE:—Items 1 to 57 are from the Archives of the Society for the Propagation of the Gospel in Foreign Parts; Items 58 and 59 are from the Fulham Palace collection. The same have been transcribed or photofilmed for the Library of Congress, and these reproductions are accessible in the Manuscript Division of that Library.)

(1) 1702, Nov. 24. To Richard Gillingham. S. P. G. A-Series, I., #LVI.

(2) 1703, Apr. 10. To Richard Gillingham. S. P. G. A-Series, I., #CXIX.

(3) 1703, May 3. To Richard Gillingham. S. P. G. A-Series, I., #CXX.

(4) 1704, Sept. 1. To John Chamberlayne. S. P. G. A-Series, I.,
    #CXXV.
(5) 1704, Apr. 7. To John Chamberlayne. S. P. G. A-Series, I.,
    #CLXXXI.
(6) 1704, Oct. 20. To George Keith. S. P. G. A-Series, II., #XXIII.
(7) 1704, Oct. 22. To Mr. Whitfield. S. P. G. A-Series, II., #XXIV.
(8) 1705, Nov. 12. From Samuel Eburne. S. P. G. A-Series, II.,
    #CXIV.
(9) 1706, March 14. To S. P. G. S. P. G. A-Series, II., #CXLII.
(10) 1707, Apr. 16. To John Chamberlayne. S. P. G. A-Series, III.,
    #XLV.
(11) 1707, June 23. To John Chamberlayne. S. P. G. A-Series,
    III., #LXI.
(12) 1707, Sept. 4. To John Chamberlayne. S. P. G. A-Series, III.,
    #CXI.
(13) 1707, Dec. 13. To John Chamberlayne. S. P. G. A-Series, III.,
    #CLVIII.
(14) 1707, Dec. 13. To George Keith. S. P. G. A-Series, III.,
    #CLXXII.
(15) 1708, Feb. 14. To George Keith. S. P. G. A-Series, III.,
    #CLXXIII.
(16) 1708, Jan. 10. To John Chamberlayne. S. P. G. A-Series, III.,
    #CLXXXVI.
(17) 1708, Aug. 20 and 24. To John Chamberlayne. 2 letters. S. P.
    G. A-Series, IV., #LI., #LII.
(18) 1709, June 30. To John Chamberlayne. S. P. G. A-Series, V.,
    #XIX.
(19) 1709, Sept. 27. To John Chamberlayne. S. P. G. A-Series, V.,
    #42.
(20) 1712, Apr. 29. From Wm. Taylor. S. P. G. A-Series, VII., p.
    262, #9.
(21) 1712, Nov. 6. From Wm. Taylor. S. P. G. A-Series, VII., p.
    286, #32.
(22) 1713, April. To the clergy of New York and New Jersey, S. P.
    G. A-Series, VIII., p. 271.
(23) 1713, Aug. 13. To Wm. Taylor. S. P. G. A-Series, VIII., p.
    181, #49.
(24) 1713, Nov. 18. Signs address of Pennsylvania clergy. S. P. G.
    B-Series, I., #152, p. 545.
(25) 1713, Dec. 18. From Wm. Taylor. S. P. G. A-Series, VIII., p.
    327, #18.
(26) (1714, May 11, covering letter.) To Gen. Nicholson. S. P. G.
    A-Series, IX., p. 208, #10.

(27) 1714, Oct. 28. To Wm. Taylor. S. P. G. A-Series, IX., p. 167, #40.

(28) 1714, Dec. 17. From Wm. Taylor. S. P. G. A-Series, IX., p. 252, #18.

(29) 1715, Apr. 7. From Wm. Taylor. S. P. G. A-Series, X., pp. 268-269.

(30) 1715, Aug. 23. From Wm. Taylor. S. P. G. A-Series, X., p. 271.

(31) 1715, Oct. 18. To the Bishop of London. S. P. G. A-Series, XI., p. 281.

(32) 1715, Nov. 13. Certificate for Rowland Ellis. S. P. G. A-Series, XI., pp. 327-328.

(33) 1715, Dec. 1. To Wm. Taylor. S. P. G. A-Series, XI., pp. 328-329.

(34) 1716, Apr. 14. To David Humphreys. S. P. G. A-Series, XI., pp. 296-297.

(35) 1716, Apr. 23. From David Humphreys. S. P. G. A-Series, XI., p. 370.

(36) (1716, May 14?) To Messrs. Walker, Talbot (and others). S. P. G. A-Series, XI., p. 373.

(37) 1716, June 11. From David Humphreys. S. P. G. A-Series, XI., p. 376.

(38) 1716, July 16. From David Humphreys. S. P. G. A-Series, XI., p. 377.

(39) (1716) (late summer) To David Humphreys. S. P. G. A-Series, XI., pp. 334-335.

(40) 1716, Dec. 5. To David Humphreys. S. P. G. A-Series, XII., p. 177.

(41) 1717, Sept. 17. To David Humphreys. S. P. G. A-Series, XII., p. 390.

(42) 1718, May 3. To David Humphreys. S. P. G. A-Series, XIII., p. 374.

(43) 1718, Sept. 4. Deposition against Thos. Haliday. S. P. G. A-Series, XIII., p. 421.

(44) 1718, Sept. 5. To David Humphreys. S. P. G. A-Series, XIII., pp. 352-354.

(45) 1718, Oct. 1. Addressed to S. P. G. S. P. G. A-Series, XIII., pp. 388-391.

(46) (1720). Petition to the S. P. G. S. P. G. A-Series, XIV., pp. 44-45.

(47) (1720). State and condition of Burlington House. S. P. G. A-Series, XIV., p. 34.

(48) 1720, Feb. 17. Certificate in behalf of Mr. Talbot. S. P. G. A-Series, XIV., p. 55.

(49) 17(20?), March 29. Certificates for Mr. Talbot. S. P. G. A-Series, XIV., pp. 151-152.

(50) 1720, June 23. Certificate for Rowland Ellis. S. P. G. A-Series, XIV., p. 148.

(51) 1722, June 30. Order for Mr. Talbot's receiving the interest of Bishop Tenison's legacy. S. P. G. A-Series, XVI., pp. 48-51.

(52) 1722, Nov. 27. To David Humphreys. S. P. G. A-Series, XVI., pp. 214-216.

(53) 1723, Sept. 14. Certificate. S. P. G. A-Series, XVII., p. 237.

(54) 1723, Sept. 20. To David Humphreys. S. P. G. A-Series, XVII., p. 237.

(55) 1723, Dec. 9. To David Humphreys. S. P. G. A-Series, XVII., p. 250.

(56) 1724, Sept. 7. To David Humphreys. S. P. G. A-Series, XVIII., p. 184.

(57) 1725, July 8. To David Humphreys. S. P. G. B-Series, I., #94, p. 347.

(58) 1714, Sept. 14. From Christopher Wilkinson to the Bishop of London. Fulham MSS., Virginia, Box I., #140.

(59) 1715, Oct. 21. To the Bishop of London. Fulham MSS., Pennsylvania, #74.

B. Allusions to John Talbot in the Manuscript Journals of the Society.

(NOTE:—The first five volumes of the S. P. G. Journals contain references to Talbot and his work, covering the years 1702 to 1725. These volumes have been photofilmed for the Library of Congress. Both the original paging of the Journals and the Library of Congress paging are given below.)

S. P. G. JOURNAL—VOLUME I.

Library of Congress paging	Journal paging	Date of meeting
80	82	Aug. 21, 1702.
83	85	Sept. 18, 1702.
84	86	Oct. 16, 1702.
87	89	Nov. 20, 1702.
101	103	March 19, 1702/3.
159	161	Aug. 18, 1704.
163	165	Sept. 15, 1704.
202	204	Oct. 19, 1705.
203	205	Nov. 16, 1705.
221	7	Feb. 28, 1705/6.
224	10	March 15, 1705/6.

Library of Congress paging	*Journal paging*	*Date of meeting*
225	11	March 15, 1705/6.
230	16	March 28, 1706.
231	17	March 28, 1706.
235	21	May 17, 1706.
240	26	June 21, 1706.
241	27	June 21, 1706.
255	41	Dec. 20, 1706.
260	46	Jan. 17, 1706/7.
261	47	Jan. 17, 1706/7.
264	50	Jan. 30, 1706/7—(*in re:* suffragan bishop for America, at time of Talbot's visit to England).
277	63	March 21, 1706/7.
282	68	Apr. 18, 1707.
285	71	Apr. 18, 1707.
287	73	May 16, 1707.
315	101	Dec. 19, 1707.
344	130	July 1, 1708.
347	133	Aug. 20, 1708.
368	152	Feb. 11, 1708/9.
454-456	238-240	Feb. 10, 1709/10.
460-461	244-245	Feb. 17, 1709/10.
471-472	255-256	Apr. 21, 1710.
558	342	Jan. 19, 1710/11.
607	(2)	A report found at the back of this volume.

S. P. G. JOURNAL—VOLUME II.

78-80	77-79	July 20, 1711.
148-149	147-148	Jan. 4, 1711/12.
248	251	Oct. 31, 1712.
268-269	271-272	Feb. 27, 1712/13.
270	273	Feb. 27, 1712/13.
315-316	318-319	Oct. 9, 1713.
318	321	Oct. 9, 1713.
341-342	344-345	Dec. 18, 1713.
351	354	Feb. 12, 1713/4.
355	—	Feb. 19, 1713/4.

S. P. G. JOURNAL—VOLUME III.

47-48	46-47	March 18, 1714/15.
51	50	Apr. 7, 1715.
60	59	June 17, 1715.
69-70	68-69	July 1, 1715.
94	93	Oct. 7, 1715.
114	113	Feb. 3, 1715/16.
116	115	Feb. 3, 1715/16.
119	118	Feb. 17, 1715/16.
157-159	156-158	July 6, 1716.

Library of Congress paging	Journal paging	Date of meeting
165-166	164-165	July 20, 1716.
175	174	Oct. 19, 1716.
207-208	206-207	Jan. 11, 1716/17.
213-214	212-213	Feb. 1, 1716/17.
274-276	273-275	Aug. 2, 1717.
291	290	Sept. 20, 1717.
299-300	298-299	Sept. 20, 1717.

S. P. G. JOURNAL—VOLUME IV.

15	14	Dec. 19, 1718.
54	53	May 15, 1719.
120	119	Sept. 11, 1720.
131	130	Nov. 18, 1720.
134	133	Jan. 20, 1720/21.
139	138	Jan. 20, 1720/21.
154	153	Mar. 31, 1721.
195	194	Jan. 19, 1721/22.

S. P. G. JOURNAL—VOLUME V.

13-14	9-10	Oct. 16, 1724.
16	12	Nov. 20, 1724.
23	19	Dec. 18, 1724.
53	49	July 16, 1725.
61	57	Sept. 17, 1725.
62	58	Oct. 15, 1725.
76	72	Jan. 21, 1725.

BOOK FIVE

GENERAL INDEX

INDEX

(Note: Pp. 3-79—Biography of Talbot; pp. 83-163—Letters and MSS. Sources; pp. 164-186—Extracts from Keith's Journal).

A.

Albany, 44.

Allen, John, 152.

Amboy. See Perth Amboy.

Amwell, Visited by Talbot, 64.

Anabaptists, settlers in New Jersey, 4, 9; books needed to answer them, 95; activities in Burlington, 115, 117.

Andrews, Jedidiah, new meeting house built for, 103; note identifying, 106.

Anglican. See Church of England.

Anne, Queen, 85, 88, 96; effect of her death on prospect of American bishop, 53; addressed concerning New Jersey act, 55; her patronage appreciated, 96.

Appoquinimy, no minister, 123.

Aqueckenonck, described, 9.

Archbishop. See Canterbury; archbishops and bishops petitioned for resident bishop, 62-63.

Atheism, growth of in East Jersey, 49.

Ayers, William, ix.

B.

Baltimore, Lord, 160.

Baptist. See Anabaptists.

Barclay, John, 170.

Barclay, Robert, governor of New Jersey, 5; mentioned, 95, 170; note identifying, 98.

Barclay, Thomas, missionary to Albany, &c., 116; note identifying, 117.

Barclay, William, missionary at Braintree, 100, 125; note identifying, 101.

Bard, Peur, 152.

Barlay, John, 114.

Barlow, Mr., 138.

Barnaby, Mr., 93.

Bartow, John, missionary in Westchester county, 124, 128, 129-130; note identifying, 129.

Bass, Jeremiah, proclamation against immorality, 8; opinion of Talbot, 51; joins in petition for bishop, 62; memtioned, 59, 104, 134; note identifying, 106.

Bass, John, 152.

Beach, Abraham, viii.

Bedford, Hilkiah, consecrated bishop, 75.

Bellamont, Earl of, 85; note identifying, 87.

Bennett, Mr., 154.

Bergen, described, 9; conditions in, 21.

Berkeley, Lord John, grantee of New Jersey, 4; sells his interest, 5.

Beveridge, William, addressed by Col. Morris, 31; his sermons, 100, 156; note identifying, 101.

Beverley, Robert, 90, 91; note identifying, 94.

Bewley, Mr., 89.

Billings, Edward, purchases interest in New Jersey, 5.

Biorck, Eric, signs petition for bishop, 39; recommended to Bishop of London, 40.

Bishop, Captain, 180.

Bishop, needed for the colonies, 32, 37-38, 48, 49, 50, 54, 62-63, 86, 104, 131, 143; efforts to secure resident bishop, 38-40, 41; why needed, 42-43, 49, 50, 54, 62-63, 86, 119, 127; jurisdiction of resident bishops outlined, 52-53; petition to obtain bishop, 62-63; failure of plan for resident bishop, 53; house provided for bishop in Burlington, 50, 51-52; falls into decay, 53-54, 64, 150; restored, 64, 65, 156, 157.

Bishop of London, addressed by clergy, 40; his authority questioned by Lord Cornbury, 47; appealed to by Talbot, 70; orders Welton's recall, 75; addressed regarding Non-Juror bishops in America, 76-77; his patronage, 96, 98; mentioned, 90, 101, 105, 108, 135, 148, 160-161.

Black, William, missionary in Dela-